Allocating the Earth

Allocating the Earth

A Distributional Framework for Protecting Capabilities in Environmental Law and Policy

Breena Holland
Associate Professor, Lehigh University
Political Science & the Environmental Initiative

OXFORD
UNIVERSITY PRESS

OXFORD
UNIVERSITY PRESS

Great Clarendon Street, Oxford, OX2 6DP,
United Kingdom

Oxford University Press is a department of the University of Oxford.
It furthers the University's objective of excellence in research, scholarship,
and education by publishing worldwide. Oxford is a registered trade mark of
Oxford University Press in the UK and in certain other countries

First Edition published in 2014

Impression: 1

Published in the United States of America by Oxford University Press
198 Madison Avenue, New York, NY 10016, United States of America

British Library Cataloguing in Publication Data
Data available

Library of Congress Control Number: 2014940453

ISBN 978–0–19–969207–1

Printed and bound by
CPI Group (UK) Ltd, Croydon, CR0 4YY

To Edith and Stephen

Preface

This book develops and applies a new theoretical framework for thinking and reasoning about the purpose, value, and social implications of environmental protection policies. I rely most heavily on a particular theory of social justice—the "capabilities approach" advanced by Martha Nussbaum—to provide the framework's guiding normative principle and basic conceptual logic. The capabilities approach has much in common with rights-based approaches to evaluating and designing policies because it treats individual-level political protections as constitutional guarantees owed to citizens living in liberal democratic societies. The individualistic focus has particular advantages for addressing the inequitable impacts that environmental policies produce, such as those that expose people to different levels of environmental harm. The approach to designing and evaluating environmental policy that I develop treats a certain level of environmental quality as an entitlement to which each individual citizen has a basic political guarantee. However, I define this individual guarantee in terms of a person's capabilities rather than a person's rights. As a conception of individual well-being and advantage, people's capabilities are preferable to rights, most simply, because the former defines a sphere of action that rights commonly protect, as well as the preconditions that make it possible for people to engage in specific forms of protected action. By extending the account of what is worthy of political protection to include these enabling conditions I hope to advance an evaluative framework that clarifies and reveals the vital role the natural environment plays in a meaningful and flourishing human life, and therefore to affirm environmental quality as a matter of basic political protection.

Environmental policy gives rise to many different kinds of questions. Those that motivate the present project concern issues of valuation, justification, and participation. How should we value the natural environment when we assess the social value of policies that protect it? On what theoretical and philosophical basis should we seek to justify environmental protection? What role should citizens, experts, and various other stakeholders play in environmental policy decisions? Because my intent is to bring a particular theoretical approach to justice to bear on answering these questions, this book is an exercise of applied political theory. I set the stage for this exercise by first introducing the contemporary environmental policy context (Chapter 1), the problems that give rise to questions of valuation, justification, and participation (Chapter 1 and Chapter 2), and the primary aims and innovations of the relevant literature on human capabilities (Chapter 3). Readers who are familiar with current practices and trends in environmental policy, such as stakeholder collaboration and citizen participation, and the use of economic analysis to assess environmental policies, may wish to skip or skim through Chapter 1 and Chapter 2, which review the problems and questions to which these trends and practices in environmental policy give rise. Likewise, readers who are familiar with the rapidly growing literature on human capabilities may wish to skip or skim through Chapter 3, where I introduce this literature—capabilities theory—as providing both a theory of well-being and the theory of justice and discuss why the theories are relevant to questions of valuation, justification, and participation in environmental policy.

It was many years ago, when I was a doctoral student at the University of Chicago, that I first began thinking about the relationship between people's capabilities and the natural environment. Since then, I have continually found the broad conception of well-being that capabilities theory offers to be productive in illuminating the unseen or unacknowledged impacts that environmental problems have on different people. While environmental degradation is increasingly recognized as bad for the planet as a whole, its impact on different people varies widely and is often difficult to measure in ways that link the actions of different people. Yet our ecological connectedness to each other is significant and inescapable—its importance has sustained my interest in developing a general framework for thinking and reasoning about the role of environmental relationships in making people capable of doing and achieving things that make their lives meaningful and good. Thus, while this book has a theoretical orientation, it is inspired by the very practical problem, which is that the laws providing protection from environmental harms and access to environmental benefits do not serve all citizens equally. Some people have an easier time avoiding environmental problems, and others have an easier time accessing environmental benefits. If the environment's value were a purely subjective matter, and if the environment contributed to people's lives in relatively similar ways, then these varying impacts might be less problematic. But environmental relationships are highly varied and some of them are objectively good for us regardless of what any person subjectively values.

In proposing a framework for designing and evaluating environmental policies that can address inequities resulting from the complexity and significance of environmental relationships, this manuscript draws heavily on theoretical ideas, but it also reasons through the practical application of these ideas to address questions of value, justice, and participation that arise in the context of environmental policy decisions. Scholarship like this, which endeavors to work back and forth between theory and practice, runs the risk of pleasing neither theoreticians nor practitioners. I have been aware of this problem from the start and settled on the goal of saying enough to convince both audiences that advancing this work in either direction is a worthwhile task. Many people have helped me in this endeavor. I cannot thank them all here, but wish to express my gratitude to those who played a significant role in helping me to complete the present project.

First, I wish to thank Jeremy Bendik-Keymer for first proposing that I write on the topic of human capabilities when we were both taking Martha Nussbaum's graduate course on Neo-Aristotelian political thought at the University of Chicago. Jeremy not only helped me conceptualize the project, he also offered critical feedback on nearly every chapter that evolved into a dissertation and then a book manuscript. Jeremy's passion for philosophical thinking and intellectual capacity can be inspiring and consuming; I am certain it sustained me through many moments of academic doubt. He has been an ongoing source of rigorous thinking, creativity, and passion for learning, from which I have benefitted in more ways than I can convey.

Second, I wish to thank my dissertation committee at the University of Chicago, which was chaired by the late Iris Marion Young. In addition to providing continual commentary and review, Iris played an important role in orienting my initial doctoral project to fit within the context of a larger research agenda that made it possible for me to continue working on the ideas long after completing the dissertation. I miss experiencing the immediacy and strength of her personality and ideas, but am so grateful to have had the chance to know her and the significant body of work she left with us. Martha Nussbaum's guidance has also been crucial to this project. Her capacity for absorbing information about environmental issues as yet another area of knowledge continues to astound and inspire me. I am lucky to have had her help in navigating the broad literature that has emerged on capabilities. I have always insisted that her work in this literature has particular advantages for questions that interest me in environmental policy, but I appreciate her patience with my speed and inelegance in demonstrating why. She has been a thoughtful and crucial source of advice throughout the drafting of this manuscript and the professional life I tried to balance while writing it. Cass Sunstein and Leigh Raymond also played crucial roles in my effort to apply capabilities theory to environmental policy. Leigh provided significant policy expertise combined with a genuine interest in normative political theory, which gave me confidence and direction in developing the ideas and bringing them down to the level of application. Cass's overall confidence in the project and his remarkable capacity to reorient and reframe my thinking about law and policy in only a few sentences cleared away some seemingly insurmountable barriers in my argument. I am immensely thankful to have had the guidance of such a talented and inspiring group of scholars.

Several other people at the University of Chicago have been central to my completion of this manuscript. Ted Steck has been a great friend and colleague who created an intellectual home for me as a graduate student and became a formidable interlocutor as he learned about my research. Murat Arsel endured the most intense stages of my initial writing, and provided a constant source of support and humor. Jennifer Rubenstein has provided essential insight at particular stages as well as ongoing friendship and inspiration. I am also grateful for the many opportunities I had to travel with John Overton, which helped me to think through the environmental dimensions of people's capabilities in many different physical and social contexts.

At Lehigh University I have been supported by a remarkable group of colleagues who have made my work life both enjoyable and meaningful. In the Political Science Department, Janet Laible, Rick Matthews, Ted Morgan, Laura Olson, and Al Wurth have all given me their time and support in more ways than I can count. Many other members of the Lehigh community have also been crucial to my finishing the book and my thinking about human capabilities. I especially wish to thank Nandini Deo, John Gillroy, Seth Moglen, Judy Lasker, Dork Sahagian, John Savage, and Joan Ramage.

Off campus I have many colleagues in the environmental political theory community who have made time to read and comment on my work amidst busy schedules and competing demands. I owe a great deal of my progress to David Schlosberg, whose enthusiasm and challenging questions brought the ideas to life; I am so thankful for his mentorship and generosity of time and spirit. At various stages valuable feedback has been provided by Sheri Breen, Antje Brock, Chris Buck, Peter Cannavò, Lisa Ellis, Joel Kassiola, Teena Gabrielson, Cheryl Hall, Tim Luke, John Meyer, Jouni Paavola, Christopher Robinson, Fabian Scholtes, Kristin Shrader-Frechette, Kim Smith, Les Thiele, Steve Vanderheiden, Harlan Wilson, and Rafi Youatt. John Meyer, in particular, has been remarkable in always finding the time to review my work and provide professional advice; I hope that I can someday be as helpful to others as the environmental political theory (EPT) community has been to me. There are many more people who are part of this community, and I thank them all for creating a supportive, engaging, and learned intellectual community, as well as something besides warmer weather to look forward to in the spring.

Finally, I wish to thank a close group of friends and family who have put up with my writing habits, endured my neuroses, and constantly engaged me in discussing the ideas in this book. Bronwen Morgan and Dorian LaGuardia are lifelong friends who have contributed more than anyone to my academic endeavors. Juliette Beck and Susannah Peterson have both played a key role in pushing me forward with my research, and in helping me to keep it in perspective. In 2007 I was lucky to meet Amy Linch, who generously welcomed me into her already busy life, and continues to provide ongoing support, intellectual guidance, and the best kind of friendship a person can imagine finding. She has read more of this manuscript than anyone; her breadth and depth of knowledge in political theory has provided significant clarity on the theoretical ideas and written text. The book would be much better if I could have addressed all of Amy's comments. A great debt of gratitude is also owed to Damon Aherne, who has been an important part of my life throughout the drafting of this manuscript as a book. His ongoing encouragement and partnership has meant everything to me, and his passion for environmental politics has sustained my belief that advocacy for environmental protection is worthy of extended commitment. Lastly, I wish to thank my wonderful family for giving me the time to write this book. Sandy Collier, J'Nelle Holland, Damian and Bryant Gover, Mary Ellen Hewsen, David Morton, and Addie and Mike Revetta have all grounded me and encouraged me at crucial times. Most importantly, I am forever grateful to have had the extraordinary support, friendship and guidance of my parents, Edith and Stephen, whose tales of magic and meaning taught me of the wisdom born in wild places.

Contents

List of Abbreviations

CAA	Clean Air Act
CAIR	Clean Air Interstate Rule
CARR	capabilities approach to regulatory rulemaking
CBA	cost–benefit analysis
CBO	Congressional Budget Office
DMV	deliberative monetary valuation
EAB	Environmental Appeals Board
EBM	ecosystem-based management
EPA	Environmental Protection Agency
FIFRA	Federal Insecticide, Fungicide, and Rodenticide Act
GDP	gross domestic product
GHG	greenhouse gas
GNP	gross national product
IPCC	International Panel on Climate Change
NAAQS	national ambient air quality standards
NEPA	National Environmental Policy Act
OECD	Organisation for Economic Co-operation and Development
OMB	Office of Management and Budget
RCRA	Resource Conservation and Recovery Act
RIAs	regulatory impact analyses/assessments
SDWA	Safe Drinking Water Act
SIP	state implementation plan
SUVs	sports utility vehicles
TEV	total economic value
TSCA	Toxic Substances Control Act
VMT	vehicle miles travelled
WTA	willingness to accept
WTP	willingness to pay

1

Introduction: Economic Analysis, Democratic Procedure, and Distributional Assessment in Environmental Policy

1.1 Establishing a Role for Distributional Assessment in Environmental Policy

How should we value the natural environment when considering the impact of environmental policies on individual people? What normative principles should we appeal to in determining an environmental policy's overall contribution to society? Should these principles guide the design and implementation of environmental policies, or should environmental policies take shape through political processes, in which various stakeholders deliberate and come to agreement about policy design and implementation? On what basis can a democratic society protect nature when citizens are not willing to support this goal? Why does the environmental crisis facing contemporary society call for redefining the role of both citizens and experts in making environmental decisions? This book addresses each of these questions in the context of its broader aim to develop and defend a new normative framework for evaluating environmental policies.

In contemporary environmental law and policy, economic analysis provides the dominant theoretical framework for thinking and reasoning about environmental protection. Broadly speaking, this framework involves evaluating environmental protection with respect to the goal of producing economically efficient policies, and valuing specific environmental resources with respect to their success in satisfying the subjective preferences that people express as consumers making market choices. Various laws and executive orders require this kind of analysis, and advocates of both weaker and stronger environmental protection often draw on such analyses to influence the public debate in ways that support their favored view of policy decisions.[1] While economic analysis is not the only type of assessment that policy practitioners employ, the significant legal and political influence of economic analysis in the area of environmental protection inspires much of this book's effort to advance a different framework for evaluating and justifying environmental protection.[2]

The normative criterion that grounds the framework that this book advances is social justice. The idea that public policy should be guided by concerns of social justice rather than economic efficiency arises in various forums of legal and political reasoning about the distributional impacts of environmental protection. A law setting national standards for air quality, for example, will require polluting industries to invest a certain amount of money in pollution control, and it will benefit citizens that would otherwise breathe polluted air. But the impact of pollution control is much more complicated than this, for there will be significant variation in the air quality the beneficiaries experience. For instance, enforcement of environmental protection laws will vary depending on the racial composition of communities in which environmental laws have been violated.[3] Likewise, a given pollution control standard will be violated more often in certain geographical locations.[4] A given standard will also provide fewer absolute benefits to people who cannot or do not avoid the worst exposures, such as people who work or exercise outdoors. If exposure to air pollution results in medical disorders, such as asthma or other respiratory illnesses, then people who cannot afford medical treatment will get fewer overall benefits from an established level of air quality.

These differential impacts describe just some of the various inequities that characterize the distribution of environmental protection in contemporary society. As environmental justice scholars have shown, personal conditions, as well as broader political and legal contexts, can significantly influence who will benefit from environmental protection, and by how much. A lack of environmental protection may compound existing disadvantages in a way

[1] Federal laws, such as the Toxic Substances Control Act (1976), the Federal Insecticide, Fungicide, and Rodenticide Act (1972), and the Safe Drinking Water Act (1996) require agencies to set regulatory standards by calculating and comparing the economic costs and benefits those standards will produce so that those for which costs exceed benefits can be identified as unacceptable. Other laws require regulatory agencies to consider whether standards are "feasible" or "achievable" as defined by the extent to which the economic costs they impose on industry will produce significant business failures. See *AFL-CIO v. OSHA* 965 F.2d 962, 980 (11th Cir. 1992). Additionally, various presidential executive orders require that regulatory agencies complete regulatory impact analyses (RIAs) for major regulations involved in implementing laws. These RIAs evaluate the economic costs and benefits of the regulation and must be approved by the President's Office of Management and Budget (OMB) before agencies can implement them.

[2] Even environmental organizations now rely on economic analysis as a way of making the case for environmental protection more compelling. See Kraft (2007:218–219).

[3] See Kuehn (1994:27–28) and Lavelle and Coyle (1992).

[4] Lazarus (1993).

that further constrains how these disadvantages limit people's choices. For these reasons, policies that seek to provide equal protection and prevent the furthering of disadvantage must account for various conditions that determine the ultimate impact of their implementation. This will require a framework for designing and evaluating policies that is grounded in ideals of social justice. These ideals, as defined contemporarily, are concerned with treating the interests of different people equally.

As scholarly interest in environmental policy has grown over the last several decades, many academics have endeavored to develop ethical principles and political theories that can guide and justify efforts to address the inequities that public policies produce. For example, Kristin Shrader-Frechette develops the "Principle of Prima Facie Political Equality" to guide efforts intending to remedy unequal exposures to environmental harms.[5] Likewise, some laws, such as the National Environmental Policy Act (NEPA) appeal to an ideal of equality in calling for the federal government to "assure for all Americans safe, healthful, productive, and aesthetically and culturally pleasing surroundings."[6] At the level of practical policy tools, there are also some methods for evaluating policies with respect to other social values besides economic efficiency, such as David Weimer and Aidan Vining's social welfare function, which draws on the ideas of justice defined by the famous political philosopher, John Rawls.[7]

Unfortunately, growing evidence of inequities in the area of environmental protection suggests that these laws and assessment tools have had limited success.[8] This may be a consequence of the significant political influence held by those wielding numbers and alleging the enormous economic costs of environmental regulation.[9] If regulation producing more equitable outcomes is also more costly, then those who bear the costs may exert considerable effort to dramatize the negative economic consequences of environmental protection policies. Perhaps less evident, the failure to address inequities may be due to limitations in the theory and practice of existing non-economic approaches to policy evaluation, for these non-economic approaches lack an equivalent level of theoretical and analytic refinement.[10] Consider that

[5] See, Shrader-Frechette (2002:24–27). Daniels (1985) develops John Rawls's liberal political theory to address inequities in health care policy.

[6] See NEPA section 101 (b)(2).

[7] See Weimer and Vining (1989:134–146). I discuss the limitations of Rawlsian political thought as a basis for policy evaluation in Chapter 5.

[8] See Cole and Foster (2001) for an annotated bibliography of initial research documenting the disproportionate impact of environmental hazards on low-income and/or minority communities. Also see Swanston (1999:546–549) and Lazarus (1993:792–806).

[9] McGarity and Ruttenburg (2002) discuss this tendency to exaggerate the costs in advance of regulations.

[10] For example, Randall (2002) seeks to refine the theoretical foundations of cost–benefit analysis, and Cropper (2000) reviews various refinements in the analytic tools necessary for measuring benefits in cost–benefit analysis.

use of the currently dominant economic approach to evaluating public policies—cost–benefit analysis (CBA)—dates back to the 1930s, when the Army Corps of Engineers applied it to assess federal projects requiring large financial investments in waterways, harbors, and flood protection.[11] With nearly a century of use behind it, CBA's predominance has benefitted from significant development and widespread recognition in the policy community.

Yet there remain important limitations in how CBA measures a policy's impact, and in how it determines whether a policy is worth implementing. These limitations, as I (and others) argue, ultimately emerge from CBA's reliance on a flawed view of what is valuable to individual people and on a contestable account of what is good for society. Thus, while non-economic approaches to evaluating and designing policies may lack equivalent refinement and use, some of the limitations that confront the current economic approach to policy evaluation are theoretical, and therefore cannot be overcome through further development and refinement at the level of application. Creating policies that treat the interests of different people in different circumstances as equally worthy of protection from environmental harms will require a different theoretical approach to conceptualizing the environmental impacts that matter and to determining what makes a policy justifiable.

By developing a theoretical framework for systematically evaluating and addressing the distributional impacts of policies protecting the environment, I hope to further justify non-economic approaches to policy analysis and design. I also hope to lay out what would be involved in evaluating and designing policy in a way that treats the interests of the different people a policy impacts as equally important. The performative success of such a framework hinges, in part, on its potential to systematically define the range and depth of environmental impacts analysts should consider in designing and evaluating policies. The political viability of such a framework depends on its potential to relate these impacts to political values, such as social justice and political equality, which often conflict with the pursuit of economic efficiency. To put this point differently, the ultimate contribution of the framework of policy evaluation this book advances will depend on the extent to which it connects questions concerning what environmental impacts matter in the lives of individual people with questions concerning why those impacts bear on important non-economic social and political goals. Policies safeguarding the environmental conditions that make it possible for each person to pursue goals that are widely recognized as socially and politically protected should be defended as such. Not only would this

[11] Guess and Farnham (2000:304) and Gramlich (1981:7).

push economically efficient policies to meet even stronger justifications, it would also provide a way of systematically accounting for instances in which economically inefficient policies are equally justifiable.

To advance such a framework, I draw on a body of literature that has already done much to improve how economists, political theorists, and policy practitioners think about the impacts and goals of public policies. This literature, which I will refer to as "capabilities theory," starts from the basic premise that human well-being should be understood in terms of people's *capabilities* to do and achieve different things. Originally, Nobel-prize-winning economist Amartya Sen built on this basic idea to critique and improve economic methods and principles that have shaped international development policies. Likewise, Martha Nussbaum, who is a philosopher by training, also built on this basic conception of well-being to theorize the philosophical underpinnings of an ethical framework for problematizing and redirecting the goals and practices of international development. Drawing on the Aristotelian philosophical tradition, capabilities theory advances ideas that often stand in sharp distinction to those emerging from utilitarian thinkers, who provide the philosophical grounding for much contemporary economic thought. Although Sen and Nussbaum both continue to develop and build on their respective projects, today a diverse group of scholars and practitioners are developing and applying their foundational work.[12]

A distinct advantage of this literature for policy analysis is that it views humans as developmental beings with the potential to flourish in many different ways and in the context of many different life activities. People are conceptualized as agents capable of engaging in economic interactions, as well personal, social, and political activities that are equally valuable and relevant to evaluating the goals and methods of government activities. Conceiving of humans in this way is especially helpful when it comes to assessing the distribution of environmental protection. Specifically, a broad view of the various activities that make up a good human life can expand how contemporary policy analysis understands the environment's role in relation to the variety of conditions and achievements that people value. Nature, in the context of a rich and meaningful human life, becomes much more than a mere commodity to be bought and sold; it is the basis of meaningful personal, familial, and communal relationships that cannot be valued accurately in economic terms. Likewise, the material conditions of such a life require an ecological context that can support and sustain these various meaningful interactions, and not simply the economic interactions through which people meet a subset of their material needs. In these ways, a more accurate view of the diverse

[12] See <http://hd-ca.org/> for an introduction to and an overview of "capabilities theory." See Chapter 3 for citations to published introductory readings.

experiences and relationships that a good human life involves can provide a fuller view of the natural environment's value, and of how environmental degradation can undermine individual well-being.

The literature on capabilities is also a fruitful basis for constructing an effective framework for policy analysis because of how it engages the relationship between politics and justice. In particular, capabilities theory treats the quality or condition of human life as something that is central to one's ability to freely make choices about the purposes or ends that one values. This functions to forefront questions about substantive conditions of human well-being that must be met if political procedures are going to treat people fairly or justly. In the context of policy evaluation and design, it makes the political legitimacy of public policy contingent upon the protection of certain substantive material and social conditions. These substantive conditions therefore become the starting point for the possibility of having procedures through which politically legitimate public policies must emerge. Thus, more generally, by focusing on human experience in its material and social context, capabilities theory recasts the possibility of liberal politics as something contingent on the protection of substantive conditions, rather than mostly about constraining certain forms of intrusive government action.[13]

The limitations of procedural approaches to preventing environmental degradation and exploitation are an additional inspiration for drawing on capabilities theory to improve the evaluation and design of environmental policies. While much of the formal evaluation of environmental policy is, on the one hand, driven by economic analysis, there is, on the other hand, a more recent trend toward devolving national-level regulatory authority over environmental protection to the state, regional, or local level. With respect to this latter trend, the goal is to transfer authority over resource management to a level of decision-making that corresponds more closely to the boundaries of the ecosystems sustaining particular resources and absorbing the impact of their use by society. At the "ecosystem-scale," all of the interested stakeholders can also collaborate and deliberate about issues of acceptable access, use, and impact. However, as I discuss in Section 1.2, while the turn toward collaboration and deliberation offers many advantages over the conventional framework of regulatory authority, in the non-ideal form in which it often plays out (and perhaps even in the ideal form), it poses significant barriers to environmental protection. In particular, collaboration and deliberation at the ecosystem-scale can sometimes allow for more environmental degradation than control at the federal level

[13] See Leeson (1979) for a discussion of why the liberal political tradition's emphasis on the importance of limiting government authority poses specific challenges to contemporary efforts intending to prevent ecological disaster.

would otherwise permit. Likewise, recent efforts to value environmental resources through deliberative rather than economic processes remain committed to certain features of economic valuation that produce an inaccurate representation of environmental values. For this reason, a primary task I take up in this book is exploring how the substantive protections of an alternative framework of policy evaluation might also serve to identify conditions that should constrain outcomes emerging from these collaborative and deliberative approaches to environmental management and valuation.

Thus, while the framework for policy evaluation that I develop is first and foremost a response to the influence of economic analysis on environmental policy, and particularly to the failure of current policy evaluation to account for the disproportionate distribution of environmental goods and harms, it also responds to problems that confront one important solution to highly technocratic approaches to making environmental policy decisions. I argue that recent efforts to transplant decision-making authority from the influence of technical (and often economic) experts at the federal level to collaborative and deliberative decisions among stakeholders at a more local level are not an adequate way of constraining the problems that confront the role of expertise in democratic governance. Instead of putting environmental decisions in the hands of collaborating and deliberating stakeholders, I argue that such decisions should emerge from a political process in which stakeholders and experts have different and narrowly defined roles, and in which policy outcomes are constrained by certain substantive standards. This implies that policy decisions should be driven neither by narrowly economic technical analyses, nor optimistically democratic processes of collaboration and deliberation. Instead, policy decisions should be informed by distributional assessments and should emerge from a democratic process in which substantive ideals specify the boundaries of what expert and stakeholders can agree to do. For those already engaged in carrying out distributional assessments of environmental policy, I hope to propose and defend a theoretical framework that can make such assessments innovative, illuminating, and more justifiable, even if they at first appear less democratic and more economically costly.

The remainder of this chapter provides a broader context for this overall project. I first discuss the trend toward economic analysis and the trend toward deliberative monetary valuation and ecosystem-based management in contemporary environmental policy (Section 1.2). I then highlight how the literature on human capabilities can respond to some of the problems to which these trends give rise (Section 1.3). Finally, I review how the remaining chapters of the book will draw on different literatures to develop a new normative framework for addressing these problems (Section 1.4).

1.2 The Rise of Economics and Democratic Procedure in Environmental Policy

The widespread use of economic analysis as an approach to valuing environmental resources and justifying environmental protection emerged in the latter half of the twentieth century, when economists developed and applied the ideas and methods from economic science to a broad array of environmental problems.[14] Seminal works such as Howard Barnett and Chandler Morse's *Scarcity and Growth* and Francis Christy and Neal Potter's statistical analysis of historical trends in natural resource use set the stage for a budding environmental movement to trigger development of environmental economics as a distinct field within the discipline of economics.[15] The new field drew heavily on Arthur Pigou's work on externalities, which provided the theoretical basis for addressing pollution damage as a non-priced negative effect on third parties.[16] Likewise, John Hicks's and Nicholas Kaldor's prior contributions in welfare economics provided justification for an approach to evaluating public policies in terms of their economic costs and benefits.[17] These ideas, alongside Siegfried von Ciriacy-Wantrup's original suggestion to elicit information about the price of non-marketed environmental goods through questionnaires, have become a mainstay in contemporary environmental policy analysis in the USA.[18] Sophisticated "stated" and "revealed" preference techniques of resource valuation have made it possible to quantify and compare how much people are willing to pay for environmental goods that, under normal circumstances, are not traded in markets.[19]

Although these economic methods of valuing environmental resources later came under strong criticism, many welcomed and continue to appreciate the rise of economics to this position of prominence in environmental policy.[20] Amidst a political process often characterized by chaotic struggles for resources and power, pricing environmental resources has made it

[14] Edwards (1987), Oates and Cropper (1992), Tietenberg (1992, 1998), and Turner, Pearce, and Bateman (1993) provide good illustrations of how the ideas and methods of economic science are applied to environmental issues. Pearce (2002) provides an excellent intellectual history of the contributions of these and other economists referenced in this chapter. Criticisms of this approach will be discussed throughout this book. Sagoff (1988a), Aldred (1997), Bromley and Paavola (2002), Foster (1997), Dore (1996), and Gowdy and Olsen (1994) all provide a good introduction to the basic normative problems. Also see *Environmental Values* 9/4 (2000), which devotes the entire issue to this topic.

[15] Barnett and Morse (1963), Christy and Potter (1962).

[16] Pigou (1920).

[17] Hicks (1939b, 1943), Kaldor (1939).

[18] Ciriacy-Wantrup (1947).

[19] "Revealed preference" approaches to valuing environmental resources assess one's preferences for non-marketed goods by assessing one's preferences for other, marketed goods. In "stated preference" approaches to valuing environmental resources, questionnaires are used to assess individual preferences that reflect the value of an environmental resource. See Chapter 2 for further discussion of these methods of economic valuation.

[20] For example, see Miller (1989) and Morgenstern (1997).

possible to subject decisions about the allocation of publicly owned goods to rational analysis. For example, by pricing the environmental resources that public policies protect, policy analysts can then balance the monetary worth of these resources against the cost of protecting them, providing an economic account of a policy's "net benefits" to society.[21] As I have previously mentioned, such weighing of economic costs and benefits has become a primary method for defining the extent to which policies protecting the environment promote the overall welfare of society. Those who advocate heavier reliance on economic justifications for policy decisions claim that this approach yields a more efficient and equitable allocation of resources. They argue that greater efficiency is achieved by allowing the market's pricing mechanism to determine which policies will satisfy the most preferences at the least cost. The approach is assessed as achieving more equitable outcomes because it incorporates the policy preferences of each citizen rather than only the preferences of those who have enough political power to compel public officials to address their interests.[22] Furthermore, because the marginal utility a person gains from a given environmental resource will decrease as a person attains more of it, transferring resources from those who have more of them to those who have less would (in theory) simultaneously produce greater overall gains and a more equal distribution of resources.

Despite various technical advances in economic valuation techniques, the influence of environmental economics on policy evaluation has come under increasing criticism, as I discuss in Chapter 2. Critics charge that efforts to base the value of environmental resources on the subjective preferences people express in market interactions are deficient because people are often uninformed about the ecological importance of resources, and they are sometimes subject to unjust circumstances that distort their subjective perspectives.[23] Likewise, critics charge that welfare-maximizing techniques, such as CBA, emphasize the social value of economic efficiency while ignoring other goals of environmental policy; for example, social justice and sustaining the ways of life that certain cultures and communities value are not captured by this approach despite the extent to which these goals depend on environmental protection.[24] These critics argue that policy evaluation

[21] For an optimistic account of the role that economic analysis can play in environmental policy, see Fraas (1991) and Morgenstern (1997:25–27).

[22] Stokey and Zeckhauser (1978:158), West (1983), and Smith (1984).

[23] See Spash and Hanley (1995) for a discussion of uninformed preferences. For a discussion of the relationship between preferences and unjust circumstances see Elster (1982), Sen (1985b:29), Sunstein (1993:177), and Nussbaum (2000a:114).

[24] In comparison with the idea of "justice," the idea that policies ought to protect particular "ways of life" is less widely referenced. Chiesura and de Groot (2003) discuss how ecological context contributes to non-economic practices, such as spiritual experiences and culture. More generally, Fischer and Hajer (1999) emphasize the social and cultural implications of environmental policy. Also see Macnaghten et al. (1998).

should be based on a broader understanding of why and how the environment contributes to individual people and to society. A more comprehensive conceptualization of this relationship would facilitate a more nuanced account of environmental value and clarify the relevance of environmental factors to a broader set of social and political goals. As I discuss in Chapters 2 and 6 respectively, although the contemporary trends toward "deliberative monetary valuation" and "devolved collaboration" in environmental policy have emerged as routes for making progress toward these goals, they remain tethered to an insufficient account of environmental value and a failure to sufficiently constrain the pathologies of democratic procedure. Thus, while promising in many respects, these contemporary efforts to improve the evaluation and design of environmental policies remain insufficient for transforming environmental outcomes in ways that are necessary for protecting the conditions of both democracy and justice.

Over the last several decades, a series of arguments in favor of increasing public participation in environmental decision-making have emerged alongside this critique of economic reasoning and decision-making tools. The instantiation of these arguments in practices such as "deliberative monetary valuation" and "devolved collaboration" are process-based in that they focus on changing the processes of valuing environmental resources and making environmental management decisions so that these processes allow for a greater exchange of knowledge and views about the natural environment's value to people and society. Deliberative monetary valuation, or DMV, which Chapter 2 will discuss in further detail, seeks to infuse normal monetary valuation techniques with communication and dialogue among those who value environmental resources, as well as with experts who can answer questions about the scientific value of these environmental resources to the earth's ecology and human health. This communication and dialogue is intended to create more informed and reflective preferences regarding the environment's value, and therefore, to result in more accurate quantitative characterizations of its value to individuals and society. While allowing for the expression of (and communication about) a broader range of values and commitments, deliberative valuations remain entirely subjective: the account of environmental value that ultimately gets associated with the environment is that which emerges from this process of deliberation, transformed into a monetary figure. In this sense, DMV does not recognize any objective notion of the environment's instrumental value to human life apart from what results from the deliberative process.

The recent interest in DMV can be viewed as part of a broader trend in environmental policy that prioritizes democratic procedure as a way of addressing problems that arise in narrowly economic and technocratic approaches to environmental decision-making. Because I return to cover the topic of

DMV in greater detail in Chapter 2, I set it aside for now and turn instead to the rise of devolved collaboration as an instantiation of this trend. Devolved collaboration is a decision-making model that is like DMV in its aspiration to create a context for the exchange of knowledge and expertise by bringing the public into the decision-making processes. However, in this form of decision-making the goal is not to collectively define the value of particular environmental resources in quantitative terms; instead, it aims to devolve regulatory authority from the federal government to state and local governments, where all the relevant stakeholders can be brought into the process for making environmental management decisions.

As I have suggested earlier in this chapter, efforts to localize or regionalize regulatory authority in this way are partly a reaction to the broader turn toward economic analysis in designing, assessing, and justifying environmental policies. In particular, economic analysis of environmental protection has produced a considerable amount of data documenting the economic costs of federal-level environmental protection measures that were enacted during the 1970s, such as those regulating air quality, water quality, and the disposal of toxic waste. Drawing on such data, some critics of current environmental regulation claim that its costs are simply too high, and therefore, that government can and should create environmental regulations that cost less and still save lives.[25] Other critics argue that funding for environmental protection would save more lives if it were reallocated to an entirely different (and non-environmental) area of investment in social welfare.[26]

The devolution of regulatory authority away from the federal level has also been fostered by the claim that federal-level rules are uniform and rigid in ways that make them insensitive to local circumstance and incapable of responding to the complex and diffuse character of modern environmental problems.[27] According to many who advance this critique, the "command and control" form of federal regulation tends to stifle industry creativity. Alternatively, incentives could encourage polluters to find effective and inexpensive ways of complying with environmental protection standards.[28] Furthermore, some critics claim that the conventional approach to setting pollution control and disposal standards at the federal level is driven by technocratic experts in an administrative process that excludes meaningful public input and citizen involvement while relying on adversarial methods of enforcement and dispute resolution.[29] From this perspective, localized, consensus-based approaches to environmental decision-making will create

[25] For example, see Morrall (1986) and Tengs (1995). For a critique of these arguments about costs, see Heinzerling (1998, 2002), and Ackerman and Heinzerling (2004).

[26] See Tengs and Graham (1996).

[27] See DeWitt (1994:10) and Kuehn (1996).

[28] See Freeman (1997:14–16).

[29] See Jones (1997:26), Wondolleck and Yaffee (2000:13), and Layzer (2008:17–18).

more of a role for citizen input, and be more likely to produce decisions with which industry and other economic development interests could agree.

While, on one hand, fostering the devolution of federal-level regulatory authority, these critiques of federal-level regulatory authority are, on the other hand, also apparent in the movement in environmental policy toward "ecosystem-based management" (EBM). The EBM approach to environmental management "entails purposefully bringing stakeholders together on a subnational but supralocal level to devise a single, holistic plan that is tailored to the conditions within a specific region."[30] By addressing environmental problems at an ecosystem, watershed, or regional scale, by engaging in collaborative planning, and by relying on flexible and adaptive implementation, advocates of EBM claim to offer an approach to environmental protection that is more durable and effective than the conventional, federal-level regulatory framework. Central to EBM is the idea that there should be collaboration among stakeholders, wherein parties that an environmental decision impacts engage in face-to-face deliberation in order to arrive at an agreement regarding how to address a specific environmental problem. In contrast to the distrust and cynicism resulting from the adversarial politics that characterizes the federal-level regulatory framework, deliberation in the context of EBM promises to foster trust and respect among stakeholders, as they discover shared values and transform their own interests or otherwise find areas of common agreement.[31] Advocates of EBM claim that it will produce policies that correspond to the geographical scale of resources the policy will protect (i.e. ecosystem-scale or landscape-scale environmental resources), and that are supported by the best scientific knowledge and implemented without challenge (i.e. due to pre-implementation agreement among interested parties, which will minimize adversarial relationships among stakeholders). For these reasons, stakeholder collaboration and deliberation have become central in recent efforts to instantiate a more effective and durable approach to environmental protection.

Unfortunately, like the trend toward economic analysis, the trend toward collaboration and deliberation in the EBM approach to environmental protection faces significant problems. While collaborative planning at the ecosystem scale does produce less adversarial relationships between and among various stakeholders, this often comes at a significant cost. Among the downsides of this approach are weaker or watered-down environmental protection goals, the exclusion of environmental protection advocates that do not demonstrate a certain willingness to compromise, and agreement on vague goals

[30] Layzer (2008:20).

[31] Layzer (2008:26–27); Beierle and Long (1999:10,402); Applegate (1998:921); Williams and Matheny (1995:190).

that allow polluters to evade compliance during the implementation stage of the agreed-upon policy.[32] Such problems do not demonstrate that a more localized and deliberative approach to environmental protection is incapable of producing effective and durable policies, but they do suggest a meaningful gap exists between some of the claimed advantages of current approaches to devolving federal regulatory authority and the actual environmental outcomes this devolved authority produces.

A meaningful gap also exists between the alleged objectivity and impartiality commonly attributed to economic analysis and the political values its application actually involves. Consider, for example, how one microeconomics textbook presents economic analysis:[33]

> ... judgments on [economic] efficiency grounds can be objective, but those on equity grounds contain subjective elements, and are thus not conclusive. While the economist can set up generally accepted standards of efficiency, neither the economist, nor other scientists, can set up universally accepted standards of equity.

This view resonates with those who claim that economic analysis is somehow beyond the reach of political influence or bias because, in determining how much people value a particular policy outcome, it accepts as given whatever values people happen to have, and merely seeks to add up their quantified expression in people's market transactions.[34] According to this reasoning, economic analysis is a value-neutral means of evaluating policies.[35] It provides a method for policy assessment that is unaffected by either the personal values of the policy practitioner or larger political pressures.[36]

Additionally, in stating that standards of economic efficiency are "generally accepted," the extract's description of economic analysis suggests that an apparent consensus among economists is sufficient to establish the legitimacy of particular criteria for policy analysis. According to this line of reasoning, an equity criterion that conflicts with economic efficiency presumably lacks this legitimacy because equity can mean different things depending on a given practitioner's subjectively selected view of *what* is being equalized and among *whom*.

Unfortunately, neither the methods of assessment, nor the acceptance of economic efficiency as the relevant normative standard among economists, demonstrate that economic analysis is objective or impartial. As I will discuss in Chapter 2, pricing unpriced resources can involve multiple methodological

[32] Layzer (2008); Duane (1997:789–795). [33] Cohen (2001:2).
[34] See Trumbull (1990:204). [35] Sagoff (1988:42–43).
[36] See Buchanan (1959:127) for a strong statement of this position.

judgments that shape the conclusion of an efficiency analysis in ways that work either for or against a particular outcome. Furthermore, just as the equity criterion will identify policies that contribute to greater equality of some sort, the efficiency criterion will identify policies that contribute to the maximization of an overall good of some sort. Indeed, equity and efficiency are different goals and will often point society in different directions. What determines whether one of these goals is more legitimate than another in a liberal democratic society that embraces a capitalist economic system is the source of much debate. For example, the civic republican tradition in constitutional thought would propose that what makes one of these goals more legitimate than the other is the strength and political persuasiveness of the reasons offered for why the goal should be a public priority.[37] This contrasts with those who favor using CBA as the ultimate criterion of policy choice, for they must ultimately hold the view that society should pursue policies that will produce the greatest overall amount of preference satisfaction.[38] In light of such alternatives, the argument that economic efficiency should be the most important social goal only makes sense if one assumes that economic efficiency provides the best definition of what is good for society, and therefore, the best criterion for evaluating public policies.[39]

Unlike the economist who assumes economic efficiency should be the criterion for policy evaluation, this book adopts a more *egalitarian* perspective. By this I mean that the criteria for policy evaluation should require assessing differences in how public policies impact different people—that is, policy evaluation should assess how public policies distribute the benefits and burdens of environmental protection. I do not assume that these benefits and burdens should be distributed equally among people, as some egalitarian theories might require.[40] Rather, I am simply asserting that a distributive ideal of some sort is relevant to policy evaluation and the consequent political decisions, and that such an ideal therefore should be incorporated into our assessment of policies that protect the natural environment. This is a central claim of the environmental justice movement, it is an implicit goal of President Bill Clinton's Executive Order on Environmental Justice (which requires that all federal agencies engage in various activities to make environmental justice a

[37] See Bessette (1992) and Sunstein (1993).

[38] See O'Neill, Holland, and Light (2008:28).

[39] For example, see Okun's (1975) classic defense of economic efficiency as a superior social goal.

[40] Here I follow Wolff and de-Shalit (2007:3–4) in holding that various different egalitarian theories would converge on the general policy prescription that steps should be taken to identify and improve the condition of the worst off in society. Thus, rather than defend a particular view of egalitarianism, I am adopting the more modest position that policies should be concerned with identifying and improving the conditions of the worst off in society, not just with improving economic efficiency.

part of their mission), and various other formal legal protections.[41] It is, furthermore, as I will argue throughout this book, a basic condition of a social justice understood as a political justifiable normative ideal. Of course, what it means to create environmental policies that impact people in more equitable ways will depend on how policy evaluation conceives of people, their relationship to nature, and the environmental impacts that the evaluation treats as consequences that are relevant to policy assessment. This book will propose a particular approach to conceiving of these different components of environmental policy. In doing so, the overarching aim is to develop a normative framework that can address some of the well-documented problems with the prevailing economic approach to evaluating and designing environmental policies. As discussed earlier in this chapter, the proposed framework also seeks to overcome the limitations of democratic deliberation and collaboration in the context of environmental valuation and more localized decision-making about environmental protection.

Although this book does give attention to the problems in both economic and process-based approaches to thinking and reasoning about environmental protection, I do not suggest that information about economic costs and benefits of environmental policy should be excluded from policy evaluation and decisions. Nor do I reject the importance of citizen involvement and understanding in addressing environmental problems. Rather, my claim is that when the environment is understood in terms of its comprehensive impact on human life, the consequences of its degradation call for stronger environmental protections. But these consequences will only become apparent if policy evaluation is more accurate and ecologically informed than economic analysis permits. Furthermore, the relevance of stronger environmental protections will only become apparent if policy evaluation systematically analyzes a policy's impact on social values other than economic efficiency. While both more accurate and socially relevant, such evaluation will also illuminate why it is necessary to have more environmental protection than collaborative decision-making and deliberative valuation sometimes deliver. With this in mind, the proposed framework is advanced in an effort to put forward a direction for improving analysis of environmental protection at the federal level, and for providing a safeguard against the pathologies that compromise process-based approaches to valuing and managing environmental resources.

[41] See Cole and Foster (2001) for a discussion of the environmental justice movement, which includes an annotated bibliography of the literature and research studies describing and discussing the disproportionate distribution of exposure to environmental harms and benefits. Also see, Executive Order 12,898, 3 C.F.R. 859 (1995) and Gerrard and Foster (2008) for a discussion of current legal protections that have implications for addressing environmental inequities.

1.3 Capabilities Theory as a Normative Basis for Policy Evaluation and Design

Central to the arguments I make in the chapters that follow is the assumption that environmental policies are the product of social institutions—such as the legislatures, courts, bureaucracies, and local governance boards/councils—and are therefore subject to evaluative standards by which we judge those institutions. In practice, such evaluative standards ultimately derive from theories about the nature of political order, or about the legitimacy of a particular form of government. For example, as Chapter 2 will discuss, the current economic approach to evaluating environmental policies employs a standard derived from utilitarian political thought, which dominated political thinking from the late eighteenth century to the mid-twentieth century. Utilitarian thinkers such as James Mill and Jeremy Bentham idealized a society in which government would produce "the greatest good for the greatest number of people" by maximizing the aggregate or total amount of pleasure or happiness in society.[42] Contemporary efforts to evaluate the extent to which public policies maximize net economic benefits seek a similar good—importantly, one that replaces the maximization of happiness with the maximization of preference satisfaction.[43]

The rise of process-based methods of valuing and managing environmental resources in deliberative approaches to monetary valuation and devolved collaboration, on the other hand, finds its theoretical justification in democratic political theory rather than in utilitarian political thought. Here, face-to-face deliberation among interested parties is modeled on an ideal of inclusive and unconstrained egalitarian dialogue. Stakeholders engage in fair and rational discussion about questions of collective value and common purpose.[44] What matters is that all parties participate in this dialogue, and that they express their interests publicly, in a language that others hear and can understand. In such a context, decisions about environmental value and protection presumably would not result from strategic bargaining among self-interested actors. Instead, stakeholder preferences are expected to transform as stakeholders recognize and reflect on the interests of others involved.[45] The policies that result, therefore, are more likely to meet the interests of citizens. For

[42] See O'Neill et al. (2008:13–30). I will discuss the relationship between economic analysis and utilitarianism, as well as the relationship between economic analysis and aggregative models of democracy, in Chapter 2.

[43] O'Neill et al. (2008:21–23).

[44] Shapiro (2003:21–34) provides a summary of recent theoretical literature on deliberative democracy as a model of political practice, which he contrasts with aggregative models of democracy. Also see Benhabib (1996:69; 1992:29), and Eckersley (2004:116).

[45] See Miller (1992) and Phillips (1995).

those who advocate the model of valuation and decision-making actualized in DMV and EBM, the ideal of democratic deliberation has the advantage of bringing the voices and information of many people to bear in solving environmental problems while simultaneously institutionalizing mutual recognition and respect among citizens. Because such deliberation also puts environmental policy more in the domain of popular control, rather than in the hands of unaccountable expert authority, it can purportedly generate more legitimate and trustworthy forms of environmental governance.[46]

While the utilitarian and democratic ideals that underlie trends toward the use of economic analysis and democratic decision-making have much to offer environmental policy, they bear out their own limitations. A crucial problem with the utilitarian goal of maximizing preference satisfaction is its disregard for *whose* preferences are satisfied. Increasing the total amount of happiness or preference satisfaction in society does not mean that each member of society will be happier, more satisfied, or generally better off. Most basically, this is because aggregate gains can accrue while there are small losses to many, or large losses to a few.[47] On these grounds, many non-utilitarian political thinkers reject utilitarian political ideals and turn instead to the ideals of social justice or political opportunity. To give a specific example, if we follow John Rawls in taking "justice" as "the first virtue of social institutions," then evaluating policies produced by those institutions will involve assessing the impact of particular policies on different people (or groups of people).[48] Rawls's theory of justice, like many others, concerns how society can achieve a fair or just allocation of the benefits of social and economic cooperation. However, in contrast to utilitarian political thought, and the goals of preference aggregation and maximization that justify the current economic approach to evaluating policies, Rawls is principally concerned with maximizing individual rather than aggregate good. In Rawls's theory of justice "Each member of society is thought to have an inviolability...which even the welfare of every one else cannot override."[49] From this perspective, a policy is not politically legitimate if it merely increases the total amount of satisfied preferences, for this may come at the cost of unacceptable losses that affect the separate lives of individual people.[50]

[46] See Graham Smith (2003:61–66) for a summary of the reasons why democratic deliberation offers a model of political practice that is environmentally appealing.

[47] See O'Neill et al. (2008:50–52). [48] Rawls (1971:3). [49] Rawls (1971:28).

[50] In this sense, the idea of justice has a great deal in common with individual rights, the protection of which also requires scrutiny at the individual level. However, in evaluating environmental policies, individual rights are less instructive than justice because individual rights cannot account for benefits that extend beyond the boundaries of what a person owns. Unlike privately owned goods, many environmental benefits are public goods, open to use (and depletion) by all members of society.

Like any plausible approach to justice, Rawls's theory recognizes that an account of individual well-being must refer to things besides people's subjective preferences, such as their actions, opportunities, and rights. Rawls's theory, however, does not go far enough in accounting for how the material and social context of human life determines the extent to which people realize these other dimensions of their well-being.[51] For this reason, the account of well-being that this book advances for assessing the natural environment's value and making environmental policy decisions refers to people's *capabilities* to do and achieve different things. A person's capabilities consist of various internal and external conditions of individual enablement that make up and therefore determine a person's real opportunities. They include basic material needs, such as adequate nutrition and shelter, as well as basic forms of social interaction, such as personal, social, and political affiliations. As I mentioned previously, economist Amartya Sen and philosopher Martha Nussbaum originally brought attention to the policy implications of defining human well-being in terms of people's capabilities to do and be different things, particularly by focusing economic thinking and decision-making tools used to address problems in international development policy.[52] Many of the ideas that they and others have developed in the literature I have referred to as "capabilities theory" have implications for improving the theory and practice of environmental policy, but few scholars (including Sen and Nussbaum) have considered these implications and none have done so systematically.[53]

My effort to bring the ideas and insights from capabilities theory to bear on evaluating and designing environmental policies will involve theorizing the relationship between people, nature, and social justice. This is necessary for developing a framework that is comprehensive and coherent in accounting for the importance of the natural environment to material and non-material dimensions of well-being, as well as to economic and non-economic social goals. In particular, the work of Sen and Nussbaum, as well others who are developing and applying their ideas, can improve how policy analysts define *what* environmental impacts matter and for *whom*. For the purpose of constructing a normative framework to guide the evaluation and design of environmental policy, capabilities theory is a starting point because it can address specific deficiencies in both a purely economic framework for evaluating

[51] See Holland (2008b) for this critique of Rawls.

[52] Chapter 3 provides an overview of Sen and Nussbaum's work.

[53] Not to overstate the case, in Chapter 4 I will discuss the extent to which Nussbaum and others do address the environmental dimensions of human capabilities. Nussbaum, for example, does defend certain personally meaningful relationships to nature as central to leading a minimally decent human life. More recently, she has also argued that her capabilities approach to justice can be applied to non-human animals such that their ends are recognized as among those that society should promote. For example, see Nussbaum (2006:325–407).

environmental policies and in the deliberative processes some propose for overcoming them.

With respect to the limitations of a purely economic framework, for several decades many ethical critiques of economic approaches to valuing resources have focused on elaborating and justifying nature's intrinsic value.[54] While the natural environment's intrinsic value is certainly something that economic valuation cannot accurately reflect, economic analysis also fails to accurately value nature's non-economic instrumental value. Specifically, because nature's non-economic instrumental value (e.g. its contribution to our experiences of family and culture, and our conditions of physical health and emotional well-being) is not fully valued or well supplied by economic markets, it is not accurately accounted for by the dominant economic approaches to valuing environmental resources.[55] Although various literatures in other disciplines elaborate and justify the importance of these non-economic dimensions of the environment's instrumental value, they have not produced a theoretical framework for capturing these values that is both generalizable and reproducible. I draw on capabilities theory to develop such a framework because the theory of well-being that it posits as fundamental to any theory of justice illuminates essential, non-economic dimensions of human life that proceed from the natural environment. Thus, as a framework for policy evaluation, the theory can make it possible to account for nature's instrumental value in a way that moves beyond assessing its contribution to the satisfaction of subjective preferences, while remaining sympathetic to the policy prescriptions that theorists of intrinsic value favor.

In addition to providing a better account of what environmental impacts matter, capabilities theory is also better than alternative frameworks at illuminating for whom those impacts are relevant. As I have previously discussed, in seeking to maximize net benefits, the currently dominant cost–benefit approach to evaluating environmental policies fails to address how a policy distributes the benefits and burdens a policy produces. Unfortunately, the most prominent liberal theories of justice—from which a framework for distributional evaluation might be constructed—provide an insufficient conceptual basis for correcting this problem because they have failed to recognize and theorize the role of nature as a basic condition of justice. As I argue in Chapter 5, contemporary efforts to green these theories remain encumbered by a conception of individual well-being that neglects the importance of various social and economic protections that enable basic civil and political freedoms.[56] In contrast, the capabilities theory that Sen,

[54] Early and influential pieces include Routley and Routley (1980), Rolston (1988), Callicott (1989, 1999).

[55] See O'Neill (1993, 2007), Norton (1986), and Holland (2006).

[56] See Miller (1999) and Bell (2004) for efforts to green liberal theories of justice.

Nussbaum, and others advance, relies on a conception of well-being that incorporates one's social and economic circumstance. This makes it possible for the theory to account for whether people are actually able to translate the things that they have into outcomes they value. Nussbaum's liberal theory of justice, in particular, recognizes the importance of defining justice in a way that gives equal importance to the social and economic protections that are necessary preconditions of civil and political freedoms. For my purpose, which concerns assessing the distributional implications of environmental protection, Nussbaum's focus on one's social and economic circumstance is especially important. Specifically, because the natural environment often has its most direct impact on these social and economic dimensions of individual well-being, Nussbaum's capabilities approach to justice provides a better theoretical framework for evaluating policies in a way that accounts for environmental inequities—that is, for who benefits and is burdened by environmental policies.

Capabilities theory is also relevant to problems that confront the deliberative processes that some scholars propose for overcoming these deficiencies in the dominant economic framework of policy evaluation and design. Those who wish to rely on democratic deliberation as a means to establish environmental policy focus on increasing the fairness and inclusivity of the decision-making processes from which environmental policies emerge. However, like efforts to achieve better environmental policies by improving economic methods of measurement, efforts to improve access and voice within deliberative political processes cannot promise that achieving this will produce socially just environmental policies. Especially in the area of environmental protection, which is plagued by problems of scientific complexity and uncertainty, even the most ideal deliberative processes can fail to produce outcomes that secure levels of environmental protection that a minimally decent life requires. This is an important reason why I argue (in Chapter 6) that the role of democratic deliberation and technical expertise must be recast in the context of an approach to environmental decision-making that checks the well-known pathologies of both. The theory of well-being that Sen and Nussbaum articulate can provide the basis for such an approach to decision-making because it reveals that the environmental protections at stake in democratic deliberation are often essential to the capabilities of populations affected by the resulting decisions. Thus, the capabilities (and their environmental preconditions) that define well-being also define what is necessary for ensuring the fairness of deliberative processes. Here, capabilities theory can help to advance justice as a politically legitimate normative ideal that requires protecting the environmental conditions that neither economic analysis nor the best forms of democratic deliberation can promise to secure.

To fully bring these advantages of capabilities theory to bear on evaluating and designing contemporary environmental policies, this book will elaborate the environmental dimensions of the theory of well-being that Sen and Nussbaum advance. In developing a normative framework for policy evaluation and design, the book will also show that assessing the impact of public policies on the environmental dimensions of people's capabilities will involve going beyond current economic analysis to systematically assess a wider range of policy outcomes, and to account for those outcomes in ways that will often defy monetization. Furthermore, evaluating these impacts with respect to the goal of social justice rather than economic efficiency will require accounting for the fundamental advantages and disadvantages that get conferred from interactions among people, particular environmental resources, and large-scale ecological processes that connect people in vastly different geographical places. I will show why policies that minimize the negative effects of these interactions serve goals of social justice. To prioritize these goals, even when democratic deliberation yields outcomes that conflict with them, is to protect the conditions of deliberation that a procedurally just democracy requires. In advancing a framework that can, in these ways, value and justify protecting the multiple ways in which the natural environment confers well-being, the book will show how capabilities theory can help to produce policies that create a more environmentally just society.

1.4 Synopsis of Chapters

The normative orientation of this project consists of two central arguments about the theory and practice of policy evaluation. First, I argue that the value of the natural environment should be understood in terms of a relationship between the natural environment and people's capabilities to do and achieve things. Second, I argue that a policy's contribution to society as a whole should be based on the extent to which a given policy will support or undermine the environmental conditions of social justice.

These two arguments provide a response to the problems of valuation and justification that arise in a purely economic approach to evaluating and designing environmental policies. Chapter 2 discusses these problems by reviewing the role subjective preferences play in the dominant economic approach to environmental valuation, and the role of economic efficiency as the criterion for establishing the social value of environmental policies. First, drawing on various critiques of current economic approaches to valuing resources through assessment of people's "willingness to pay" for environmental goods in the context of market exchange, I argue that people's subjective preferences are an insufficient basis for environmental valuation because they fail to account for or accurately represent important dimensions of well-being to which the environment makes crucial contributions. Here I highlight the conceptual and practical limitations of this approach, which erroneously treats the natural environment as an *object* of individual choice. Subsequent chapters address these limitations by outlining an alterative approach to resource valuation, one that treats the environment as a *basis* of choice.

Although my primary emphasis in Chapter 2 is on the problems with standard economic analysis of the environment, in recent years practitioners have sought to improve environmental valuation by turning to deliberative methods of value assessment, which endeavor to determine the environment's value in the context of communicative democratic processes rather than in the context of market exchange. These deliberative methods increase the range and accuracy of environmental valuation at the value-articulation stage of the valuation process, but I argue that they remain problematic in treating the environment as an object of choice, albeit of collective rather than individual choice.

Chapter 2 then turns to the problem of policy justification, first focusing on the priority that the current cost–benefit approach to evaluating environmental policies accords to economic efficiency as a social goal. Policies meeting goals of economic efficiency confront the same problems that have made utilitarian political thought an unattractive political ideal. Specifically, like utilitarianism, current policy analysis seeks to maximize the total or aggregate amount of some benefit or good that a policy (or government more generally) produces, regardless of how those aggregate gains are distributed among individual people. Consequently, policies justified with respect to the ideal of economic efficiency do not ensure equal consideration and protection of citizens' basic interests. The more recent deliberative approaches to valuation appeal to different political ideals, such as equality of political opportunity and procedural neutrality, but ultimately these ideals provide an insufficient justification for policies that protect the environment because they still monetize the environment's value so that policies can be evaluated in the standard cost–benefit framework. Furthermore, I argue that even if such deliberative assessments of environmental value were not forced into the monetary terms that CBA requires, we would still have reason to question them on distributive grounds. Specifically, democratic processes do not ensure that any particular conditions of substantive justice are met, and thus, they allow for an inequitable distribution of environmental protection. Public policies should be assessed with respect to goals of fairness and equitable treatment, acknowledging the environment's value as a basis of both individual and collective choice.[57]

[57] The book provides the most pointed response to these problems in Chapter 5 and Chapter 6. Chapter 5 responds to problems that challenge the utilitarian justification of policies

After problematizing current policy analysis with respect to how it values environmental resources and justifies environmental protection, Chapter 3 introduces Amartya Sen and Martha Nussbaum's "capabilities theory" as the basis for an alternative theoretical framework for thinking and reasoning about how the environment contributes to individual well-being and broader social goals. I explain how capabilities theory conceives of individual well-being and I consider the conceptual advantages of this view of well-being for valuing the environment and justifying environmental protection. Specifically, with respect to valuation, I argue that a capabilities-based conception of well-being expands the dimensions of human life to which environmental protection can be made relevant, while also contextualizing the environment's role as a basis of individual choice. This can provide a more accurate account of the environment's non-economic instrumental value.

With respect to policy justification, this view of well-being can reveal the channels through which environmental policies have disproportionate impacts on different people. For this reason, a capabilities-based conception of well-being lends itself to assessing a policy's distributional impact, and thus, a policy's implications for social justice rather than for economic efficiency. Respectively, these advantages provide the reasons why we should value the environment in terms of its contribution to human capabilities, and why we should assess the distributional implications of environmental policies by assessing their impact on the various capabilities that make up different people's overall capability to function and flourish as human beings. These arguments about environmental valuation and policy justification are developed further in Chapter 4 and Chapter 5, respectively.

Building on Chapter 3's argument for why we should value the environment's contribution to human capabilities, Chapter 4 more fully theorizes a capabilities approach to environmental valuation by addressing *what* to value with respect to the environment when we assess its instrumental contributions to human capabilities. This involves considering the many ways and levels at which the environment contributes to the irreducibly plural dimensions of human well-being that human capabilities define. Central to my discussion of these instrumental contributions is the idea that human capabilities should be understood in the context of ecological systems and interactions that provide important goods and ecosystem services to people. These systems and interactions tie humans together because it is through them that one person's activities that impact an environmental good or ecosystem service can degrade the environment in ways that undermine another

as economically efficient. Chapter 6 responds to the democratic justifications that have been claimed to underlie the current economic approach to valuing and making decisions about the management of environmental resources.

person's capabilities. In this context I argue that protecting human capabilities requires protection of an "ecological meta-capability" that includes the broad contribution of an ecologically functioning natural environment to individual well-being. An ecological meta-capability refers to the ecological conditions that make humans capable of living a decent and dignified human life. Chapter 4 conceptualizes this ecological meta-capability as a human capability that makes it possible for people to pursue the various activities and achievements that capability theorists seek to protect. For this reason, including it in the capabilities-based conception of well-being can improve capabilities theory as a theory of well-being and make it more applicable to the central question of environmental valuation, which is *what to value.*

Chapter 4 then takes up the question of how to value the environment when it is understood as a meta-capability of humans. Here I propose a process of environmental valuation that separates the task of value identification from the task of value measurement. While the former task of value identification requires citizens to specify the abstract list of human capabilities that Nussbaum proposes as central to a good human life, the latter task of value measurement is more in the domain of experts, who must assess how changes in environmental quality (resulting from environmental policies) will impact these specified capabilities. Here, environmental valuation should provide a systematic and empirically verifiable account of a policy's relative impact on different people. Toward this end, I argue that a capabilities approach to environmental valuation can compare a policy's impact on different people with respect to distinct capabilities, but it cannot (and should not) seek to make these impacts commensurable across the different capabilities of different people.

Having proposed that we should value the environment in terms of its contribution to human capabilities (in Chapter 3), and *what* this requires valuing with respect to the environment (in Chapter 4), Chapter 5 addresses how we should justify environmental protection as a social goal. I argue, specifically, that we should value certain environmental protections as preconditions of social justice. I make this argument by building on Nussbaum's "capabilities approach" to justice. Nussbaum's capabilities approach offers an account of what justice requires in the context of social, political, and economic institutions that organize a liberal democratic society, and why such a society should pursue justice as a social goal. The theory of justice I develop from Nussbaum incorporates her philosophical commitment to human dignity and to providing a threshold level of capability protection for each person that due respect to human dignity would require.

However, because Nussbaum has not fully theorized how environmental conditions relate to human capabilities, I assume the account of environmental value elaborated in Chapter 4 to develop Nussbaum's theory of justice in a way that requires protecting the environmental preconditions necessary for maintaining (a threshold level of) human capabilities. Here I argue that when the capability *thresholds* that Nussbaum seeks to protect as constitutional guarantees are understood in the context of large-scale ecological interactions that span across vast geographical spaces, Nussbaum's theory of justice also requires establishing capability *ceilings*. Specifically, these ceilings should be defined partly in terms of the limits of ecological systems (or "ecological thresholds") and they are necessary for determining politically legitimate tradeoffs that must be made when protecting one person's capabilities degrades the environmental conditions that are necessary for protecting a threshold level of another person's capabilities. Applying this theoretical framework to an analysis of clean air policy, Chapter 5 explores the distributive implications of what respect for human dignity requires in the provision of environmental protection.

In Chapter 6 I return to the broader trend toward process-based decision-making in environmental policy that I have discussed in this introductory chapter. Here I explore how a capabilities approach to evaluating and designing environmental policies can address problems that arise in contemporary administrative rulemaking, which often entail devolving decisions about policy implementation to a regional or local level, where stakeholders can engage in deliberation and collaboration about how to manage the relevant resources. This "deliberative" or "collaborative" response to what many perceive as an overly technocratic (i.e. expert-driven) and often economistic approach to making environmental decisions at the federal level gives rise to important procedural problems that a capabilities approach can address. In particular, these more localized approaches to making decisions at the ecosystem-scale can produce outcomes that undermine the environmental conditions that are necessary for protecting human dignity, and that are necessary for participation in the environmental decisions determining one's well-being.

To address such problems, I use the account of justice developed in Chapter 5 to develop a "capabilities approach to regulatory rulemaking," which I refer to as a CARR. The CARR is a model for making decisions in the administrative context of policy implementation. Like the approach to environmental valuation that I develop in Chapter 4, it remains committed to providing substantive protections to citizens, but it also incorporates a commitment to democratic processes, particularly for the purpose of determining why the environment is valuable to people, and therefore what level of environmental protection is necessary for ensuring people are capable of leading the kind of lives that liberal democratic societies seek to put within a person's reach. The approach to administrative rulemaking I propose involves recasting the role of citizens and experts in environmental decision-making. While experts are necessary for defining how it is that a given policy outcome will undermine the capabilities of citizens, citizens must work with experts to specify the content of the capabilities that a given policy outcome threatens. In this context I argue that the CARR can and sometimes should operate as a mechanism for *determining* policy outcomes rather than simply as a mechanism for *generating information* that can inform public and political debate about acceptable levels of environmental protection.

The final chapter of the book, Chapter 7, summarizes the basic ideas of the capabilities approach to evaluating and designing environmental policies developed in the preceding chapters and then considers how the approach might be further theorized for application to questions of policy at the international level, focusing on questions of justice arising in the current discussion of global climate change. Thus, although this book addresses environmental policy from a domestic perspective, the capabilities approach to social and environmental justice I advance has advantages for addressing environmental problems that require collective action at the international level. I argue, first, that it can provide a framework for defining how carbon emissions shares ought to be allocated among parties to a global climate agreement. Second, I argue that in a more applied context, the capabilities approach to social and environmental justice might be combined productively with the procedural account of capabilities justice advanced by David Schlosberg. This would entail incorporating forms of expert accountability into the mapping and design of climate adaptation policies in highly varied local contexts. Third, I argue that the philosophical grounding of the capabilities approach in a notion of human fellowship and cooperation rather than self-interest and mutual advantage provides a compelling basis for a theory of global climate justice. Furthermore, if this theory includes the ecological meta-capability theorized in Chapter 4, then it can also overcome certain deficiencies in the theories of global justice advanced by John Rawls and Charles Beitz, as well as the theory of climate justice advanced by Steven Vanderheiden.

Finally, throughout the book, I clarify ideas and arguments by applying them to actual or hypothetical policies regulating environmental quality. Chapter 3 and Chapter 5 demonstrate the salutary effect the proposed approach to policy evaluation would have on public decisions about air quality. Chapter 6 focuses on land-use management policy, a context in which ecosystem-based management is commonly used. In many single instances I refer to the implications of the ideas and arguments for water quality and natural resource management more generally. Before turning to these specific areas of policy, let us first consider limitations in the currently dominant economic approach to policy evaluation, which gives rise to the alternative approach I develop in later chapters of this book.

2

Valuation, Justification, and Participation in Contemporary Environmental Policy

2.1 Introduction

Valuing environmental resources and justifying their protection are central features of contemporary environmental policy analysis. Generally speaking, policy analysis, or policy evaluation (as I will also refer to it), entails assessing a proposed or existing public policy for the purpose of determining whether government ought to adopt or implement it. When the subject of this assessment is a policy that protects the environment, the evaluation must provide an account of what is valuable about the protection provided and why that protection is justifiable as a political goal. Questions concerning *what* to value and *why* are therefore implicit in contemporary thinking and reasoning about environmental protection. Different approaches to policy analysis will answer these questions in different ways and, consequently, they will introduce different information into the various political and administrative decisions that shape policy design and implementation. For instance, if the approach to policy analysis assumes that achieving an economically efficient allocation of resources is the reason why an environmental policy is valuable, then the analysis will require information about the environment's value as commodity for which consumers are willing to pay a price. Such an analysis may ignore or inaccurately represent other information about what is valuable, such as the environment's contribution to activities and experiences that go on outside market interactions; for example, in the context of people's culture, family, religion, emotional experiences, and so on. Because different approaches to evaluating policies can, in this way, shape what legislators and administrators understand and treat as relevant to policy decisions, the political legitimacy of the policies these evaluations support hinges on their success in relating the value of environmental protection to justifiable political goals.

This chapter problematizes current approaches to evaluating environmental policies in order to set the stage for introducing capabilities theory—and especially an expanded version of Martha Nussbaum's capabilities approach to justice—as an alternative theoretical framework for valuing the environment and justifying its protection. In identifying the problems that challenge current forms of policy analysis, I focus on the themes of environmental valuation and policy justification. I argue, first, that an approach to valuing the environmental resources and conditions policies protect should treat the environment as a *basis* of individual choice. By this I mean that we should understand the natural environment as a condition of human life and political action. Its basic ecological functioning should be viewed as a necessary context from which human choice proceeds. As such, components of ecological processes are objectively valuable regardless of the subjective views of individual valuers. This view of the environment contrasts with current approaches to environmental valuation that treat the environment as an *object* of individual or collective choice. As an object of choice, the natural environment can have a highly variable value, depending on the values individual people subjectively ascribe to it. I argue, second, that environmental policies should be justified with respect to their actual impact on individual people, and specifically, on the potential for people to pursue and achieve the kind of lives that liberal democratic societies aim to make possible.[1] Furthermore, I argue that policy should be justified with respect to this goal independent of whether it also meets standards of economic efficiency or emerges from democratic decision-making processes. Thus, by critiquing current approaches to evaluating policies, my overall aim in the present chapter is to lay the basis for proposing a capabilities approach to environmental valuation and policy justification in the chapters that follow. As a theory of justice that can be applied to value the environment and justify its protection through government intervention, the capabilities approach has distinct advantages as an alternative and more comprehensive approach to policy design and evaluation.

In this chapter I will proceed as follows. In Section 2.2 I explain how the dominant economic approach to policy analysis values the environment and justifies its protection. Section 2.3 takes up the topic of environmental valuation, explaining how standard economic valuation treats the environment as an object of individual choice, and why this provides an insufficient account of environmental value. Section 2.4 considers the contemporary alternative to standard economic valuation, which is known as "deliberative

[1] In treating environmental valuation as a matter of individual choice, for present purposes I am setting aside—but not denying—the environment's value as a condition of community or collective choice.

monetary valuation," and addresses why its treatment of the environment as an object of collective (rather than individual) choice also remains insufficient as a method of accounting for environmental value. In the remainder of the chapter, I then turn to the topic of policy justification. Section 2.5 problematizes efforts to justify the dominant economic approach to policy evaluation as an instantiation of utilitarian political ideals, and focuses particularly on the distributional inequities that this justification neglects to address. In Section 2.6 I then address efforts to justify contemporary policy evaluation in relation to aggregative and deliberative theories of democracy, and I argue that these justifications remain limited on both procedural and substantive grounds.

2.2 Environmental Valuation and Policy Justification in Current Practice

Environmental valuation refers to the process or method by which a particular kind and/or quantity of value is ascribed to an environmental resource that a given policy will protect.[2] For instance, a policy might protect a wetland, a river, or a park by putting constraints on the use of a particular place where these resources are found. Likewise, a policy might protect a particular resource (e.g. a river's water) or environmental media (e.g. air quality) according to an updated regulatory standard by lowering the amount of permitted pollution that can be emitted into it. In order to evaluate such policies, policy analysts will have to determine what is valuable about changes in the quantity or quality of environmental protection provided. While many environmental laws reference and adopt secondary standards that establish specific protections for plant life and other non-human components of the natural environment, the primary standards, and those that dominate the political debate, are those that protect people.[3] For this reason, environmental valuation, as I discuss it here, will concern what is valuable about human relationships to the natural environment. Different approaches to environmental valuation define (or permit the definition of) what is valuable about these relationships in different ways, and consequently, the approach that

[2] For an introduction and overview of environmental valuation as currently practiced, see the chapter on "Valuing Concern for Nature" in Turner, Pearce, and Bateman (1993:108–128), and the chapter on "Valuing Impacts through Surveys" in Boardman et al. (2001:358–390).

[3] For example, the Clean Air Act requires the Environmental Protection Agency to set National Ambient Air Quality Standards for pollutants that are harmful to public health and the environment. The Clean Air Act's "primary standards" set limits on pollution that are intended to protect the public health of people, while its "secondary standards" set limits that protect public welfare more broadly conceived, including protection against decreased visibility, damage to animals, crops, vegetation, and buildings. See, 40 C.F.R. Part 50.

policy analysis adopts will significantly influence what views about the value of environmental protection will get considered and factored into policy decisions.

In contrast to the topic of environmental valuation, the topic of policy justification concerns why the account of value emerging from a particular approach to environmental valuation is justifiable to broader society as a political goal. At the level of policy justification, the important issue is not what is valuable to people about the natural environment, but rather why a policy protecting the environment should be understood as worthwhile to the many individuals that make up society as a collective endeavor. The justification for an environmental policy will vary depending on the collective goals and purposes that a given approach to policy analysis assumes.[4] For instance, if an approach to policy analysis assumes that the goal of public policy is to produce government actions that mimic interactions occurring in private markets, then policies that achieve an economically efficient allocation of resources will be treated as politically justifiable. In contrast, if an approach to policy analysis assumes that the goal of public policy is to produce government actions that reflect a consensus among citizens that emerges from citizens' reasoned deliberation and reflection, then policies tracking this consensus will be treated as politically justifiable.[5]

Both of these kinds of justifications for environmental protection are implicit in the approaches and methods that policy analysts currently use. For example, cost–benefit analysis, or CBA, which is the currently dominant approach to policy analysis, evaluates policies based on the extent to which they demonstrate that government actions will mimic the "efficiency" of the free market.[6] From the economic point of view that CBA adopts, most environmental resources are "public goods," which means they are open to use by all members of society but not priced by normal mechanisms of private ownership.[7] As unpriced goods, the market's allocation of environmental resources through the free interplay of supply and demand does not fend off

[4] While there may be a plurality of policy justifications for protecting the environment, here I emphasize the political justifications that provide the rational for normatively legitimate government action.

[5] Section 2.6 and Section 2.7 of this chapter discuss both of these approaches to policy justification, respectively.

[6] Several environmental laws and executive orders require or authorize agencies to complete these analyses. For example, the Toxic Control Act of 1976, the Federal Insecticide, Fungicide, and Rodenticide Act of 1972, and the 1996 Safe Drinking Water Act currently authorize CBA. Beginning with Jimmy Carter, presidents in the United States have issued and/or upheld executive orders requiring CBA as part of the "regulatory impact assessments" (RIAs) that the president's Office of Management and Budget requires federal agencies to complete when they plan to promulgate new and expensive environmental rules. For this characterization of CBA as seeking to produce government actions that mimic the interactions of the free market, see Gillroy and Wade (1992:7).

[7] See Turner, Pearce, and Bateman (1993:25–26).

threats to their underproduction and non-sustainability, ultimately leading to market failure.[8] Environmental economists admit that government intervention through policy is necessary to correct such problems, thereby allocating environmental resources to their most highly valued uses, and maximizing overall social welfare.[9] In this context CBA is a tool for evaluating whether government intervention through particular policies will achieve this maximizing goal. It does this, first, by pricing currently unpriced environmental goods, and, second, by assessing whether the aggregate prices that people are willing to pay for environmental protection of particular resources outweighs the aggregate economic costs resulting from a policy providing this protection.[10] Policies for which aggregate benefits outweigh aggregate costs are treated as economically efficient in the sense that those who benefit from a policy could pay off or compensate those who the policy burdens, such that there are net gains remaining. When policies produce these gains, they can be supported by the claim that if environmental resources were priced and exchanged, people would be motivated to exchange them in ways that result in the same allocation of resources that the policy does in fact produce. In other words, policies that pass a cost–benefit test by producing net benefits are justifiable as a form of government intervention because they achieve what markets under more ideal circumstances would produce.

While this economic goal that CBA adopts is the subject of much controversy, the particular way CBA measures the policy benefits it seeks to maximize is also contentious. Specifically, CBA defines the value of environmental goods that policies protect in terms of the prices people are willing to pay for these goods in real or hypothetical markets.[11] With respect to the former, valuation techniques that provide a "true" measure of individual welfare attempt to capture individuals' revealed or expressed preferences as a way of gauging how citizens themselves view the worth of a resource. In some economic valuation methods, policy analysts look at an individual's *actual market behavior* to determine their "willingness to pay" (WTP) for an environmental resource.[12] For example, a policy analyst might determine the value of clean air by considering differences in the prices people pay for property in areas that are subject to different levels of air pollution but otherwise similar.[13] Policy analysts can also make this

[8] See Farley (2008). [9] See Turner, Pearce, and Bateman (1993:77–81).

[10] Formally, this condition is referred to as Kaldor–Hicks efficiency, which I discuss in further detail later in this chapter. For a general overview of CBA see Turner, Pearce, and Bateman (1993:93–107).

[11] See Turner, Pearce, and Bateman (1993:94–96).

[12] Although "willingness to accept" (WTA) values are often assumed to be more accurate or valid than WTP values, for the purpose of providing a general characterization of economic environmental valuation I will refer only to WTP in characterizing a person's monetary valuation of the relevant resource.

[13] Here analysts must try to hold all other influences on the price of property constant, such that the only way in which the homes differ is in the quality of air that surrounds them. Since the

kind of indirect estimate by considering the expenditures households save on services such as laundry, cleaning, building upkeep, health care, and so on, in neighborhoods with cleaner air or water. Similarly, since people do not pay for national parks, analysts can indirectly estimate the value of the recreational benefit of parks by looking at how much people pay in travel costs to get to park locations.[14] In each of these instances, the "market-based" valuation technique bases the monetary value of a resource on actual choices people make.

In contrast, other kinds of economic valuation techniques rely on a person's *hypothetical market choices* to determine what she is willing to pay for a resource. For example, a survey questionnaire might present the value of clean air in terms of different hypothetical prices from which a person can select the one that best represents its worth to her; more open-ended questions ask people to come up with their own monetary figure, rather than select one among predefined options.[15] In addition to these ways of measuring the *use* value of environmental resources, policy analysts also rely on hypothetical market choices to determine "option" and "existence" values. The option value of a resource is the maximum amount (above use value) a person would be willing to pay to ensure he will have access to an environmental amenity at some date in the future.[16] In contrast, the existence value of a resource is the amount a person is willing to pay to preserve a resource that she has no intent to use, ever. For example, existence value might reflect the value non-users put on a resource because they benefit from the pleasure of another person or future generation's access to it. Thus, while some market valuation techniques attempt to calculate the amount individual people do pay or would pay to *use* a resource, other techniques—that is, those assessing option and existence values—attempt to determine the monetary worth of a resource's *non-use* value to people living today, perhaps because they wish to preserve a resource for people living in the future.[17] Environmental value in this latter context expands the use value of a resource to include the intertemporal value of both use and non-use of a resource.

These forms of economic valuation make it possible for CBA to directly translate information about individual people's willingness to pay for environmental resources into an estimate of a policy's overall social value. Determining social value simply involves adding-up (or aggregating) what each individual is willing to pay, and then situating these benefits within

houses typically differ in many ways, it can be difficult to isolate the effect of air quality on property prices. See Turner, Pearce, and Bateman (1993:120) and Ward and Duffield (1992:247–56).

[14] This is referred to as a "hedonic pricing method"; see Turner, Pearce, and Bateman (1993:116–120) and Smith and Kaoru (1990).

[15] See Turner, Pearce, and Bateman (1993:122).

[16] See Turner, Pearce, and Bateman (1993:113).

[17] See Menell and Stewart (1994:83 and 1192).

the broader balancing framework of CBA by comparing them to a policy's aggregate costs, which generally refer to the amount of money it will cost the regulated industries to comply with the policy.[18] If policy analysts are using survey methods of valuation to construct hypothetical markets, characterizing the overall value of a resource requires calculating the average WTP among (surveyed) respondents and then multiplying this by the total number of people that use or access the resource.[19] To complete the calculation of a policy's "net social value"—and hence, determine whether and to what extent it will achieve goals of economic efficiency—the costs are subtracted from the benefits or the benefits are subtracted from costs (depending on which is lesser).[20] The resulting estimate provides the basis for comparing one policy to alternative policy options or to the option of pursuing no policy intervention.

While the logic and advantages of this approach to policy analysis may be straightforward, CBA has been the subject of much criticism, refinement, and overall debate concerning the nature and purpose of environmental protection. With respect to the valuation component, critics have challenged how CBA both defines environmental value and quantifies its worth to individual people and broader society. Consequently, in more recent years, alternative methods of defining and quantifying environmental values have been developed; however, as I discuss in this chapter and those that follow, these alternatives remain limited in some significant ways. With respect to the justification component of CBA, critics have challenged its implicit commitment to utilitarian political ideals, as well as the viability of proposed alternatives to CBA that are modeled on democratic politics. Consequently, although policies bearing the stamp of democratic approval may appear to have a compelling justification, I argue that more substantive justification is necessary where environmental matters are concerned. In the remainder of this chapter I will discuss these problems of valuation and justification in turn. My goal is to bring out reasons why policy analysis should value the environment as a basis of individual choice and why it should justify protecting it on instrumental grounds—as a condition of social justice—independent of whether doing so is also economically efficient or agreed upon in the context of democratic decision-making procedures.

[18] In theory, the costs that analysts include in a policy analysis can range widely. Jaffe et al. (1995:139) provide a taxonomy, but explain that "most analysts...would identify the capital and operating expenditures associated with regulatory compliance as the fundamental part of the overall costs of the regulation." The US Congressional Budget Office (CBO) (1985) explains problems that challenge the measurement of compliance costs for environmental regulations.

[19] See Turner, Pearce, and Bateman (1993:122).

[20] See Boardman et al. (2001:7–17) for a more detailed overview of the post-monetizing steps involved in CBA, such as discounting costs and benefits and performing a sensitivity analysis.

2.3 Valuing the Environment as an Object of Individual Choice

A key feature of economic valuation as conducted in standard CBA is that it defines what is valuable in terms of the subjective preferences people reveal in market choices. As discussed in Section 2.2, the practical goal of economic valuation is to determine what people are willing to pay for environmental protection in the context of real or hypothetical market exchange. When people select a price they are willing to pay for use, access to, or protection of a particular environmental good, CBA assumes they indicate whether and by how much the protection of that good serves the ends or aims that define their well-being. Preferences, in this context, stand as proxies for individual ends or aims, connecting environmental resources to the choices people value.[21] A central advantage of structuring environmental valuation in this way is that it gets people to reduce complex judgments about why they value those particular ends or aims into a choice that reflects the environment's value to whatever a person values most among the available options. Thus understood, the environment is an object of individual choice that may or may not serve a person's purposes.

The problem with this understanding of environmental value is that it disregards the environment's value as a basis of individual choice—that is, as a condition of human choosing, and therefore, as more objectively valuable than what people's subjective preferences may reveal when they are making choices among fungible goods. By objectively valuable, I do not mean to suggest that the environment has intrinsic value as an end in itself, independent of its worth to humans.[22] Establishing various components of the environment as the subject of intrinsic value has been one prevalent response to the narrowly instrumental approach to environmental valuation on which CBA relies. Instead of treating the environment as a means to human ends, intrinsic value theorists assert the environment's value as an end in its own right, independent of its relation to other things people value.[23] This provides a compelling alternative to economic valuation at the level of ethical theory, but its impact on policy remains limited due to the practical implication of adopting a principle to respect forms of non-human life and systems. As

[21] Richardson (2002:121) and Anderson (1993:193); Taylor (1981) presents the opposing view, which is that features of the non-human natural environment are intrinsically valuable, independent of people's subjective valuations.

[22] Following Trainor (2006:4), I do not understand the environment's value as an objective property that inheres in resources, broader ecological systems, or "nature."

[23] While biocentrists focus on the intrinsic value of non-human things that are the "subject of a life," ecocentrists seek to establish the intrinsic value of both living and non-living components of the non-human world that make up whole ecological systems; see Taylor (1981) and Leopold (1949:201–226), respectively.

Kenneth Goodpaster puts it, the operational problem with such a principle is that "one cannot *live* according to it."[24] Because an important component of the present project is to advance a more applicable alternative to economic valuation, my reference to the environment's objective value should not be understood as a reference to its intrinsic value. Rather, by objective value, I mean that the environment has instrumental value that is independent of both what people happen to know about it and therefore reveal in their subjective preferences, and of the non-ideal circumstances to which people's subjective preferences may adapt.

Characterizing the environment's value in this way, as something that is partly independent of people's knowledge and circumstance, is important because these two factors can make people's subjective preferences unreliable as indicators of what contributes to the ends or purposes that define their well-being. As background to this point, it is important to understand that the modern theory of neoclassical economics on which economic environmental valuation is based makes two important assumptions that bear on the role and definition of preferences in policy analysis. First, it assumes that individuals know what is best for them and that they have sovereignty over all judgments regarding their self-interest.[25] Here, a person's preferences explain her choices; they are like desires that combine with a person's beliefs to provide an explanation of her action.[26] It follows that the preferences people reveal in choices provide an account of people's values that can claim to be grounded in people's own thoughts and judgments, telling us (as I have mentioned earlier in this chapter) about the ends that people value given how they conceive of their interests, well-being, goals, and so on. Second, modern neoclassical economic theory assumes that people act rationally and that their preferences are consistent, such that if a person prefers option *a* over option *b*, and option *b* over option *c*, then the person prefers option *a* to option *c*.[27] Here the relevant assumption is not that a person's preference explain her choices, but rather that her preferences are simply revealed in them. Preferences, therefore, allow us to study patterns of individual behavior, even if they do not convey a psychological reality explaining what a person thinks is best.[28]

Both of these assumptions about individual preferences are questionable, giving us reason to interrogate their role in environmental valuation. The second assumption, that preferences are consistent and reflect rational

[24] Goodpaster (1978:324). [25] Mishan (1982:33).

[26] See Nussbaum (2000a:120), who links this conception of what a preference is to the writings of Gary Becker and Amartya Sen.

[27] See O'Neill (1998:35).

[28] See Nussbaum (2000a:119), who links this conception of what a preference is to the writings of Paul Samuelson, John Hicks, and more generally, to the behaviorist movement in psychology.

action, treats a person's preferences as indistinguishable from a person's actions. Specifically, in assuming that choices are rational actions revealing well-ordered preferences, the theory that underlies economic valuation provides no basis for understanding whether patterns of behavior that appear irrational and inconsistent—thus contradicting the theory—really are so.[29] Making sense of patterns of behavior people exhibit will, therefore, require reference to something besides what people choose, such as the "objectives or values" that people are pursuing when they make choices.[30] Of course, if this kind of information is really what is necessary for understanding what matters to people, then it is unclear why preferences should provide the basis for assessing environmental value in the first place.

With respect to the first assumption about preferences, here the problem is that preferences are understood as providing information about what people subjectively perceive as relevant and valuable to their own well-being. Although preferences may reveal a person's subjective perspective, both cognitive limitations and a lack of information lead people to make mistakes about what is good for them.[31] This is especially the case when we are talking about complicated environmental processes, about which people have little information and knowledge.[32] For instance, a person with allergenic skin sensitivity to the sun or plants may express a low willingness to pay for a policy protecting a park, simply because she has no intention to use it for recreational purposes. However, due to the park's role in broader ecological dynamics, it may provide many additional benefits that are valuable in contributing to ecological conditions that support human life, such as sequestering carbon, stabilizing soil, recharging groundwater, and so on. If a person lacks information and knowledge about the park's role with respect to these broader ecological conditions, her willingness to pay for the park's protection will reflect only a portion of the park's actual instrumental value to her.

Thus, a crucial problem with economic valuation of the environment is that it treats the environment as a matter of mere preference, when in fact, the resources it assesses are bound up with and contributing to broader ecological relationships that are much more central to human well-being than people's subjective preferences are likely to reveal. What matters here is not

[29] See Sen (1982a, 1982b). [30] See Nussbaum (2000a:120) and Sen (1982b).

[31] See Spash and Hanley (1995). Sophisticated defenses of preference-based accounts of individual welfare therefore link individual welfare to what people would in fact value if they were competent to make the required judgments and be fully informed. See Brandt (1979), Griffin (1986), Harsanyi (1996). O'Neill (1998:47–49) and Johansson-Stenman (2002:112–115) for brief arguments opposing these efforts to defend preference-based accounts of welfare.

[32] See Arrow and Costanza (1995:520–521) explaining that, on average, people do not understand the importance of scientific matters such as the resilience of entire ecological systems; also see Spash and Hanley (1995) for data suggesting that people lack an understanding of even basic ecological concepts such as biodiversity.

just that the ecological relationships to which a park contributes determine whether a person will have a park for recreation, although the value people ascribe to the park when they express their WTP for its recreational purposes may indeed fail to account for the park's broader ecological value to their own conditions. More important in the present context is that the ecological relationships to which the park contributes also determine whether a person will have a stable climate, drinkable water, a home that is safe from flooding, and at the broadest or most primary level, an ecological context that creates the possibility for human and other forms of life.[33] These ecological contributions to human life are crucial components of the park's instrumental value, but they are contributions that people may not even treat as relevant to questions of valuation when they are asked about willingness to pay for the use of it. In short, when policy analysts measure the market value of easily bounded environmental resources (e.g. trees, parks) without accounting for their ecological contribution at this primary level of life support, they can end up with *partial* (or even arbitrary) valuations—that is, valuations that do not account for a particular resource's value as part of a larger life support system.[34]

Before further elaborating this problem, it is important to highlight the overriding point: what economic valuation studies fail to capture is that particular sections or components of the natural environment for which these studies seek to establish a subjectively determined price have a connection to human well-being that precedes individual choice. The environment makes objectively good contributions to well-being because its various components contribute to a set of ecological relationships providing the basic conditions for humans and other forms of organic life on which humans are also dependent. It is by virtue of this connection that the environment should be understood as a condition from which human choice proceeds—that is, as basis of individual choice, not merely an object of individual choice. However, treating the environment and its components as something that makes objectively good contributions to human well-being is not something that economic valuation can easily accomplish. Part of the problem, as I have

[33] Odum (1993) explains the functional interactions among organisms, processes, and resources in the environment that provide the "life-supporting ecosystem" that is of primary value to humans.

[34] See Brauman et al. (2007:69) and d' Arge (1994). In making a related point, Vatn and Bromley (1994:137) argue that ecological systems involve webs of "functional relations between different entities" that are not "precisely demarcated" objects and therefore defy "precise valuation." O'Neill and Spash (2000:527) also discuss the difficulty of separating resources (as distinct units) from functional ecological relations. Scholars such as van den Bergh and van der Straaten (1994:224) explain this problem by analogy to market relationships: just as one cannot calculate the price of a good in a market interaction without knowing the prices of all other interdependent goods, one cannot determine the price of one element of an ecological system without determining the prices of all the interdependent elements of an ecological system.

suggested earlier in this chapter, is that economic valuation seeks to base environmental value on people's subjective preferences, and people's subjective preferences may be highly uninformed about how a particular component of the environment, such as a wetland, contributes to broader and crucial ecological relationships. These relationships, as I have discussed, are difficult for people to comprehend and absorb because they are dynamic, long term, continuous, and involve multiple scales and complicated feedback loops.[35]

Also problematic to economic valuation of the environment is the highly adaptive nature of people's subjective preferences. By this I mean that both what people value and how much they value it can be determined by largely lived experiences that deny them an effective opportunity to develop preferences for things that make objective contributions to their well-being.[36] This problem has much to do with what Cass Sunstein refers to as the "phenomenon of endogenous preferences." As Sunstein explains, people's preferences often are not "fixed and stable" in the way that economic analysis assumes. Rather they "adapt to a wide range of factors—including the context in which the preference is expressed, the existing legal rules, current information, past consumption choices, and culture in general."[37] In the context of environmental valuation, the problem of adaptive preferences most relevant here is that even if people attain information about how the environment contributes to their life in ecologically important ways, their preferences may still adapt in ways that lead them to disregard this contribution, simply because by doing so they are responding to broader social norms, or are better able to cope with circumstances they experience as threatening or beyond their control.

A prime example of this problem occurs when residents in low-income communities are offered jobs at highly polluting facilities located near their homes. Some of these residents may register a low valuation for the level of environmental quality that would prevail in their own community if the polluting facilities were located elsewhere, suggesting that the polluting facility has what residents consider to be a negligible environmental impact. However, the low valuation may be due to residents' experience of

[35] See Cowling et al. (2008:9485).

[36] The literature on adaptive preferences is vast. In the present context I am focusing on how opportunity and (unjust) circumstance shape people's preferences, although there are many additional reasons why the economic assumption that people's preferences are stable and fixed can be brought into question. For instance, specific to environmental valuation, individual expressions of willingness to pay are sensitive to both the context in which willingness to pay survey questions are asked and the respondents' views of their social importance; see Schkade and Payne (1994) and Schuman (1996). Likewise, Slovic (1995) and Vatn (2004) have shown that the environmental values people express are sensitive to how the relevant issue is framed and the information to which the process of valuation brings attention.

[37] See Sunstein (1993:164).

a level of basic deprivation so extreme that having a job (even one that will increase one's health problems) is more immediately crucial than maintaining cleaner air or water.[38] Put differently, if some residents of such communities think it is politically impossible to have both economic opportunities and a healthy environment, they may reveal preferences that undervalue the latter. Preferences that are born of such extreme vulnerability are adaptive in the sense that they reflect what a person tells herself in order to cope with an unjust situation, not what a person would want under conditions of genuine autonomy.[39] To the extent that people's preferences are adaptive in this way, or uninformed, as I have explained earlier in this chapter, the values they express through their willingness to pay may be irrational and inconsistent with their ultimate ends or aims in life.[40] Most important to my purposes here, a person's subjective preferences may not reflect the environment's objective ecological contribution to human well-being, as a condition from which human life, health, and choice proceeds.

Ecological economists—broadly defined as a group of scholars attempting to integrate ecology and economics—provide one powerful response to the general failure of economic valuation to account for the ways in which particular environmental resources are bound up with broader ecological conditions that support human well-being.[41] To capture this kind of environmental value, ecological economists have established "natural capital" as distinct from human-made capital but of crucial importance to economic activity. Specifically, natural capital is the stock of earth's natural ecosystems, which produces a flow of ecosystem goods and services. For instance, natural capital yields both particular goods, such as timber for building and wood for fuel, as well as services such as carbon sequestration, water purification and recharge, nutrient cycling, and soil protection and regeneration.[42] These ecosystem goods and services are dependent on ecosystems that function as a whole, which requires that they have a certain structure and diversity. To ensure their continued provisions, ecological economists therefore focus on

[38] See Shrader-Frechette (2002:58–59), who characterizes choices made under such threats of serious harm as non-voluntary or compulsory.

[39] See Sen (1985a:191) as well as Elster (1983), Sen (1987a:10–12, 1990), and Sunstein (1993:162–194) for a discussion of the problem of adaptive preferences. In light of the tendency for people to adapt their preferences to fit their circumstances, we might also follow Sunstein (1993:177) in questioning the subjective preferences of a person who lacks an interest in visiting a natural park for even aesthetic or recreational reasons; these preferences may simply be the result of the person's lived experience in highly industrialized urban areas that provide no opportunities to experience non-industrialized nature as an escape from the danger and chaos of urban life.

[40] As Bullard (1993:201) notes, "it is usually a community's business and political elites (not ordinary residents of the community) who seek waste facilities as an economic development program."

[41] See Prugh (1995) for a highly accessible introduction to the basic ideas in the field of ecological economics. See Liu et al. (2010) for an historical account of the field of ecological economics.

[42] See Folke et al. (1994:4).

issues such as the *scale* of the economy relative to the ecological conditions that sustain it, and the *volume* of materials flowing from the environment through the economy and back to the environment as waste.[43]

By treating this broader ecological context as a form of capital that supports economic activity, ecological economists have made it possible to provide an economic account of the environment's ecological value, even if the market does not price ecosystem goods and services, and even if people lack knowledge about how broader ecological conditions relate to particular components of the environment that they subjectively value. For instance, in order to value a park's ecological functioning, ecological economists might determine the amount of groundwater that the protected area recharges on a yearly basis and then consider what it would cost to produce that same amount of water through non-natural means, such as human-created reverse osmosis filtration systems that turn dirty water into clean water.[44] The cost of producing this water reflects components of the park's value that individual people may not recognize and therefore choose to value in their expression of willingness to pay for access to it. By accounting for the economic value of ecosystem services that particular resources such as a park provide, ecological economists can supplement what people express in their uninformed or adaptive preferences with a monetary figure that reflects at least some of the environment's value in providing the basic life support functions that are the basis for human life and choice.

Although such efforts to place an economic value on ecosystems tend to yield strikingly high outcomes, they remain insufficient in two important respects.[45] First, in order to determine the market price of a currently unpriced ecosystem good or service, the good or service must replicate or contribute to something that is in fact directly marketed. In the example just given, the ecological value of a natural area is based on its water purification capacity. This accounts for some of the area's ecological value, and it is possible to assess this value because there is a market value for purified water, but this natural area also makes additional ecological contributions that the cost of water purification does not capture. For example, it does not capture the area's role in carbon sequestration or in supporting the earth's biodiversity.[46] These latter services are an important component of what the natural area (or the watershed it subsumes) does for humans, but they are not accounted for

[43] See especially ecological economists who argue for a "steady state economy," such as Daly (1991) and Czech (2006).

[44] For example, see Chichilnisky and Heal's (1998) discussion of the Catskill Watershed, which provides water to New York City.

[45] For example, see a study by Costanza and D'Arge (1997) that endeavored to measure the total economic value of the earth's ecosystems.

[46] See Heal (2000:27) discussing this in reference to economic valuation of the Catskill Watershed.

in the value of any easily bounded market good. For this reason, as Geoffrey Heal explains, such valuations are likely to be incomplete: "There are usually services provided by natural ecosystems for which there are no markets and so no market prices. These therefore will be omitted from the calculations. At best therefore we will compute lower bounds for the values of these natural systems."[47] Thus, one crucial problem with efforts to impute prices in a way that captures the full or total economic value (TEV) of ecosystems for their role in contributing to ecosystems' aggregate life support capacity is that the resulting valuations are likely to remain incomplete.[48]

However, even if all the goods and services that ecosystems produce could directly be related to goods for which there are market prices, the ecological economists' approach to capturing the environment's ecological value remains limited in a second way: it cannot accurately represent the environment's non-economic instrumental value to people. Most basically this is because the environment's ecological value is instrumental to many non-economic dimensions of human life such as culture, family, and community that are organized by non-monetary currencies. It is worth emphasizing that the language of "ecosystem services" that ecological economists have developed in describing the multiple ways in which ecosystems contribute to human well-being does recognize these non-economic contributions. For instance, many scholars who might be loosely described as ecological economists recognize the value of "cultural services" as a distinct category of ecosystem services supporting culturally specific non-economic practices and norms that people value.[49] In the present context, however, making ecological economics relevant to the current cost–benefit approach to policy analysis requires translating accounts of the environment's ecological value into monetary terms compatible with economic valuation. Such translations remain insufficient for assessing the environment's contribution to many areas of human life that people do not and cannot value accurately in dollars.

The practice of monetizing the value of specific environmental resources is the subject of a long-standing critique of the economic approach to environmental valuation, and these critiques are no less powerful when it comes to valuing ecosystem services in monetary terms. With respect to the latter, the problem with pricing ecosystem services (even if the pricing is complete as opposed to partial) is that monetary pricing does not convey the total value of ecosystem goods or services in a social or philosophical sense any more than economic activity contains everything that is of social and philosophical value. To put this point differently, the environment contributes to human life in ways that have non-quantifiable and non-monetary

[47] See Heal (2000:26). [48] See Turner, Pearce, and Bateman (1993:113).
[49] See Millennium Assessment Panel (2003:133).

value, and these contributions are therefore beyond the descriptive capacity of economic terms. For instance, some attachments to the environment are so strong that losing them cannot be reduced to any price a person (or community) can or would pay (or accept compensation for).

Andrew Dobson exemplifies the problem well in providing the following vignette about a village's relationship to a yew tree:[50]

> Think of a village green with a yew tree in the middle of it. The yew tree has been there for 200 years, and has become a symbol of village life. The road system around the village green is complex and dangerous, though, and it is proposed to remove the green to make the roads safer. This means removing the yew tree too. The villagers protest that the tree is important to them and they are offered compensation. In effect they are offered a sum of money that the authorities regard as *equivalent* to the symbolic value of the yew tree to the villagers. The villagers say that nothing can compensate for the loss of the tree, so the authorities offer to buy them another yew tree. The villagers protest again, on the grounds that the new yew tree is not *the same* as the old one. So the authorities propose moving the old one to a new site, instead of chopping it down or replacing it with a new one. Then it turns out that the site of the old yew tree was an important part of its value to the villagers, so moving it somewhere else is also unacceptable.

In this vignette, the yew tree has something that we might describe as an "irreducible originality"—it is bound up with practices that are "ineluctably local, indivisible from their instruments and their encasements."[51] As such, the yew tree can only do what it does for the villagers in the context of their connection to a history that they built through consistent cultural practices involving the tree. To remove the tree is to irrecoverably sever that connection. Ex post compensation for loss of the tree is impossible in the sense that once the damage to the tree is done there is no compensation that can make up for it.[52] More generally, to treat such resources as fungible goods that can be defined and traded in terms of money is to degrade their value in ways that destroy their meaning.[53] For the same reason, the instrumental value of ecosystems and broader ecological relationships to the provision of particular resources and physical settings in which people pursue non-economic practices quite consequential to their history, culture, and lived experience of a place are equally suspect when treated as the subject of monetary valuation.

[50] Dobson (2003:172). [51] Geertz (1983:4). [52] See O'Neill (2007:34).
[53] See Kelman (1992:160).

This problem also arises in efforts to assess the environment's value in contributing to earth's life support services. Ecosystems and ecological relationships are indeed a prerequisite of human life, but just as we cannot represent the value of having or losing a human life in monetary terms, we cannot capture the value of having or losing an ecological life support system in monetary terms. Money expresses the economic value of things to the ends or purposes in life that money can buy us. The environment contributes to these things, but also to things money cannot buy, such as meaningful social relationships, spiritual realization, and actual health (as opposed to medical care for coping with health problems, which is how economists might cast this value). Because money cannot reflect the personal and social importance of these relationships and conditions to human life, it cannot accurately value them; neither can it describe the extent of losses that people would suffer if the environment failed to provide the ecosystem services that put these ends and aims within our reach.[54]

The non-compensable and non-monetizable dimensions of environmental value are often discussed in relation to the problem of value incommensurability.[55] Two things are said to be incommensurable when they cannot be accurately measured along some common scale that uses a single metric of value.[56] While some of the philosophical debate about value incommensurability centers on conflict between the environment's intrinsic value as an end in its own right and the environment's instrumental value that economic valuation seeks to capture, value incommensurability is also relevant to valuation of the environment's non-economic instrumental value. Specifically, the environment has non-economic forms of instrumental value that are also incommensurable in monetary terms.

Sarah Trainor elaborates this problem by distinguishing different "realms of value" in which it is possible to categorize the various values people ascribe to their use of, interaction with, and/or relationship to natural resources or non-human nature.[57] Different realms of value are defined by the different ways in which people value things. Each realm, on Trainor's account, contains different notions or concepts regarding what it means to value something.[58] For instance, in studying the various values associated with protection of a national monument known as the Grand Staircase-Escalante in southern Utah (USA), Trainor finds that people's aesthetic valuation of the canyons in this protected area entails recognizing their beauty, while people's economic valuing of the canyons entails assessing a marketable commodity within

[54] Heal (2000:28).

[55] For example, see Chang (1997), Sagoff (1988:99–123), Anderson (1993:190–216), Espeland (1994).

[56] See Anderson (1993:55) and Chang (1997).

[57] Trainor (2006).

[58] Trainor (2006:9).

them. The values that are of interest to Trainor, like myself, are those that are the result of a human valuing process that occurs in different contexts of human life, related to people's experiences of culture, history, religion, family, and various other dimensions of their lives in which they experience meaning or personal fulfillment.[59] The content of values in each of these different realms of value in fact may be unique and irreducible, but standard economic valuation seeks to express each distinct form of value in common economic terms; specifically, in marginal increments of monetary units, as revealed in people's willingness to pay.[60] The problem is that treating the environment as a matter of individual economic choice will inevitably omit values people attach to the environment that cannot be made commensurable in economic terms.[61]

More specifically, within distinct realms of value it may be possible to compare values with respect to some goal—that is, with respect to what Ruth Chang refers to as a "covering value"—such as recognizable beauty or spiritual growth, and therefore, to rank values within distinct realms. For example, we might be able to say that a protected canyon is more valuable to a person's spiritual realization than it is to her need for having marketable commodities.[62] But quantifying values relevant to non-economic realms of value along the cardinal scale of monetary units can misrepresent what valuable things mean to people, and therefore, it can produce decisions that fail to represent the values people actually hold. For example, because the value of canyons in the Grand Staircase-Escalante to Native American spiritual traditions cannot be measured alongside the dollar or commodity value of minerals in those canyons, both succumbing to market valuation and refusing to value the canyons in those terms will render these values external or tangential to the values that get counted in the policy analysis.[63] Thus, while ecological economists are unlikely to account for the total economic value of all ecosystem services that any particular environmental resource or place contributes to human life, the single metric of monetary value that economic valuation requires cannot account for the environment's value to non-economic goals and purposes that define distinct realms of value.

In contrast to this critique of how economic valuation conceptualizes the environment's instrumental value, some scholars focus on problems with how economic valuation conceives of humans. Mark Sagoff, in particular,

[59] These values do not refer to objective properties that inhere in nature, requiring that humans respect nature or treat it with consideration on moral grounds.

[60] See Trainor (2006:15).

[61] Sunstein (2002:124), for instance, argues that we might therefore supplement WTP studies with a qualitative description of the goods involved; a description conveying that resources "are not merely commodities, [and] that people do not value these goods in the same way that they value cash."

[62] See Chang (1997:4).

[63] See Grove-White (1997:24–29).

provides an early and compelling argument that economic valuation treats people as individual consumers, failing to consider what people value as citizens and how this might differ from what they value as individuals engaged in market interactions.[64] Sagoff argues that when people are treated like consumers expressing their willingness to pay for environmental goods in settings of market choice, they will assess the environment in relation to what is good for them as individuals, endeavoring to maximize their own self-interest. In contrast, when people are asked to value the environment as citizens in a collective decision-making context, Sagoff argues that they will conceive of environmental value in less self-interested ways, considering what is valuable for society as a whole, as members of a political community. In this respect, standard economic valuation turns a policy question that should concern what we want as a community into a question about what I want as an individual consumer.

I raise this point here because although the theoretical literature on environmental value often focuses on elaborating and defending the importance of treating the environment as intrinsically valuable, at the level of practice, environmental valuation has recently been suffused with an effort to create a valuation context in which what people value as citizens can be expressed and determined. For example, as I discuss in Section 2.4, the contemporary turn to a more democratic and deliberative approach to assessing the environment's value has begun to advance the practice of environmental valuation in significant ways. However, while making some progress in dealing with the expression of incommensurable values, this approach to valuation ultimately remains committed to treating the environment as an object of choice, albeit of a collective rather than individual choice.

2.4 Valuing the Environment as an Object of Collective Choice

Deliberative monetary valuation of the environment, or DMV, is an approach to valuing the environment that engages citizens in a process of collective discussion and reflection in order to arrive at a decision about the value of an environmental good or service. While there are several different models by which the process of value articulation, deliberation, and value assignment proceeds, this approach to environmental valuation has its roots in the same principles of democratic deliberation that underlie ecosystem-based management (EBM), which I discussed in Chapter 1.[65] In the context of DMV, the goal

[64] See Sagoff (1988b).

[65] While both EBM and DMV are grounded in theories of deliberative democracy, EBM seeks to arrive at an agreed-upon decision outcome, such as a specific policy or environmental

of the deliberative setting is to arrive at an account of environmental value through decision-making procedures modeled on democratic dialogue and discussion rather than on market exchange. As Arild Vatn explains, "communicative rationality" is the basic idea behind the deliberative process:[66]

> It demands the involvement of citizens. It is about the creation of understanding through dialogue and the force of the better argument. It is a form of common reasoning where mutual learning, understanding and preference changes are all elements of the process.

Thus, ideally, DMV instantiates an approach to environmental valuation grounded in the ideals of mutual understanding and learning, preference transformation, and collective agreement. It produces an account of environmental value that is based on the strength of reasons that support different conceptions of value, rather than on the strength of people's preferences or the strategic exercise of political power.[67]

In relation to the problems discussed in Section 2.3, DMV has some significant advantages. To begin with, DMV establishes forums for collective dialogue and discussion about environmental values rather than a mere market registering of preferences. This means that when citizens hold non-economic values for the environment, they can initially express and debate these values in their own terms, rather than in the monetary metric of market exchange.[68] Crucial here is that the initial process of value articulation does not necessarily privilege values that are well represented in monetary terms while ignoring or sidelining values that citizens cannot accurately characterize in this way. Specifically, whereas standard economic valuation requires the initial expression of an environmental good's value in monetary terms, the initial expression of value in DMV does not require citizens to treat the environment as something fungible or suitable for trading with things that may matter much less. Instead, for the purpose of defining and assessing the environment's value, citizens can debate both economic and non-economic values based on the reasons deliberative participants offer for why particular values ought to be privileged as political goals. This means that citizens who value the environment as an economic commodity must come face to face with citizens that value it as something they understand to be priceless.[69] Likewise, to the extent that deliberative participants understand the

management decision, while DMV seeks to arrive at a collectively agreed-upon characterization of the monetary value of a resource. Although I discuss EBM as a form of collaborative and participatory decision-making in Chapter 1 and Chapter 6, here my focus is on DMV as an approach to environmental valuation rather than an approach to making policy decisions. See Spash (2008) for an overview of the four primary models of DMV and the limitations of each.

[66] Vatn (2009:2212). [67] See Sagoff (1998b). [68] See Trainor (2006:18).
[69] See Jacobs (1996:220).

functional importance of ecosystems that are bound up with particular features of the environment, they can articulate the ecological value of these features in terms that characterize the various non-economic contributions they make, not merely in terms that characterize something that is of direct market value.[70]

Building on this latter point, in addition to permitting a more accurate representation of incommensurable values, DMV also creates a context for learning about the ecological importance of particular resources. This is because experts in ecological science can participate in deliberative processes by providing information and answering scientific and technical questions.[71] For instance, in deliberating about the value of a watershed, natural scientists can provide information and answer questions about why and how continuing human impacts on the watershed will reduce water supply below expected demand. This information, and the opportunity to have scientific experts answer relevant questions, may have more meaning to citizens than ecological economists' estimates of the reduction in monetary value of all the watershed's ecosystem goods and services that will result from the same human impacts.[72] As Matthew Wilson and Richard Howarth explain, even without experts playing a specified role, group-based valuation (as opposed to individual valuation) "should bring more intellectual resources to bear and, hence, increase the probability that more information about an ecosystem service will be generated and a higher quality valuation will result."[73] In this sense, DMV creates a context for ecological learning about environmental value that citizens would otherwise lack, increasing the probability of collective choices that are more informed than any individual member's isolated choice.[74] Thus, in comparison to standard economic valuation, DMV is more likely to reflect the value of particular goods or services to earth's broader life support system, and therefore, to reflect the environment's role as a basis—rather than mere object—of choice.

Notwithstanding these significant advantages for addressing the problems of value incommensurability and uninformed preferences in standard economic valuation, producing a monetary characterization of the environment's value remains a crucial feature of the deliberative valuing process in DMV. The deliberative context is intended to increase the validity of stated preference methods of economic valuation, but the various methods and decision processes do result in a monetary valuation of the resources citizens deliberate about. This produces some internal contradictions, as Vatn notes,

[70] See Leinhoop and MacMillan (2007a) for an explanation of a DMV study in which non-economic values arise in the deliberative context.
[71] Trainor (2006:19). [72] See Cowling et al. (2008:9485).
[73] Wilson and Howarth (2002:438–439); see also Kaplowitz and Hoehn (2001).
[74] See Alvarez-Farizono and Hanley (2006) and Wilson and Howarth (2002:439–440).

because "it mixes collective reasoning and consensus building over principles and norms with individual trade-off calculations."[75] Of course, there are different models of DMV, and these models involve different approaches to translating group deliberation into monetary values. For instance, in the "charitable contribution" model of DMV, citizens engage in a process of discussion and social learning about the relevant environmental resource before they are asked to express their individual WTP in monetary terms. Here the deliberative features that allow citizens time to discuss and reflect on the environment's value function to increase the validity of the resulting individual WTP measures, but ultimately, an aggregation of these individual monetary values is what defines the net value of the relevant resource.

In contrast, the "fair price" model of DMV does not aggregate individual values after group deliberation, but instead requires the group to deliberate about what a justifiable disaggregated individual WTP value should be. Here the deliberative forum is a vehicle for the group to make a collective decision about what an average individual should be willing to pay for a valued resource or willing to accept as payment for its loss or degradation. Likewise, in the "arbitrated social WTP/WTA" model of DMV, the deliberative process produces an aggregate annual income tax that deliberating citizens think protecting the relevant resource is worth, with a process of majority voting that comes into play if deliberation does not produce a consensus about how high the tax ought to be.[76] While these latter two forms of DMV require citizens to discuss issues of collective responsibility and fairness that align the valuation process more closely with the theory of deliberative democracy in which DMV claims its justification, ultimately the environment's value as a collective good is eventually "forced" into the metric of monetary units, so it can be made commensurable with other monetized things.[77] For this reason Vatn describes DMV as combining an approach to environmental valuation that is "based on capturing incommensurability with one that is focused on commensurability."[78]

An additional problem with DMV is that while it does offer the potential for arriving at environmental valuations that are more informed about the ecological role and importance of particular environmental goods and services, it does not promise that the monetary value emerging from the deliberative valuation process will ultimately reflect this importance. In part this is because, in the absence of consensus among deliberators, the models of DMV that require collective decision-making permit the use of majority voting to close down debate.[79] This opens the door for those in

[75] Vatn (2005:360–361).
[76] Spash (2008) summarizes these and other models of DMV.
[77] See Spash (2008:483). [78] Vatn (2005:360–361).
[79] Spash (2008:471) and James and Blamey (2005).

the majority to strategically avoid consensus for the purpose of eventually imposing their valuations on the minority through a vote. In this way, DMV may permit a self-interested majority to impose an unecological understanding of environmental value on those who make up a minority of deliberators. Furthermore, even in the absence of a majority rule closure requirement, the deliberative process is no panacea. Deliberative processes, as I discuss in the context of resource valuation in Chapter 4 and in the context of collaborative rulemaking procedures in Chapter 6, are subject to various well-known distortions and abuses, such as inequality among deliberators with respect to skill, time, recognition, strategic capacity, and various other factors that prevent people from articulating their interests on an equal footing with others.[80] Refining the structure and content of the deliberative process can diminish these pathologies to greater or lesser degrees, but the more general problem with DMV is that leaving questions of environmental value entirely in the domain of collective choice procedures does not promise to ensure the environment is accurately valued and therefore protected as a basic condition of human life and choice.

Thus, far from ensuring the environment is valued for its contribution to human well-being as a basis of choice, DMV treats the environment as an object of choice, albeit one that is either informed by or subject to collective rather than individual decision procedures. These procedures pose problems in the context of justifying environmental policies (as I discuss in Section 2.5), not just in the context of valuing environmental resources. With respect to the present discussion of environmental valuation, my primary aim has been is to explain why DMV, on its own, is insufficient for assessing the natural environment's non-economic instrumental value. Like standard economic valuation, DMV ultimately reduces environmental value to a monetary price and therefore only deals with the problem of value incommensurability at the level of value articulation and discussion. While this promises to improve the validity of preference-based approaches to environmental valuation that standard economic analysis uses, it does not promise to produce valuations that accurately reflect the environment's substantive contribution to human life, and the very conditions of life from which human choice proceeds. Without systematically accounting for this component of the environment's substantive contribution in policy assessment—independent of what people subjectively value as a matter of individual or collective choice—there is nothing to ensure that policy assessment will provide the information necessary for justifying protection of the environment's non-economic instrumental values. Furthermore, as I now discuss, while

[80] See Young (2000:52–57).

economic approaches to policy assessment fail to justify environmental protection with respect to non-economic political goals, deliberative approaches to environmental valuation fail to justify environmental policies as a matter of substantive democratic commitments.

2.5 Aggregating Preferences as Justification for Environmental Protection

Unlike environmental valuation, which concerns what and how we value the environment for the purpose of making policy decisions, the topic of policy justification concerns *why* information about environmental value should lead us to adopt, reject, or alter policies that protect the environment. For example, CBA offers a framework for evaluating environmental policies that justifies them with respect to the goal of economic efficiency, defined as a condition in which a policy's consequences produce net economic benefits that are greater than its net economic costs. As I have discussed in Section 2.2, a policy meeting this condition is efficient in the sense that those who benefit from it *could* compensate those who are burdened by it and still be better off than they were prior to the policy's implementation.[81] However, as critics of CBA commonly point out, in the actual practice of CBA, the requirement that a policy make at least one person better off without imposing uncompensated costs on others is only hypothetical. Thus, in order for a policy to satisfy the evaluative criterion of CBA, it need not actually redistribute benefits to those who suffer from the policy's negative consequences. CBA deems a policy justifiable if the benefits outweigh the costs because under these conditions such redistribution is possible through further political decisions.[82]

When the justification for the cost–benefit approach to policy evaluation is understood independent of any real commitment to compensating those who will suffer a policy's negative consequences, CBA merely requires policies to produce (and/or maximize) aggregate economic benefits that outweigh aggregate economic costs. This goal aligns CBA with the utilitarian tradition in political thought, which, contemporarily, is a highly controversial political theory about what government should do.[83] Generally speaking, the original utilitarian political thinkers held that government should make decisions

[81] See Hicks (1939a) for the original formulation of the Kaldor–Hicks criterion, and Stavins, Wagner, and Wagner (2002:5), who explain it as the foundation of modern CBA.

[82] More technically, if a policy's impact were to meet this condition of making no person worse off, then it would meet the stronger justifying criterion of being Pareto efficient; i.e. of meeting conditions of Pareto efficiency.

[83] See Sen and Williams (1982:1–21) for an overview of utilitarianism and its problems.

producing the greatest amount of "utility" or welfare among affected agents, thereby maximizing human pleasure or happiness and minimizing pain or suffering.[84] Much of the philosophical debate about this theory concerns how individual utility or welfare is defined within this project of maximizing the total amount of it. For example, as I have discussed earlier in this chapter in relation to environmental valuation, in CBA, the satisfaction of people's subjective preferences is what defines the utility or welfare a policy should maximize. Although preference satisfaction is worthy of discussion because it offers a questionable account of human well-being, the practice of aggregating preferences is more central to the topic of policy justification. In particular, CBA determines the total amount of welfare a policy will produce by summing up each individual's willingness to pay for policies that will satisfy their preferences. It is this practice of aggregating the impacts of a policy on different people for the purpose of calculating and/or maximizing the policy's net benefits that reflects the utilitarian political goal of producing the greatest overall amount of utility.

The problem with these aggregating and maximizing goals is that they combine people's utilities together in a way that ignores the separateness of individual people. By this I mean that they ignore how a policy with net positive or negative impacts distributes those impacts across different citizens.[85] For example, utilitarian goals may be met under conditions in which relatively few people benefit a great deal from an environmental policy producing net positive impacts, while a great many suffer. Alternatively, a large portion of a population may benefit in modest ways from a policy with net positive impacts, while relatively few suffer tragic consequences. In these ways, policies producing the greatest amount of preference satisfaction ultimately may leave some members of society highly unsatisfied and even worse off than they were prior to the policy intervention. Some members of society, in other words, can be sacrificed for the sake of producing the greatest aggregate good.[86]

This is why CBA can be said to justify policies irrespective of their distributional impacts. If a large number of people are willing to pay money (and hence register a large quantity of preference satisfaction) to dispose of their trash in a place where it will pose significant burdens, but only for very few people, then CBA will view the policy as economically efficient, and therefore

[84] Bentham (1789) and J. S. Mill (1861) provide the foundations of utilitarian political thinking. O'Neill, Holland, and Light (2008: 11–87) offer a detailed philosophical account of the ways in which modern CBA can be understood as an application of utilitarian political thought.

[85] As Persky (2001) explains, this is a problem about which even the original proponents of the Kaldor–Hicks criterion were aware, and which motivated them to proceed cautiously in applying the CBA to policy evaluation.

[86] See O'Neill, Holland, and Light (1998:49–53).

as worthy of implementation. It is these inequities, however, that give rise to claims that environmental policies are unjust, violating both democratic norms and substantive legal and political commitments. Especially for advocates of the contemporary environmental justice movement, CBA has been insufficient for preventing the implementation of policies that disproportionately burden low-income minority communities that may have too little purchasing or political power to fend off locally unwanted land uses and other hazardous environmental exposures.[87]

Thus, the distributional consequences that result from policies maximizing net benefits (or economic efficiency) are foremost among the challenges confronting the utilitarian justification that underlies CBA. These policies ignore the significance of impacts that can accrue to individual people, and therefore, they can fail to treat the interests of people equally. As John Rawls famously claimed in developing his own response to utilitarian political thought, "Each person possesses an inviolability founded on justice that even the welfare of society as a whole cannot override."[88] While Rawls, and many who follow him in theorizing social justice as a political goal for democratic societies, does not account for the natural environment as a basic condition of social justice, he does offer an alternative basis for thinking and reasoning about substantive democratic political goals that are grounded in ideals of justice, fairness, and conditions of political equality.[89] Policies meeting these ideals will often differ significantly from policies meeting CBA's standards of economic efficiency. For instance, the approach to policy evaluation that I develop in later chapters of this book justifies policies based on the extent to which they protect each person's basic capabilities to do and achieve different things that are central to living a decent and dignified human life. Policies providing these protections may also satisfy people's preferences, but that is not the basis of their justification. In the capabilities approach to justifying environmental policies that I advance, certain environmental protections are a basic condition of social justice. Likewise, the approach to policy evaluation that I advance does not assess whether the basic capabilities to do and achieve things are maximized across people, rather it seeks to assess whether the capabilities are protected at a threshold level, for each individual

[87] See Been (1992), Bullard and Hendrix (1986), and Hamilton (1993:115–118); for more general characterizations of the environmental justice movement see Cole and Foster (2001), Timmons and Toffolon-Weiss, and Shrader-Frechette (2002).

[88] Rawls (1971:3).

[89] For instance, Charles Anderson (1992:131) argues that social justice should be taken as the paramount criterion for evaluating policies. Likewise, in Gillroy and Bowersox (2002:45), Bowersox argues that a democratic society committed to minimizing coercion must at least act in ways that people perceive are fair when policies require them to give something up that was previously permitted or subsidized. See Holland (2008b) for a discussion and critique of Rawls's account of the natural environment in relation to his two principles of justice.

person, for this is necessary to respect the dignity—or basic human worth—of each person.[90] As such, in later chapters I advance the idea that environmental policies are justifiable to the extent that they enable people to pursue a variety of activities and accomplishments that are central to the human form of a flourishing life.

Before further elaborating an approach to policy evaluation that is justified with respect to this ideal, let us first consider the non-utilitarian justifications for CBA. These justifications are grounded in a commitment to democratic procedures. While having certain advantages, appeals to procedure as a way of justifying both CBA and DMV remain problematic because they can also disregard the importance of impacts suffered at the level of individual people.

2.6 Democratic Deliberation as Justification for Environmental Protection

Many contemporary scholars view efforts to ground CBA's justification in democratic theory as far less contentious than CBA's grounding in utilitarian political thought. Let us first consider those who view democracy as a set of procedures for aggregating people's preferences so that policies can reflect them effectively.[91] Those adopting this "aggregative view" of democracy treat majority voting as the essence of the democratic exercise, and they assume it should reflect people's preferences as they are given. Thus, rather than engaging paternalistic projects, such as making citizens into good or virtuous people by cultivating particular desires or habits of character, the aggregative view of democracy assumes that government actions should seek merely to satisfy citizens' wants.[92] CBA is an instantiation of this "liberal" form of democratic politics because the WTP studies it uses to measure environmental values function as ballots through which people cast "dollar votes" that communicate the level of environmental protection they are willing to support (i.e. through taxes or some means of market trading).[93] As such, the policies

[90] The formulation of the evaluative criterion I propose is most closely associated with Martha Nussbaum's (2000, 2006, 2011) "capabilities approach" to justice.

[91] See O'Neill (1993:83–101).

[92] See Shapiro (2003:3). See Dryzek (2000:33–36) for a discussion of why rational choice theorists treat views of democracy that rely on voting as a collective choice mechanism as meaningless, arbitrary, and unstable, and therefore point toward more minimalist views of what government ought to do.

[93] See Arrow et al. (1993:20). Pearce et al. (1989:55) advocate, further, that "[T]he attraction of placing money values on these preferences is that they measure the *degree* of concern...Such measures automatically express not just the fact of a preference for the environment, but also the intensity of that preference. Instead of 'one man one vote', then, monetization quite explicitly reflects the depth of feeling contained in each vote."

CBA approves can claim to reflect government actions that remain neutral regarding how citizens ought to live their lives; for example, without appealing to any particular account of what human well-being consists in when identifying policies that reflect the "general will" of the people.[94]

An important set of problems emerging from this view of democracy concerns the vulnerability of aggregation mechanisms such as "majority rule" to strategic manipulation by powerful political interests that dominate contemporary democratic politics. For instance, a simple majority rule voting system can produce a "tyranny of the majority" and therefore confront the same substantive problems that make utilitarianism a contentious political philosophy. More specific to the justification of CBA as an instantiation of aggregative democracy is the fact that the application of this tool cannot convincingly claim to remain procedurally neutral with respect to the values of different people. CBA measures people's preferences by assessing their WTP for the outcome they desire. Presumably, this has the advantage of accounting for the intensity of a person's preferences. However, one important problem is that WTP may reflect people's "ability to pay" rather than the intensity of their preferences. For instance, a wealthy person may be willing to pay a lot for a policy outcome that is of little value to her, while a poor person may be able to pay very little for a policy outcome that is of great value to her. Because those who are willing to pay the most for environmental protection can have the greatest impact on the benefits a policy is understood to confer, CBA allows those who are able to pay a lot to have a larger voice within the benefit calculation process, even if their valuations are low compared to those who can pay very little. As John O'Neill has argued, in treating the prices expressed in WTP as equivalent to votes, CBA allows "the preferences of a few to have a disproportionably high influence, simply in virtue of their [presumed] intensity."[95]

It is for this reason that the aggregate theory of democratic politics, as instantiated through the use of CBA, fails to meet the conditions of procedural neutrality on which its justification hinges. Some people's values do count for more than others, making it possible for the preferences of a few to have disproportionately high influence on the policies that CBA defines as economically efficient.[96] While this poses significant problems as a matter of democratic procedure, there is also an important substantive problem: CBA's falsely claimed procedural fairness will mask the unfairness of policies producing environmental inequities. Specifically, if the existing distribution of income is not accounted for in the assessment of people's WTP,

[94] See O'Neill (1993:83–84). Also see Shapiro (2003:10), who links this view of democracy to a reading of Jean-Jacques Rousseau's notion of the "general will."

[95] O'Neill (1996:756–757). [96] O'Neill (1996:757).

policies for which benefits outweigh costs may produce highly unequal levels of environmental protection or unequal access to environmental goods, but the inequities will be explained away as a reflection of people's preferences for different kinds of relationships to the environment. Some advocates of CBA have responded to this problem by devising strategies for weighting the WTP of poor people more than the WTP of rich people in the final tally of a policy's net benefits; however, finding a non-arbitrary method for assigning these weights remains a significant challenge.[97] In short, CBA's justification as an instantiation of aggregative democracy fails to meet ideals of both government neutrality and distributive fairness.

Those who advance the deliberative approach to valuing environmental resources—DMV—that I have discussed in Section 2.4 of this chapter, claim that CBA can address both of these problems. With respect to distributive fairness, for instance, DMV adopts procedures that allow citizens to articulate and consider values besides economic efficiency, such as how the benefits of a policy ought to be distributed across citizens.[98] Most basically, DMV does this by creating a space for citizens to articulate non-economic individual values and collective goals, and by creating a communicative context in which these values and goals can be the subject of collective discussion and debate. Minimally, this makes it possible for those who lack resources and political power to confront those who do not, forcing the powerful to provide a public defense of why their values should prevail and at what costs. In the idealized deliberative context, the strength of reasons would prevail, not the ability to pay of those wielding more income and political power. Thus, in providing a forum for democratic reasoning that calls on citizens to reason together rather than simply register their preferences, the deliberative approach to environmental valuation creates a space for the distributional implications of environmental policy to play a more central role in determining a socially acceptable characterization of the environment's monetary value. Here, DMV not only helps to meet the ideals of procedural fairness that are central to the democratic justification for CBA, it is also renders CBA more likely to produce outcomes that are substantively fair.[99]

With this in mind, we might think of DMV as lending two kinds of justification to the standard cost–benefit framework in which the collective and deliberatively informed monetary values are eventually balanced against costs. First, DMV relies on a deliberative model of democracy, idealizing a set of procedures that involve ongoing reasoned engagement among free and

[97] See Boardman et al. (2001:44–45). [98] Ward (1999:88) and Spash (2008:472).

[99] In advocating the application of DMV to ecosystem services, Wilson and Howarth (2002:441) characterize this context as one in which "new techniques for measuring economic values and understand[ing] fairness dilemmas over ecosystem services will be revealed." Also see Howarth and Wilson (2006).

equal citizens that move toward identifying a consensus about what is good for society. Government, therefore, is not a crude aggregating machine, but rather, implements policies that are a product of reasons that survive public scrutiny.[100] Those having the highest ability to pay will not necessarily control the valuation that determines a policy's worth, for they must provide reasons that compel others to agree that the policies they support serve the collective good. In this way, DMV increases the democratic legitimacy of the monetary valuations that get factored into CBA. The second way in which DMV helps to justify CBA is more substantive than procedural. Specifically, DMV provides a context for addressing distributional issues at the level of monetary valuation. If people do in fact discuss a policy's distributional implications, and if this does prevent those with resources and power from determining the collective decision that results, then DMV will likely improve the substantive outcome of CBA. For instance, citizen deliberators may agree that policies meeting goals of distributional equity are indeed worth a lot of money, ultimately outweighing the costs to which they are compared.[101] In this context, the fair procedures that DMV aims to incorporate would function to produce more fair or equitable outcomes.

While DMV does have the potential to deliver these procedural and substantive advantages, and therefore improve the democratic justification of CBA, the problem is that in actual practice it can promise neither the procedural fairness nor equitable outcomes that would lend it this legitimacy. Part of the difficulty, as I have previously discussed, is that DMV is not a form of genuine democratic deliberation because it employs valuation processes that are highly constrained by the goal of arriving at a monetary account of the environment's value. To reiterate, while the goal of the DMV process is to arrive at a group consensus about the monetary value of the environmental change a policy will produce, in the absence of attaining that consensus, majority voting serves as an acceptable way of closing down the debate.[102] This reintroduces the problems associated with aggregate models of democracy, such as "tyranny of the majority" and it opens the door for deliberators to behave strategically. For instance, some deliberative participants may refuse to agree to a monetary valuation that conflicts with their interests—regardless of the strength of reasons offered—simply because they know that a majority of the remaining participants share their own perspective, and that they will therefore be in the majority if they can stall the discussion long enough to force

[100] See Sunstein (1993:162–166), who connects this deliberative view of political procedures to the Madisonian view of democracy.
[101] See Dryzek (1987:200–215) and Miller (1992), who argue that deliberation makes it more difficult for individual people to put undue weight on positions that privilege their interests or those who share them.
[102] See Spash (2008:471) and Brown, Peterson, and Tonn (1995:254–255).

a vote. Clive Spash notes that this potential for strategic behavior among deliberators justifies some facilitation of the deliberative process (i.e. so citizens can engage in more genuine and reflective forms of deliberation); however, if this reveals a genuine conflict among values, citizens' preferences may not transform—nor should they. For instance, a conflict among deliberators may reveal a socially important fact, especially if it is a consequence of past or present injustices that some deliberators fail to acknowledge.[103] Unfortunately, it remains unclear how such conflict should be handled in the context of an approach to policy evaluation that idealizes collective dialogue as a process in which citizens overcome self-interested behavior in favor of what is good for broader society.

The deliberative justification for CBA is further undermined by the eventual requirement of conforming people's non-economic values to a market model of valuation and exchange. This has led some practitioners to remove monetary values that reflect citizens' efforts to express non-economic values in the context of DMV. For instance, one DMV study that adopts what Clive Spash categorizes as the "charitable contribution" model, sought to assess the value of goose conservation in Scotland by preceding the individual expressions of WTP with two one-hour meetings with all participants, separated by a week, in which the participants had time to exchange information, reflect on tradeoffs, and pursue further research.[104] Various aspects of this study's statistical analysis posed problems, but the one most relevant to the present discussion concerns the practitioners' effort to remove any WTP valuations that were based on the participants' concerns for fairness.[105] Apparently those who were conducting the DMV study treated the post-deliberation expression of WTP values that were based on respondents' concerns for fairness as exemplifying strategic behavior. Consequently, while on one hand acknowledging that the study's participants might use the additional time and information created by the deliberative context to calculate what they consider to be a "fair" donation for conservation goals, rather than their maximum WTP, on the other hand, the study's practitioners recommend applying "appropriate checks and protocols to minimise the risk of it [i.e. the expression of a fair donation value] occurring are essential."[106]

Spash argues that practices such as these (i.e. that seek to eliminate WTP bids that are based on fairness) are a way of forcing reality into a preconceived economic model.[107] Rather than finding ways to incorporate non-economic values into their decision-making method, DMV practitioners have sought

[103] See Ward (1999:84) and Spash (2008:471–472).
[104] See Macmillan et al. (2002).
[105] See Spash (2008:474–475) for a critical review of the study.
[106] Macmillan et al. (2002:57). [107] Spash (2008:483).

to remove them, labeling them as based on biased and preconceived views or on insufficient participant experience.[108] This undermines the democratic justification for DMV because participants holding non-economic values are not treated equally to those holding values that conform well to the preconceived model of market valuation in which the deliberatively expressed values are ultimately forced. Furthermore, it suggests that outcomes reflecting people's non-economic commitments to a fairer or more equal distribution of environmental benefits and burdens will be unlikely to result from DMV, even if the participants express the value of these commitments.

The problem, therefore, is not just that DMV is committed to a set of procedures that fail to ensure that the substantive outcomes achieve environmental equity; rather the problem is that making sense of deliberatively informed values may mean simply removing any values that conflict with economic goals and commitments. Outcomes resulting from this process are unlikely to meet distributional goals, such as ensuring that each person has a level of environmental protection and access that is necessary for living the kind of life that a socially just society seeks to put within the reach of its citizens, which includes equal treatment and opportunity. DMV does not require that policies achieve such substantive commitments, and when participants are committed to such values at least some deliberative models seek to eliminate their impact on the monetary valuations that the assessment ultimately factors into the broader cost–benefit framework.

For these reasons, while DMV lends some credibility to CBA, it is insufficient for justifying CBA on either procedural or substantive grounds. With respect to the former, to the extent that DMV lends to the democratic legitimacy of CBA, it must confront a range of problems that make the deliberative process non-ideal. With respect to the latter, to the extent that DMV introduces non-utilitarian, distributive values into the valuation process, it can too easily remove the impact of these values on the ultimate monetary assessment, and it otherwise fails to prevent a maldistribution of environmental benefits and burdens. Some economists endeavor to correct these inequities by weighting the valuations of those who have a low ability to pay more than those have a high ability to pay, but a variety of technical difficulties make it difficult to assign weights without making subjective judgments.[109] For these reasons, standard economic valuation, even if more equitably determined through deliberative valuation methods, does not ensure that environmental policies do in fact protect each person's basic interest in environmental

[108] See Leinhoop and MacMillian (2007b).

[109] See Boardman et al. (2001:456–472) for an overview of these difficulties and Harberger (1978) for an original characterization of how distributional weighting in CBA can lead to inefficient projects and above-market price payments.

protection. These approaches to valuation only ensure that people have some opportunity to express how and how much they value the environment as a matter of individual or collective choice. Furthermore, while the utilitarian justification of CBA permits normatively problematic inequities, democratic justifications for CBA either permit similarly problematic inequities or instantiate a false procedural neutrality without ensuring that the conditions or goals of genuine democratic deliberation are met. The current approach to policy evaluation does not account for the environment's value as a basis of individual or collective choice, and it does not justify its protection as such.

2.7 Conclusion

The problems of environmental valuation and policy justification that I have reviewed in this chapter are only a portion of those discussed in the extensive literature on CBA. My aim has been to bring out problems that highlight some central limitations in the current economic approach to determining what is valuable about the environment and to justifying environmental protection as a political goal. The dominant cost–benefit approach to policy evaluation, as well as the deliberative approaches that have emerged as a way of validating the monetary value of environmental resources, provide an inaccurate account of environmental value and an insufficient justification for environmental protection. In treating the environment as an object of individual or collective choice, contemporary approaches to environmental valuation fail to account for the environment's value as a basis of individual choice.

Whether modeled in the context of market exchange or democratic deliberation, environmental valuation does not capture the crucial importance of environmental protection to the ecological relationships and conditions that support human life and the other forms of life on which human life depends. I have argued that while ecological economists have made significant progress in capturing this value, they remain tethered to a model of market valuation that makes their assessments incomplete for conveying the environment's ecological value to non-economic goals and purposes. Building on this point, I have connected the problems of monetization and value incommensurability often discussed in the environmental valuation literature to the ecological values that ecological economics cannot capture. While deriving the ecological value of particular environmental resources from goods that have a market value is unlikely to convey the total economic value of those resources, the problems of incommensurability that arise in putting monetary values on environmental resources render any such analysis insufficient for capturing the non-economic values to which those resources contribute, and hence for conveying their ecological value in supporting the non-economic goals and purposes that make up human life. Although deliberative approaches to environmental valuation permit the articulation of non-economic values in terms that better reflect what the environment means to people, this approach to valuation remain saddled with a commitment to monetization that reproduces many of the same problems.

The theoretical justifications for relying on CBA and DMV to make political decisions about environmental protection are insufficient when it comes to addressing matters of fairness and equality that are central to broadly accepted views about democratic governance. Some still link CBA to utilitarian political goals of maximizing the aggregate utility that government action produces, but the distributional implications of this goal are problematic, not to mention the fact that there are various other reasons why utilitarianism, as a political philosophy, has few contemporary adherents. The aggregative and deliberative democratic justifications for CBA link it to values of procedural neutrality and political opportunity, but ultimately this does not solve the potential for distributional inequities, even when deliberative approaches to monetary valuation are used in place of narrowly market-based approaches that assess people's WTP. Protecting the environment as a basis of choice for each person extends beyond what aggregative and deliberative theories of democracy can promise to deliver, suggesting the need for a new framework for valuing and justifying environmental protection.

In the framework I advance in the following chapters, the environment is treated as having a variety of non-economic instrumental values that make it possible for people to live flourishing lives—lives that are worthy of human dignity. By treating the environment as a condition of human capabilities rather than as an object of preference satisfaction, I argue that environmental values can be made comparable (but not commensurable) along different dimensions of well-being to which the environment contributes. This comparability of values is sufficient for environmental valuation because rather than justifying policies in terms of their maximization of satisfied preferences, I propose an approach to policy analysis that justifies policies in terms of whether they protect minimal conditions of human well-being for each person, which is required as a matter of basic justice. This imposes substantive standards on policy outcomes, even in the context of collaborative and negotiated decisions made in the administrative rulemaking process. Contemporary efforts to democratize this rulemaking process appeal to the same procedural ideals that justify the forms of deliberative monetary valuation discussed in this chapter, and although they do not seek to make values commensurable in monetary terms, these processes confront the same problems of strategic behavior and power inequalities that can emerge in DMV. In proposing an approach to policy evaluation that values and seeks to protect the each person's capabilities, I hope to recast environmental value as a condition of human living and choice, and to recast environmental protection as a matter of basic justice. Toward this end, let us first consider why the theory of human capabilities holds distinct advantages for addressing questions in environmental policy.

3

Capabilities, Well-Being, and Social Justice

3.1 Introduction

What theoretical framework should guide assessments of the natural environment's value and the justification for policies that protect it? Should an individual's "willingness to pay" (WTP) for use of environmental resources be the basis for determining the benefits of environmental policies? How can we assess the distributional impacts that these policies produce? Chapter 2 considers various reasons why individual WTP provides an inaccurate measure of the environment's contribution to individual well-being. In treating individuals as consumers and the environment as a commodity, WTP accounts only for the environment's value as an object of choice—its worth is based on the preferences people reveal in real or hypothetical market exchanges in which their existing knowledge and interests motivate them to choose among whatever options the market makes available.

Critics argue that this approach to valuation assumes a very narrow conception of individual well-being, and, thus, of how the natural environment contributes to it. Not only does much of the richness of human life and experience take place outside of market transactions, the environment also has value in these contexts that WTP measurements cannot capture. For these reasons, an accurate account of the environment's value requires a more nuanced view of the dimensions of human well-being to which the environment contributes, as well as an account of the various environmental values that are not expressible through monetization. This would improve assessment of the environment's instrumental value, and reveal the dimensions of human life for which environmental protection is most vital, making it more possible to identify and account for the real distributional impacts of environmental protection.

This chapter introduces the "capabilities theory" of Amartya Sen and Martha Nussbaum as the basis for a framework of policy evaluation that can overcome these and other problems that challenge the current economic approach to thinking and reasoning about environmental policies. Sen's "capability approach" and Nussbaum's "capabilities approach" are related but distinct research projects. In this chapter I discuss their ideas together, as composing a single "capabilities theory", because, when taken together, their work can be understood to advance both a theory of well-being and a theory of justice. In the remaining chapters of this book, I will build on these theories and show why and how they can provide the basis for an alternative framework for evaluating and designing environmental policies.

Thus, while my goal in the present chapter is to simply introduce capabilities theory and present two conceptual advantages it offers, I do this with an eye toward fuller elaboration of both a theory of well-being and a theory of justice in the following two chapters. Specifically, in Chapter 4, I develop the application of capabilities theory as a theory of well-being to questions of environmental valuation; in Chapter 5 I develop the application of capabilities theory as a theory of justice to questions of policy justification. This further elaboration and development of Sen and Nussbaum's work in the two following chapters is necessary because neither Sen nor Nussbaum has systematically considered how the natural environment bears on human capabilities as either a component of well-being or a condition of social justice. Thus, before engaging in this task, I will first show why the conception of well-being central to their work is a potentially powerful basis for improving how we value environmental resources and justify environmental protection.

I argue, first, that capabilities theory provides a conception of individual well-being that is broad enough to reveal the natural environment's various non-economic contributions to human life. The theory rests on the Aristotelian premise that humans are beings with the potential to flourish in many different ways. It views a good human life as composed of many different conditions and life activities, of which engaging in market transactions may be only one. Given this view of what makes up a person's life, the theory also focuses on the internal and external conditions that enable people facing very different life circumstances to make self-defined choices about the activities or forms of flourishing they find valuable. Specifically, Sen and Nussbaum argue that evaluative judgments should focus on the conditions and states of enablement—the capabilities—that make it possible for people to freely form and express preferences without the various distortions and adaptations that social context and individual circumstance can create. This focus on the conditions that enable people to pursue—and thus to choose to pursue—various life activities and achievements is crucial to improving environmental valuation. Its distinct advantage over the WTP model is its potential to treat the environment as a basis of individual choice.

Second, I argue that the broad and nuanced conception of well-being that capabilities theory introduces can illuminate inequities that remain invisible in the WTP model of environmental valuation, which assesses impact with respect to values expressed by citizens interacting in a real or hypothetical market process. Capabilities theory does not posit an ideal consumer exchanging market goods. Instead it views humans as embedded in personal, social, and economic circumstances that determine the extent of their formally protected civil and political freedoms, and even their freedom to choose among market options. These social and economic circumstances encompass human health, mobility, social and cultural affiliations, material resources, a variety of emotional experiences, and various other dimensions of well-being that make one's life better or worse. Environmental protection (or the lack of it) has an impact on these various dimensions of human life. When the capabilities-based view of well-being is expanded to include the environmental context in which human life is inevitably embedded, it can reveal the channels or paths through which environmental protection has disproportionate impacts. Therefore, if expanded as I propose in later chapters, the conception of well-being that capabilities theory introduces can help policy evaluation to shed light on the extent to which people experience very different benefits from the same level or standard of environmental protection.

In bringing attention to these conceptual advantages of Sen and Nussbaum's capabilities theory, this chapter makes two arguments regarding the problems of accuracy and distributional assessment that Chapter 2 discussed in relation to the topics of environmental valuation and policy justification, respectively. First, given that the capabilities-based view of well-being can capture the environment's role as a basis (rather than just an object) of choice, when we value environmental resources that public policies protect, we should value them in terms of their contribution to human capabilities. Second, because the capabilities-based view of well-being is broad enough to capture the natural environment's role in shaping the conditions and possibilities determining what people are able to do and achieve in their lives, when we assess a policy's distributional implications—and hence its contribution to goals such as equality or social justice—we should assess its impact on people's capabilities. Thus, by introducing capabilities theory, and offering two arguments for why it should be brought to bear on the evaluation of environmental policy, this chapter shows why this body of ideas can provide a basis for an approach to policy evaluation that is both accurate and politically justified.

The chapter will proceed as follows. First, I introduce the capabilities theory of Amartya Sen and Martha Nussbaum and explain the way in which it can be understood to offer both a theory of well-being and a theory of justice.

Second, after elaborating the primary features of both theories, I highlight the way in which they can help to reframe how policy analysts commonly understand the relationship between the natural environment, individual well-being, and choice. In particular, I argue that capabilities theory provides an expanded view of individual well-being, which makes it possible to capture an expanded view of the environment's contribution to well-being. Third, I argue that this broader view of well-being can reveal the pathways through which environmental protection policies have unequal impacts, introducing the occurrence of fundament conflicts between the capabilities of different people. Drawing on both of these arguments, the final section of the chapter summarizes why a capabilities-based conception of well-being and justice can improve the accuracy and justification of policy evaluation.

3.2 Capabilities Theory

The body of literature that I have referred to as "capability theory" emerged from an initial effort by Amartya Sen and Martha Nussbaum to develop conceptual ideas and policy tools for improving the theory and practice of international development policy.[1] Sen and Nussbaum questioned both the dominant understanding of the goals of international development and the evaluative tools used to assess the success of international development programs. The goals, they argued, emerged from a narrow view of what it means to make an individual person's life better. Likewise, the success of a government in improving people's lives was based on a flawed view of what politically legitimate government action should be understood to involve. Responding to the first problem, their work advances a theory that defines what comprises well-being and provides an account of why we should think about well-being in the way that they propose. Corresponding to the second problem, their work (and especially the work of Martha Nussbaum) advances a theory of what politically legitimate government action should be understood to involve and why this action should be treated as a political goal in liberal democratic societies. I will discuss each of these theories below.

3.2.1 Capabilities and well-being

A central feature of Sen and Nussbaum's capabilities theory is the idea that people's well-being should be understood in terms of their "capabilities" to do and achieve different things. Capabilities are the conditions or states of

[1] See Crocker (1992, 1995) for an early overview of Sen and Nussbaum's work. For a more recent updated overview see Robeyns (2005) and Crocker (2008:104–189).

enablement that define people's real options to pursue activities and achievements they value. For example, a capability can refer to a condition in which one is able to meet one's basic bodily needs, such as being able to have adequate shelter; a capability can also refer to a more abstract capacity, such as being able to critically reflect on the planning of one's life. In either case, Sen and Nussbaum argue that a person's capabilities are what make it possible to pursue the things he or she does or might care about. Assessments of an individual's income by contrast, which is what many economists use to measure progress in international development, do not account for whether people are actually able to improve their well-being with whatever money is available to them. Likewise, assessments of people's preferences (as a measure of well-being) fail to capture how people's preferences can adapt to unjust circumstances and therefore fail to accurately reflect what is objectively good for them. Capabilities define individual well-being in a way that avoids both of these problems because they characterize what people are effectively able to do and achieve, reflecting people's real opportunities to achieve outcomes they value.

For the purpose of addressing problems in international development policy, Sen and Nussbaum offer two compelling reasons why individual well-being should be understood in terms of what people are actually able to do and achieve. First, capabilities can characterize the opportunities that make up a good life for the kinds of beings that humans really are. Second, capabilities are more accurate than other conceptions of well-being in defining what is actually necessary for living that kind of life. Let us consider each of these reasons in turn.

As elaborated most fully by Martha Nussbaum, the capabilities-based view of well-being stems, ultimately, from an Aristotelian view of humans as developmental beings with the potential to flourish in many different ways and in the context of many different life activities.[2] The acquisition of material goods and wealth, for instance, is but one component of a complete and satisfying life, and thus only one component of assessing how well a person's life is going. Indeed, in the Aristotelian view, what matters about the acquisition of material goods and resources is the contribution they make to the diverse doings and beings that make up ways of living that are fully human. Most directly, in addition to the acquisition or accumulation of goods, such a life would also involve social and political affiliations, and the activity of human reasoning involved in making genuine choices. While Nussbaum argues that there are important similarities among the kinds of activities and achievements that humans have valued across place and time, she admits

[2] Generally, see Nussbaum (1988) and Nussbaum (1990).

that there will be "plural specifications" of what these activities and achievements entail, depending on the historical, social, and physical conditions characterizing particular contexts in which people live their lives.[3]

More prominently, Nussbaum argues that it is not just the range of valuable human activities and achievements that are relevant to assessing individual well-being and therefore to assessing how much development policies are improving people's lives. How well humans are able to function in doing and being these different things in their lives also matters. A person subject to conditions of extreme deprivation, for instance, will be forced to carry out genuinely human functions in a "merely animal manner."[4] As Nussbaum explains in reference to Marx's characterization of a person who lacks choice and control over his own eating activity, "...a starving person doesn't use food in a fully human way...He or she just grabs at the food in order to survive, and the many social and rational ingredients of human feeding can't make their appearance."[5] A fully human life, in contrast, is one in which a human being "shapes his or her own life in cooperation and reciprocity with others, rather than being passively shaped or pushed around by the world in the manner of a 'flock' or 'herd' animal."[6] In other words, a truly human way of using one's body and senses requires that people be capable of making choices free from the kind of desperate conditions in which one's unique faculties to taste, enjoy, and reason about one's food become irrelevant. In this respect, to view well-being in terms of the capabilities that really make people able to do and achieve different things is to recognize what is necessary for humans to flourish as the kinds of beings that they are.

For Sen, the capability-based view of well-being emerged as part of his larger critique of efforts to measure progress in international development in terms of changes in a country's gross national product (GNP) or gross domestic product (GDP).[7] Sen argues that these measures of economic activity (i.e. GNP and GDP) do not provide enough information about whether and to what extent a country's development is actually improving the *quality* of people's lives. On one hand, increases in economic activity may not translate into other social improvements. For instance, increases in economic activity do not capture the fact that a country's success in the area of economic activity may make people better off in some ways (e.g. with respect to income) and worse off in others (e.g. with respect to family affiliations).[8] On the other hand, neither of these measures provides information about who within a

[3] Nussbaum (1990:209–211, 234–236). [4] Nussbaum (1988:183).
[5] Nussbaum (2000a:72). [6] Nussbaum (2000a:72).
[7] This theme runs through much of Sen's work. For a recent discussion see Sen (1999:70–74, 290–97).
[8] See Sen (1999) for a general introduction to his body of research on these topics, which includes references to his more technical scholarship.

country is benefitting from overall successes in the area of economic activity. For example, a country's success in the area of economic activity may make some groups of people much better off, while simultaneously worsening the lives of many others.

In the context of these distributional issues Sen takes up the challenge of comparing different conceptions of individual advantage. Noting that all lasting approaches to making ethical judgments about social arrangements have sought to assess or achieve equality of *something*, Sen has argued that equality should be assessed and/or achieved in the evaluative "space" of a person's capabilities.[9] His reasons why capabilities should be the focus for comparing how well different people are doing are straightforward and compelling.

First, Sen demonstrates that, for the purpose of assessing inequality, people's capabilities explain the most relevant differences in individual advantage. For example, comparing people in terms of the things that they have (e.g. income or goods) is inadequate because it does not account for differences in people's abilities to translate or transform the things they have into outcomes or achievements they value.[10] Consider that a disabled person who uses a wheelchair to get around cannot use a given amount of income as effectively as a person who is not disabled.[11] The disabled person will have to divert her income to the added costs of maintaining her wheelchair, to making various modifications in her home, and to her special needs for exercise and bodily care. For the same reason we can also say that in order to achieve equivalent conditions of health, in many instances a pregnant woman and a non-pregnant woman will need different amounts and kinds of nutritional intake.[12] The pregnant woman will need nutrition to feed herself and a growing fetus, while the non-pregnant woman only needs to feed herself. Simply put, to reach the same level of well-being or advantage, different people will need different amounts and kinds of material goods. This is why we cannot compare improvements in individual well-being by assessing a policy's impact on people's incomes or other material resources—there are too many interindividual differences in the physical conditions different people face.

Similarly, the influence of social factors also demonstrates why capabilities can provide an accurate basis for assessing individual well-being or advantage. As Nussbaum argues, social factors can produce or ameliorate inequalities that arise because of differences in people's personal characteristics. The mobility of a person bound to a wheelchair, for example, is

[9] Sen (1992:ix). [10] See Sen (1992:81–87). [11] See Sen (1982c:357–358).
[12] Nussbaum (1990:211).

dependent upon social provisions such as access ramps and lifts.[13] In this instance, a lack of such conditions makes a disabled person's income irrelevant to assessing well-being, for even vast amounts of personal income will not help to overcome the social barriers that prevent people in wheelchairs from using normal modes of mobility. Similarly, the role of social conditions in shaping well-being is apparent in the obstacles women confront in pursing a successful career. Relative to men, women must put extra resources into "achieving security (e.g. in single parent families), having fulfilling work (e.g. because of stereotyping of 'women's jobs'), and into establishing one's professional reputation early on in one's career (e.g. because of the asymmetric demands of family life)."[14] Here, institutional contexts and processes influence men and women differently, such that given equal resources, women are able to do and consequently will do different things than men are able to do. In order to account for how variation in the institutional contexts and processes that men and women face might pose special challenges (of conversion) for women, it is necessary to conceive of well-being as composed of capabilities that are influenced by these various social (conversion) factors.

Capabilities not only provide a more accurate account of individual well-being than a person's goods and resources can illuminate. A second reason why they provide a superior basis for comparing how well-off people are is that they avoid problems of inaccuracy that arise in efforts to measure well-being in terms of one's "subjective" values. Here Sen and Nussbaum emphasize the idea that a variety of personality traits and life circumstances can distort a person's subjective view of how well he or she is doing. For instance, in situations of extreme injustice, a person's hopes and desires can adapt such that the person stops wanting what he or she cannot hope to ever have. As Sen explains, amidst a life of grave deprivation or oppression, people often habituate to their circumstances, adapting their preferences to a limited horizon of potential achievement:[15]

> The hopeless destitute desiring merely to survive, the landless laborer concentrating his efforts on securing the next meal, the round-the-clock domestic servant seeking a few hours of respite, the subjugated housewife struggling for a little individuality, may have learned to keep their desires in line with their respective predicaments. Their deprivations are gagged and muffled in the interpersonal metric of desire fulfillment. In some lives small mercies have to count big.

[13] See Nussbaum (2003:56, fn.4) and (2001) for a fuller discussion.
[14] Sen (1992:113). [15] Sen (1985a:191).

The susceptibility of preferences to adapt in this way leads capability theorists (and many others) to question the reliability of subjective accounts of well-being.[16]

Assessing a person's capabilities, in contrast, requires facts about a person's situation, which remain stable amid the flux of immediate and potentially fallible judgment.[17] Assessing a person's capabilities might involve gathering empirical data on how many hours a person actually works instead of soliciting the person's own point of view about whether she thinks she works too hard. Alternatively, such assessment might involve identifying a person's options for achieving alternative means for meeting her basic needs, in order to determine whether the person has a real option to work less. By documenting observable outcomes rather than focusing exclusively on subjective states of mind, we can empirically verify certain components of well-being. Thus, in addition to providing a more accurate assessment of individual well-being than one's income and resources can convey, capabilities lend themselves to less subjective (and therefore, potentially less distorted) forms of well-being assessment.[18]

To summarize: the view of well-being that Sen and Nussbaum advance defines well-being in terms of the conditions and states of enablement—the capabilities—that make it possible for people to pursue and to choose to pursue a wide variety of activities and achievements. In addition to providing a view of well-being that is more accurate and less subject to distortion than common approaches to assessing and comparing it, capabilities can also describe the components of human living in a way that distinguishes humans as developmental beings whose activities and achievements take a specifically human form. Taken together, these components comprise the basic features of a theory of well-being that defines both what comprises well-being and why, thus conceived, it can improve well-being assessment as theorized and practiced in international development policy. Before discussing the implications of this theory of well-being for the evaluation of environmental policy, let us first consider how capabilities theory has been advanced as a political theory that specifies and justifies the boundaries of politically legitimate government action.

3.2.2 Capabilities, social justice, and self-defined choice

Although Sen and Nussbaum's capabilities theory has sought to address theoretical and practical problems in international development policy, it is

[16] The problem of "adaptive preferences" is discussed more completely in Elster (1983); Sen (1987a, 1990).

[17] Sen (1992:43).

[18] As Alkire (2002) has shown in the context of assessing micro-development projects, more objective assessments are also likely to follow from processes of self-evaluation that are thoughtfully structured and well-facilitated.

strongly engaged with the "liberal" tradition of political thought.[19] At a basic level, this tradition is concerned with the definition of individual liberty (or freedom) and with the nature of a political order and structure of government that can adequately and legitimately protect it. In this context, liberal political theorists tend to treat ideas such as individual autonomy and individual consent in one's social relations as normatively basic. Furthermore, because political and legal authority are components of a social order that can potentially undermine individual freedom, these theorists address them as forms of authority in need of justification. While Sen's argument that capabilities provide the best conception of well-being for assessing inequality is directly engaged with liberal theories of justice, Nussbaum, who is a philosopher by training, has gone further than Sen in developing the components of a theory of justice that takes the ideas about well-being discussed earlier in this chapter as its point of departure.[20] In particular, Nussbaum advances her own "capabilities approach" as a substantive theory of justice that defines and justifies political principles that should underlie constitutional guarantees in liberal democratic societies.

Before elaborating Nussbaum's theory of justice, it is important to note that some authors, notably David Crocker (2008), Sharath Srinivasan (2007), Severine Deneulin (2005), and James Bohman (1997), have pushed Amartya Sen's ideas toward more direct engagement with political theory, and especially with theories addressing how democratic political procedures can better support the political agency of citizens. However, Sen himself, who is an economist by training, has tended to resist developing his own work as a more substantive account of justice. Likewise, even in his recent work, which specifically addresses the topic of social justice, Sen strongly criticizes theories that offer up blueprints and standards concerning what is required in a perfectly just society. Here he also emphasizes his commitment to a process of public reasoning about the institutions, policies, and particular strategies that will get us closer to such ideals.[21] In this respect his account of justice remains somewhat procedural. More generally and prior to this recent work, Sen has advanced his "capability approach" as a general framework for evaluating social arrangements and individual advantage, not as a well-defined or even partial theory of social justice. In keeping with this agenda, his

[19] Robeyns (2005:95).

[20] See Sen (2009) for his most comprehensive summary and development of the capability approach as a unique account of justice.

[21] In his most recent work on justice Sen (2009:esp. 321–415) endorses what he refers to as a "comparative approach" to justice, which differs from the "transcendental institutionalism" of Rawls and others in that it seeks to identify which among actual institutional practices and outcomes exemplify manifest injustice, rather than appealing to unrealistic and idealistic principles that would govern a perfectly just society.

capability approach is deliberately underspecified, which presumably allows for its application in many different disciplinary and applied contexts.[22]

Notably, Sen does not therefore propose or endorse a list of capabilities that academics or practitioners can use as a basis for evaluating policy outcomes. He argues that his reluctance to offer such a generalized list of valuable capabilities reflects his commitment to people's political agency, which is exercised in specific contexts, when people deliberate and reason together to define for themselves what capabilities should be relevant to political decisions or policy assessments.[23] In particular, Sen fears that relying on a "fixed list [of capabilities], emanating entirely from pure theory," will "deny the possibility of fruitful public participation on what should be included [on the list of important capabilities] and why."[24] It is the "act of reasoning" in an engaged public discussion that Sen wishes to preserve, for it leaves room for individuals to act as agents or authors of their own lives in determining what capabilities matter to them.[25] In this respect, although Sen does not advance a list of universal capabilities as background conditions of democracy that can be used as a basis for making claims on governments, he does state a strong commitment to the kind of freedom that would be involved in planning one's life or participating in democratic decision-making processes. Implicit in this view is the idea that politically legitimate government action should (at the very least) involve governmental support and respect for the capabilities that enable people to develop and advance their political agency.[26]

Because I am interested in a theory of justice that can provide substantive criteria for a generalizable approach to policy evaluation, as well as substantive constraints on democratic processes that occur within existing regulatory processes but fail to meet the idealized conditions assumed by many advocates of deliberative forms of public reasoning, the approach to policy design and evaluation that I develop in the forthcoming chapters relies more heavily on Nussbaum's account of justice than on Sen's related work. As previously mentioned, Nussbaum differs from Sen in explicitly developing a theory of substantive justice—the "capabilities approach"—that endorses a list of "central human functional capabilities"[27] that she advances as a basis

[22] See Robeyns (2005:103–104).

[23] See Sen (2004). See Nussbaum (2003) for a discussion of why Sen's capability approach lacks practical usefulness without specification of a list of endorsed capabilities.

[24] Sen (2005:157–158).

[25] Some scholars view this commitment to individual or political agency as a feature of Sen's capability approach that allows him to avoid the charge of paternalism. For example, see Crocker (2008:125).

[26] See Srinivasan (2007) for a development of this argument, and Denuelin (2005) describing political freedom as a capability.

[27] Throughout this text I will refer to these "central human functional capabilities" interchangeably with "central human capabilities" and "central capabilities."

for legitimate claims concerning what citizens in liberal democratic societies have a right to demand from their governments.[28] Specifically, the list of capabilities that Nussbaum proposes as constitutional guarantees is composed of the following:[29]

1. **Life.** Being able to live to the end of a human life of normal length; not dying prematurely, or before one's life is so reduced as to be not worth living.
2. **Bodily Health.** Being able to have good health, including reproductive health; to be adequately nourished, to have adequate shelter.
3. **Bodily Integrity.** Being able to move freely from place to place; having one's bodily boundaries treated as sovereign, i.e. being able to be secure against assault, including sexual assault, child sexual abuse, and domestic violence; having opportunities for sexual satisfaction and for choice in matters of reproduction.
4. **Senses, Imagination, and Thought.** Being able to use the senses, to imagine, think, and reason—and to do these things in a "truly human" way, a way informed and cultivated by an adequate education, including, but by no means limited to, literacy and basic mathematical and scientific training. Being able to use imagination and thought in connection with experiencing and producing self-expressive works and events of one's own choice, religious, literary, musical, and so forth. Being able to use one's mind in ways protected by guarantees of freedom of expression with respect to both political and artistic speech, and freedom of religious exercise. Being able to search for the ultimate meaning of life in one's own way. Being able to have pleasurable experiences, and to avoid non-necessary pain.
5. **Emotions.** Being able to have attachments to things and people outside ourselves; to love those who love and care for us, to grieve at their absence; in general, to love, to grieve, to experience longing,

[28] See Nussbaum (2000a, 2006, 2011) for her most recent and complete elaboration of the "capabilities approach" to justice. Although Sen is explicit in emphasizing the importance of citizens' political agency, it should be noted that Nussbaum's list of central human capabilities does include a general commitment to effective political participation, which is a component of her tenth central human capability. While critics such as Menon (2002) and Crocker (2008) argue that Nussbaum's theory of justice does not sufficiently allow for the protection and development of one's political agency, I would argue that these critiques sometimes fail to acknowledge the extent to which achieving the forms of political agency they advocate would require the kind of background political protections that Nussbaum's theory of justice seeks to establish. For example, this is the case in the non-idealized and actually existing democratic contexts I discuss in Chapter 6.

[29] Nussbaum (2000a:78–80). For ease of reference, the full list of capabilities as defined by Nussbaum is provided in the Appendix.

gratitude, and justified anger. Not having one's emotional development blighted by overwhelming fear and anxiety, or by traumatic events of abuse or neglect. (Supporting this capability means supporting forms of human association that can be shown to be crucial in their development.)

6. **Practical Reason.** Being able to form a conception of the good and to engage in critical reflection about the planning of one's life. (This entails protection for the liberty of conscience.)
7. **Affiliation.**
   A. Being able to live with and toward others, to recognize and show concern for other human beings, to engage in various forms of social interaction; to be able to imagine the situation of another and to have compassion for that situation; to have the capability for both justice and friendship. (Protecting this capability means protecting institutions that constitute and nourish such forms of affiliation, and also protecting the freedom of assembly and political speech.)

   B. Having the social bases of self-respect and non-humiliation; being able to be treated as a dignified being whose worth is equal to that of others. This entails at a minimum, protections against discrimination on the basis of race, sex, sexual orientation, religion, caste, ethnicity, or national origin. In work, being able to work as a human being, exercising practical reason and entering into meaningful relationships of mutual recognition with other workers.
8. **Other Species.** Being able to live with concern for and in relation to animals, plants, and the world of nature.
9. **Play.** Being able to laugh, to play, to enjoy recreational activities.
10. **Control over One's Environment.**
    A. **Political.** Being able to participate effectively in political choices that govern one's life; having the right of political participation, protections of free speech and association.

    B. **Material.** Being able to hold property (both land and moveable goods), not just formally but in terms of real opportunity; and having property rights on an equal basis with others; having the right to seek employment on an equal basis with others; having the freedom from unwarranted search and seizure.

In Nussbaum's account of justice, protection of these ten capabilities at a "threshold level" for each person is the bare minimum of what justice and respect for human dignity requires.[30] If people are falling short of this threshold level of capability, then they are falling short of a good human life.

Given this view of what social justice consists in, much of Nussbaum's scholarship in capabilities theory involves arguing why liberal democratic societies should treat protecting these ten central capabilities as a political goal.[31] Here, a key feature of Nussbaum's general approach to justice is that it has evolved in critical but constructive engagement with the liberal political theory of John Rawls. Rawls advanced and justified what are perhaps the most frequently referenced principles for ordering the basic structure of a liberal and socially just democratic society.[32] While his work is widely celebrated, it is also criticized for overlooking or ignoring the special circumstances that pose barriers for women, disabled citizens, non-citizens, and non-human animals. Thus, part of Nussbaum's project is to develop her own approach to justice that overcomes these problems in Rawls's theory, while incorporating aspects of his theory that she finds intuitively appealing and philosophically persuasive. She argues, in particular, that, like the content of Rawls's theory of justice, her capabilities approach should not be understood as a form of "comprehensive liberalism."[33] Instead, the list of capabilities is advanced as the core of a political conception of justice that can be used to define "fundamental political principles" or "specifically political goals" without adopting and mandating any particular view of what a good life must involve.[34]

A central argument that Nussbaum offers as to why protecting the list of central human capabilities at a threshold level for each person does not favor or prioritize any particular conception of the good hinges on the distinction between capabilities and the *functionings* they enable. Specifically, what people are effectively able to do or achieve (i.e. their capabilities) is different from what people do in fact do or achieve (i.e. their functionings). A person's "functionings" refer to a person's actual "doings" and "beings." Like the

[30] Nussbaum (2006:71).

[31] Nussbaum's burden in this regard is much bigger than Sen's, for although Sen has critically questioned liberal political thinkers for assessing the inequalities that are relevant to justice in the wrong evaluative space (as Section 3.2.1 discusses), Sen has not advanced a specific list of capabilities that are universally required as a matter of basic justice. Nussbaum (2000:11–15) describes Sen as focusing more on issues of poverty and deprivation in developing countries and on issues of quantitative analysis and the measurement of well-being and inequality. See Robeyns (2005:104), who discusses these and other differences between Sen and Nussbaum; also see Sen's (2009) effort to develop a "comparative approach" (rather than a "transcendental approach") to justice.

[32] See Chapter 5, Section 5.3, for a detailed discussion of these principles.

[33] See Rawls (1993:195–200). Comprehensive liberalism refers to a form of liberalism that threatens the possibility of maintaining "reasonable pluralism" in different views of the good that citizens can hold because it includes features such as an overall theory of value or a controversial metaphysical view of people and/or society.

[34] See Nussbaum (2000a:5, 70, 75–77). Nussbaum models the justification of her political principles on a Rawlsian method of "reflective equilibrium," which I discuss later in this chapter.

capabilities that make them possible, functionings can range "from the most elementary [achievements], such as being well-nourished, avoiding escapable morbidity and premature mortality, etc., to quite complex and sophisticated achievements, such as having self-respect, being able to take part in the life of the community, and so on."[35] However, the crucial difference between a person's functionings and a person's capabilities is that a person's functionings result from what a person chooses to do or achieve. Functionings are a product of individual choice, but it is an individual's capabilities that make him more or less free to choose his own functionings, or ends.[36] In this respect, a capabilities-based view of well-being instructs us that capabilities must precede choices, if one's choices are to be defined as genuine. It follows that assessment of a person's capabilities is central to determining whether her functioning achievements are a product of self-defined choices. If we look at people's choices rather than their capabilities, we may miss the ways in which less obvious forms of desperation or explicit forms of intimidation and harassment are shaping people's preferences.

Thus, for Nussbaum, a government that protects a threshold level of the ten central human capabilities for each person can remain neutral among competing conceptions of the good because capabilities are not about a person's ends, rather they are about the conditions of enablement that make it possible for one to define and choose to pursue one's own idea of what a good life involves. Protecting people's capabilities therefore preserves rather than denies genuine individual choice. For Nussbaum, the importance of genuine choice is precisely why the list of central human capabilities includes not just commonly accepted political freedoms (such as political speech and religious exercise), but also material and economic protections, such as being able to have adequate nourishment and the real opportunity to hold property on an equal basis with others. Nussbaum recognizes that for many people these material and economic protections must be met before one is free to choose to exercise civil and political freedoms. In short, treating people equally as a matter of justice requires protecting the capabilities that must precede self-defined choices.[37]

Nussbaum argues that protecting the central human capabilities could be the subject of an "overlapping consensus" of the kind that Rawls uses to justify the content of his own theory of justice. Central to this argument is

[35] Sen (1992:5).

[36] For these and other reasons, Sen (e.g. 1999:75) has argued that in principle we should assess well-being in terms of what people are able to do—specifically, in terms of people's capabilities, not their functionings. Gore (1997:237) discusses the evolution of Sen's work on capabilities, which first emphasized the importance of looking at objective features of well-being, and then went on to address how preferences and capabilities relate to "freedom of choice."

[37] See Nussbaum (1992:225, 2006:288–289).

the previously discussed idea that the list of capabilities is not a list of functionings, and it therefore leaves people free to choose for themselves the ethical, religious, and cultural views that will define their lives. Following Rawls, Nussbaum theorizes a political order that allows for the coexistence of a plurality of views about what a good human life involves, and she argues that people with conflicting but "reasonable" conceptions of the good could endorse the list of capabilities she proposes as constitutional entitlements.[38] However, this remains a project that is distinct from advancing a full moral conception of justice; the capabilities approach does not even advance an "exhaustive account of political justice," for Nussbaum admits that there may even be important political values closely connected with justice that her theory does not include. In this sense, Nussbaum's capabilities approach is a "partial" theory of justice that is politically liberal in that people are left free to determine the actual functionings that will make up their lives.[39]

Finally, what these arguments from neutrality and choice leave unanswered is why the particular list of capabilities that Nussbaum advances can be understood as instrumental to any individual conception of the good, such that all people would endorse the list as relevant to goals they value. Here Nussbaum offers two reasons. First, she argues that the list of capabilities enables people to do and achieve things that people in many different cultures and contexts would agree are valuable. In fact, the list was drafted over a number of years during which time Nussbaum engaged in collaborative dialogue with citizens in many different societies, wherein she has attempted to approximate the ideal of achieving a cross-cultural consensus about the capabilities that enable experiences all people would agree are worthwhile.[40] This is partly why the substance of the list of capabilities remains articulated at a "somewhat abstract and general" level, so that it can be the subject of an "overlapping consensus" among people with reasonable but conflicting views of what a good human life entails.[41] Nussbaum is advancing the list as basis for political discussion and dialogue, which will presumably leave room for specifying the capabilities differently in the context of public debate about the needs and histories of specific peoples in specific places.[42] As such, the list is also subject to revision over time. However, while Nussbaum rejects the idea that the items on the list should be subject to removal by the whims of a democratic majority that may seize power at a single point in history, she does leave room for significant change to the list that might result from democratic outcomes that are persistent and supported

[38] Nussbaum (2004) addresses several (common) confusions about the methodological and normative justification for her capabilities approach.

[39] See Nussbaum (2000a:78–80).

[40] Nussbaum (1993:78–80, 265).

[41] Nussbaum (2006:163).

[42] See Nussbaum (2006:78–79).

through sustained and reflective moral argument about what a good human life requires.

The second reason Nussbaum offers as to why her list of capabilities could be the object of agreement among people with different and perhaps conflicting conceptions of what a good life entails is that the list of capabilities can be justified according to the same method of reasoning toward a "reflective equilibrium" that Rawls uses to justify the political principles defining his account of justice. As generally understood in the context of Rawls's theory of justice, reflective equilibrium refers to the end point of a deliberative process in which people reason back and forth among (a) their considered judgments (or "intuitions") about particular instances, (b) the principles or rules that they believe govern these considered judgments, and (c) the theoretical considerations that they believe bear on accepting these judgments, principles, or rules, while revising these elements in an effort to achieve coherence among them. When there is a high degree of coherence, then the principles or rules can claim to be more legitimate or justifiable. As Nussbaum explains:[43]

> The account of political justification that I favor lies close to the Rawlsian account of argument proceeding toward reflective equilibrium: we lay out the arguments for a given theoretical position, holding it up against the "fixed points" in our moral intuitions; we see how those intuitions both test and are tested by the conceptions we examine. . .We hope, over time, to achieve consistency and fit in our judgments taken as a whole, modifying particular judgments when this seems required by a theoretical conception that seems in other respects powerful, but modifying or rejecting the theoretical conception when that has failed to fit the most secure of our moral intuitions.

In accordance with this model of political justification, Nussbaum's list of capabilities is subject to revisions according to what reasoning toward such a reflective equilibrium would produce.[44] In other words, the list is to remain

[43] Nussbaum (2000a:101–102).

[44] While adopting Rawls's reflective equilibrium as her method of political justification, Nussbaum differs from Rawls in one important respect. Whereas Rawls relies on a procedural justification—one that is modeled on the traditional social contract for establishing a just political order—to arrive at the principles that he subjects to the process of reflective equilibrium, Nussbaum takes a more outcome-oriented approach to "commend the conception [of justice] initially, before the comparative assessment begins." See Nussbaum (2004:196). Specifically, instead of arriving at the content of justice by imagining ourselves into a hypothetical state of nature in which parties agree to a social contract under a "veil of ignorance" that prevents them from knowing their potential status in the resulting political order, Nussbaum's method for arriving at the initial list involves making "intuitive arguments about what a good outcome is, in the form of an account of a minimally decent and just society." See Nussbaum (2004:197). Socratic reasoning about the basic preconditions—or capabilities—required for living a life

open for revisions that result from a society's efforts to square individual intuitions with considered judgments about what is good.[45]

To summarize capabilities theory as an account of justice and a method of political justification, Sen and Nussbaum both offer accounts of what politically legitimate government action should be understood to involve. For Sen, the account is more procedural than substantive, but can reasonably be taken to require protecting the capabilities that enable political agency for individual citizens. Nussbaum aims to give her account of justice more bite as an evaluative tool and as a justification for political and legal claims in a liberal democratic society, and she therefore defines a list of ten central human capabilities that social justice requires protecting for each individual person at a threshold level. She justifies these protections (which she understands as the basis for constitutional guarantees) as politically legitimate because they do not endorse any particular conception of what a good life involves, but rather provide protections that make people free to choose and pursue their own conception of the good; capabilities are the basis for making self-defined choices. Therefore, the list of capabilities can be the subject of an overlapping consensus among people in a society characterized by reasonable pluralism. Nussbaum has conceptualized the capabilities at a general and abstract level, such that they can be specified further through a process of political discussion and debate, and she has also composed the list through a process aimed at achieving a degree of cross-cultural consensus on the list's content. But even so, Nussbaum advances the list as subject to the constraints of reasoning toward reflective equilibrium, a process through which the list can be revised so that it will continue to reflect the political constraints and substantive commitments of citizens actually living in liberal democratic societies.

3.3 Expanding Well-Being to Include the Environment

With this understanding of the relationship between functionings, capabilities, and the protection of self-defined choice, we can now return to the questions raised at the start of this chapter concerning *how* we should value the natural environment and *how* we should assess the distributional implications of policies designed to protect it. Questions of how we should value the environment and how we should assess the distributional consequences of

worthy of the dignity of a human being would be the basis for identifying general and abstract conditions that resonate with people the world over. Political procedures would then be defined in accordance with what promotes these outcomes. See Nussbaum (2004:196–201) for a summary and review of her system of political justification.

[45] See Nussbaum (2004).

environmental protection are partly questions about *what* we should value and assess. Specifically, the questions concern what dimensions of human well-being we should consider when we value the environment's role in making a person's life go well and when we assess who benefits from environmental protection.[46] In the remainder of this chapter I will answer these questions in the context of policies that protect the natural environment.

As Chapter 2 explains, from the perspective of economic theory, we should value the environment as a commodity—as an object of consumer choice—by assessing its contribution to the satisfaction of subjective preferences people reveal in real or hypothetical market settings.[47] Capabilities theory, in contrast, would suggest that we should value the environment as a precondition of human functioning—that is, as a basis of self-defined choice—by assessing its contribution to the capabilities that make it possible for people to pursue and thus to choose to pursue those functionings.[48] Toward this end, the relationship between human capabilities and human functionings facilitates the development of a theoretical framework for valuing the environment by providing a broad conception of well-being that illuminates the activities and achievements to which the natural environment is vital. For instance, consider first the variety of relationships between people and particular natural resources (e.g. trees) that people's functionings can characterize. When children climb trees, their faces express a variety of *emotions* that convey the tree's role in the functioning achievement of *play* (which Nussbaum's ninth capability enables), even if children themselves do not recognize the value of the tree in this role. In other instances, a tree may play a role in people's "beings" rather than in their "doings." The tree may, for example, provide resources necessary for building "adequate shelter," and therefore play a role in the functioning achievement of *bodily health*, which Nussbaum's second capability enables. Likewise, because the tree will help to purify air, it will also be involved in the multitude of functionings that one's *bodily health* capability enables, such as living a physically active or mentally stimulating life.

Although a tree may be involved in various other activities and achievements, I bring attention to these particular functionings because they help to distinguish why functionings provide a more accurate category for valuing the environment than people's subjective preferences. Specifically, the

[46] An additional question concerns what dimensions of the natural environment we should consider when we assess its role in making a person's life go well. I take up this question in Chapter 4.

[47] See Chapter 2 for a discussion of both points.

[48] In Chapter 5 I will address why a society that values social justice should provide specific environmental protections; however, for the present purpose of considering the relationship between the environment and individual choice, I rely on the more general justification that environmental protection enables people to choose to pursue the functionings they value.

subjective preferences one expresses regarding the value of a tree may reflect its role in only some of these functionings. For instance, if a person cuts down the tree and uses it to build a shelter, then the person's subjective valuation will likely reflect the tree's value with respect to the goal of achieving shelter. However, a person's subjective valuation may not reflect the tree's contribution to other functionings, such as breathing oxygen, or childhood play. In these latter functionings, the role of the tree may either be unknown to people, or of such a significant value that it is not expressible in monetary terms.[49] Thus, while people's subjective valuations illuminate a narrow dimension of well-being that can reflect the importance of the natural environment to some experiences, assessing the actual functionings to which the environment contributes can convey the environment's value to the diverse forms that human activities and achievements do in fact take.

Characterizing activities and achievements involving the natural environment with respect to distinct and diverse human functionings makes it possible to understand the environment's instrumental value in a *pluralist* form. This pluralist understanding of the environment's instrumental value follows from understanding individual well-being in a pluralist form.[50] Specifically, Sen often emphasizes the importance of expanding the informational bases that inform assessments of well-being to include a wide range of changes in people's quality of life.[51] As Sabina Alkire explains in discussing the capabilities that must precede functioning achievements, the "space" that defines well-being "has quite a substantial degree of internal plurality," and can thus include material capabilities (such as being able to be well nourished) as well as more sophisticated capabilities (such as being wise or contented).[52] Furthermore, capabilities theory views the different dimensions of individual well-being as incommensurable in the sense that more of one capability or functioning achievement does not make up for the loss of another capability or functioning achievement.[53] Simply put, the multiple components of individual well-being are not reducible to a single dimension of well-being.

With respect to environmental valuation, what matters here is that when individual well-being is viewed in this pluralist form, it becomes clear that the environment's instrumental contribution to one dimension of well-being may not be commensurable with its contribution to another dimension of well-being. For example, the loss of a tree that contributes to one's *play* capability may be incommensurable with the loss of a tree that provides lumber

[49] See Chapter 2 for a discussion of the limitations of uninformed preferences and the problem of incommensurable values.

[50] Wolff and de-Shalit (2007:8); Alkire (2002:8–10).

[51] See Sen (1987b:27, 1985:176a, 1980/1).

[52] See Alkire (2002:9).

[53] See Nussbaum (2006:167, 401–403); Wolff and de-Shalit (2007:96–97).

for adequate shelter, which is a component of one's *bodily health* capability. This is because the loss of a tree that contributes to one's *play* capability cannot necessarily be made up for by the provision of a tree that provides lumber for shelter. If playing in the tree has contributed to one's attachment to a certain place, then there may be no amount of lumber that can make up for what the loss of the tree does to a person.[54] In this respect, the pluralist understanding of well-being that the categories of human functionings and capabilities characterize can block the commensuration of environmental values that renders economic valuation of them inaccurate.

Furthermore, just as functionings provide a category for characterizing activities and achievements involving the natural environment that can include much more than the monetized expression of preferences, a person's capabilities provide a category for characterizing the value of the environment to much more than a person's preference satisfaction. To put this point differently, when subsumed in the context of a capability-functioning relationship, the satisfaction component of the preference-satisfaction relationship is exposed as exceedingly narrow. Being able to have one's preferences satisfied certainly may be a valuable capability, but there are many additional conditions or states that enable a good human life. For example, the fifth capability on Nussbaum's list of central capabilities includes being able "to love, to grieve, to experience longing, gratitude and justified anger." Likewise, Nussbaum's third capability includes "having opportunities for sexual satisfaction," while her fourth capability includes "being able to have pleasurable experiences, and to avoid non-necessary pain." Some of these components of a person's capabilities (e.g. loving, longing, and sexual satisfaction) might be understood as something for which people would be able to have a satisfiable preference, but many other components of capabilities that enable a rich and meaningful human life are not well construed as satisfying people's preferences or desires (e.g. grieving and being angry).[55] Thus, although preference satisfaction may be descriptive of some dimensions of human well-being, to the extent it is, there are more descriptive ways of characterizing the richness of human experience; and to the extent that preference satisfaction is not descriptive of well-being, it misses much of the complexity that makes a person's life fully human.

People's capabilities, in contrast, can refer to many conditions of a good human life besides preference satisfaction. This is not only because capabilities expand the emotional and psychological repertoire of concepts that characterize human experience, but also because capabilities highlight the

[54] See Cannavo (2007) for a discussion of the politics surrounding such seemingly entrenched conflicts of place in contemporary society.

[55] See Nussbaum (1997a:1209–1212).

material, social, and political components of a life that meets minimal conditions of what basic respect for human dignity requires.[56] In the argument Nussbaum offers for protecting these capabilities, people should not merely be capable of experiencing both positive and negative emotional states; they should also be equipped with material resources, as well as the conditions necessary for social and communal relationships, political rights, and economic opportunities.[57] Capabilities theory, in short, relies on a conception of well-being that can identify multiple and specific conditions of well-being that matter to people—conditions besides merely being able to have one's preferences satisfied.

Thus, rather than assessing the extent to which a policy will make people more or less able to satisfy their subjective preferences, a capabilities approach to policy evaluation would seek to assess the extent to which a policy makes people more or less able to achieve different components of well-being, such as having adequate shelter, moving freely from place to place, producing self-expressive works and events of one's own choice, avoiding having one's emotional development blighted by overwhelming fear and traumatic events, engaging in various forms of social interaction, enjoying recreational activities, holding property that provides one with real opportunity, and so on. Additionally, because these and many other components of well-being are understood as essential conditions that enable people to make choices, an environmental policy's impact on them matters, even if people do not choose to pursue the functionings that these capabilities put within their reach. In this sense we should understand capabilities theory as offering the theoretical basis for an approach to policy evaluation that is less concerned with determining the extent to which a policy's impact will make people more or less able to satisfy their preferences, and more concerned with documenting *which* dimensions of well-being a policy will expand or contract, as well as *for whom*, and by *how much*.

I will return to these latter issues concerning who benefits from environmental protection in Section 3.3.1. My present purpose is to highlight why

[56] As Chapter 4 will discuss, this is one reason why Nussbaum's theory of justice improves on John Rawls's (1971, 1993) theory of justice. Nussbaum wants to protect civil and political freedoms as well as social and economic guarantees at a threshold level for each person. For Nussbaum, the latter must be protected, regardless of where one falls with respect to the least advantaged group or class in society. See Nussbaum (2006:288–289).

[57] Although some capability theorists propose central capabilities that are different from Nussbaum's, and although some propose a method for selecting those capabilities that differs from the method Nussbaum proposes, in both of these instances the list of relevant capabilities that other theorists arrive at involves more than being able to satisfy one's preferences. Even those who disagree with the content and/or justification of Nussbaum's list of capabilities tend to (a) elevate the role of political agency as a capability, (b) give a more locally specific description of capabilities (as Nussbaum often recommends is appropriate), and/or (c) add to Nussbaum's list to include even more capabilities.

conceiving of people's well-being in terms of their capabilities to function significantly expands the dimensions of well-being to which the natural environment can be made relevant. I have argued that if we assess the value of a particular environmental resource that a policy protects (e.g. a wilderness area) in relation to people's capabilities, then the assessment can include the value of the wilderness's contribution to dimensions of well-being to which people know the wilderness contributes, such as producing self-expressive works of one's own choice (e.g. when a particular image in a wilderness area inspires an artist), or engaging in various forms of social interaction (e.g. when a group of fellow hikers treks through the wilderness). But the assessment can also include the value of this wilderness area to dimensions of well-being that people do not know the wilderness enables. For instance, the role of the wilderness as a carbon sink may be important to climate stabilization, which makes the wilderness valuable to maintaining the atmosphere's chemical composition, and thereby preventing the impacts of climate change, such as loss of agricultural land in drought-ridden countries, or the fear and trauma that results from severe weather, such as many hurricane victims experience.[58]

Thus, a central advantage of treating the environment as instrumental to people's capabilities is that this relationship is broad enough to characterize the range of ways in which people are involved in relationships with the natural environment. By valuing the environment in relation to people's capabilities to function, it is possible to broaden the dimensions of well-being—beyond the mental state of preference satisfaction—to which the natural environment can be made relevant. Just as human functionings provide a more accurate representation of the activities and states of well-being in which people realize the natural environment's value as a matter of self-determined choice, human capabilities provide a more accurate account of the multiple ways in which the environment contributes to the various preconditions—or capabilities—that enable one to make those choices. Whether assessing well-being in terms of these capabilities, or in terms of the functionings a person does in fact achieve, we can arrive at a more accurate and nuanced view of the environment's value.

3.3.1 Revealing differential impacts and capability conflict

The broader conception of individual well-being that capabilities theory advances also has significant implications for improving the justification of policies protecting the environment. As Chapter 2 discusses, the problem

[58] See Holland (2012) for discussion of how Hurricane Katrina impacted the various capabilities of those who fled New Orleans, Louisiana, in August 2005.

of justification in contemporary policy analysis arises because of the failure to systematically evaluate policies with respect to values besides economic efficiency. By defining a policy's social value (i.e. its overall contribution to society) in terms of maximizing net economic benefits, current evaluation disregards how those benefits are distributed among different people, and hence, it disregards the extent to which some people suffer inadequate and unequal protection from environmental harms.[59] This potentially undermines the political legitimacy of policies that are justified in terms of the values implicit in the current economic approach to policy evaluation because such policies may violate legal rules that prevent government-funded programs from having disparate impacts, and they may ignore equally important political ideals such as political equality and social justice.[60] Assessing policies with respect to these latter ideals will require making comparative assessments of how policies impact different people.

Many academic studies document the problem of environmental inequity and find that the people who suffer the biggest burden from exposure to environmental harms are those who also suffer from other forms of social, economic, and political disadvantage.[61] For this reason, environmental inequities contribute to what Jonathan Wolff and Avner de-Shalit explain as a "clustering" of disadvantage: a distribution of disadvantage in which the same people experience low levels of attainment along multiple dimensions of their well-being.[62] "Declustering" such disadvantage requires preventing a distribution of disadvantage in which the same people do badly overall. For example, if disadvantage were declustered, it would be unclear who the worst-off people are, for people with low levels of attainment along one or two dimensions of well-being would not also have low levels of attainment along various other dimensions of their well-being. Consequently, no person or group of people could be described as worst off by multiple measures,

[59] There is a significant amount of empirical documentation demonstrating that low-income, (often) minority communities disproportionately bear the burden of exposure to various environmental harms, such as hazardous waste, air pollution, pesticides, and household toxins. Cole and Foster (2001:167–183) provide an annotated bibliography of research, documenting and describing the disproportionate impact of environmental hazards by race and income.

[60] The legal rule that most directly addresses the disproportionate impact of environmental protection in the USA is the "Executive Order on Federal Action to Address Environmental Justice in Minority and Low-Income Populations," which was issued by President Bill Clinton in 1994. See Executive Order 12,898, 3 C.F.R. 859 (1995). A memorandum accompanying this executive order also directs federal agencies to comply with the non-discrimination requirements of Title VI of the Civil Rights Act, which prohibits discriminatory effects of programs receiving federal funding. See 42 U.S.C. 2000d to 2000d-7 (1994).

[61] For example, a *National Law Journal* study published in 1992 documented that, between 1985 and 1991, the average penalties imposed for violations of federal environmental protection standards regulating air and water quality, as well as hazardous waste pollution, were 46 percent higher in white communities than in minority communities. See Lavelle and Coyle (1992).

[62] Wolff and de-Shalit (2007:103).

only as less well-off than others in some respect, and better off than others in a different respect.[63] Wolff and de-Shalit persuasively argue that if public policies are going to produce a more equal distribution of disadvantage, then they must be informed by an understanding of well-being in which "everything that affects people for good or ill can figure in an understanding of their level of advantage and disadvantage."[64]

With this in mind, in order to justify environmental policies with respect to their distributional impacts, it is necessary to conceive of individual well-being (or advantage) in a way that accounts for the multiple dimensions of well-being that environmental harms can undermine. The capabilities-based conception of well-being that Sen and Nussbaum advance is central to this goal. Because people's capabilities include dimensions of well-being with which environmental harms come into most direct contact, assessing a policy's impact on people's capabilities to function can reveal the multiple channels through which a given environmental harm—and hence, a given amount of environmental protection—will produce different impacts on different people.[65] This is an important reason why an approach to policy evaluation that adopts a capabilities-based understanding of well-being will produce information necessary for justifying environmental protection with respect to non-economic legal and political goals that current policy evaluation neglects.

However, even without relating environmental policies to non-economic political goals, at the level of well-being assessment capabilities offer a distinct advantage over preferences because they are constituted by both the internal and external conditions that determine whether people suffer harm at a given level of environmental protection. By internal and external conditions I mean, respectively, a person's personal powers and traits, such as physical and mental health, and a person's external circumstances, such as the social norms, familial relationships, and monetary resources that enable or prevent a person from pursuing otherwise recognizable opportunities.[66] Vast variation among people with respect to their experience of these conditions of well-being is especially important in assessing the social value of environmental policies. Specifically, these conditions determine *whether* and *to what extent* people will be able to avoid exposure to environmental harms. As I discuss in relation to clean air policy later in this chapter, a capabilities approach to valuing the environment can account for how these conditions make people vary in their capability to avoid exposure to environmental harms. An evaluative framework that involves assessing a policy's impact on people's capabilities can therefore reveal the extent to which environmental

[63] Wolff and de-Shalit (2007:131).
[64] Wolff and de-Shalit (2007:8).
[65] I will return to this topic in Chapter 4.
[66] See Crocker (2008:174).

protection or degradation disproportionately impacts specific people or groups of people. Let us briefly explore this point with respect to the relationship between people's capabilities and policies regulating air quality.

In the United States, the Clean Air Act (CAA) regulates ambient air pollution by establishing "national ambient air quality standards" for six "criteria pollutants."[67] Two of these pollutants—fine particulate matter and ground-level ozone—are nonetheless present in the air at levels above the national standard in many different geographical locations around the United States.[68] Because both ground-level ozone and fine particulate matter are forms of air pollution that are known to trigger asthma (in addition to furthering a variety of other respiratory disorders), failure to meet the CAA standards poses a threat to public health. Most relevant to issues of distribution and equality, the occurrence and extent of this problem will be different depending on how people vary with respect to their existing condition of bodily health. We can understand this as a variation in the *bodily health* capability of different people.

For example, when exposed to the same level of fine particulate pollution, a child who has asthma (and therefore lacks the achievement of "good health") and a child who is free from asthma (and who therefore has achieved "good health," assuming the child has no other health problems) will be able to do different things. The asthmatic child will be unable to play outside on highly polluted days and will be unable to attend school when the cumulative impact of air pollution and other triggers produce an asthmatic reaction.[69] In light of these conditions, a policy that reduces the allowable level of fine particulate matter in the air will produce more benefits for children that already have asthma. But the benefits of a policy controlling fine particulate that flow to this group of asthmatic children do not simply involve an increase in the extent of each child's *bodily health* capability. There will also be an increase in the extent of asthmatic children's *play* capability, which involves being able to enjoy recreational activities, and in the extent of their

[67] See 40 C.F.R. Part 50 (1994).

[68] For example, in 2012, over 133 million people in the United States lived in counties not meeting air quality standards for ground-level ozone, and over 28 million people in the United States lived in counties not meeting air quality standards for fine particulate matter. See Environmental Protection Agency (n.d.). "Air Trends: Number of People Living in Counties with Air Quality Concentrations above the Level of the NAAQS for 2012." Available at: <http://www.epa.gov/airtrends/aqtrends.html#airquality> (accessed April 25, 2014). For designations of non-compliance with ground-level ozone standards established in 1997, see Environmental Protection Agency (n.d.). "Areas Designated for the 1997 Air Quality Standards." Available at: <http://www.epa.gov/ozonedesignations/1997standards/statedesig.htm> (accessed April 25, 2014). For designations of non-compliance with particulate matter standards established in 2006, see Environmental Protection Agency (n.d.), "Area Designations for 2006 24-Hour Fine Particle ($PM_{2.5}$) Standards." Available at: <http://www.epa.gov/pmdesignations/2006standards/state.htm> (accessed April 25, 2014).

[69] See Nocon and Booth (1989–1990); Coughlin (1988); Donnelly et al. (1987).

senses, imagination, and thought capability, which involves being able to form and cultivate such dimensions of one's life through an adequate education.

Because people's capabilities depend on their various personal powers and internal traits, assessing capabilities provides a lens for viewing how variation in people's personal powers and traits will result in different levels of environmental protection for people living in an area meeting the same level of air quality. In the example just described, for two children with different physical traits (i.e. one with asthma and one without), evaluating the impact of a given pollution control standard from the standpoint of capabilities would show that the standard would provide greater benefits to children with asthma. Furthermore, this evaluation would also show that the benefits of an air quality standard are not merely relevant to improving one's health because areas meeting the air quality standard would also provide recreational and education benefits to children with asthma. A capabilities-based conception of well-being can, in this way, help to identify variation in people's need for environmental protection that proceeds from their personal powers and traits—that is, from the internal conditions shaping a person's overall capability to function in many different ways and for many different purposes.

A conception of individual well-being that focuses on people's capabilities also has important advantages for illuminating the way in which people's external conditions determine the extent to which they benefit from an environmental policy. Consider a slightly different example, in which two children both experience the same internal condition of having asthma, while facing different external conditions with respect to their wealth and mobility. Evaluating the capabilities that refer to or depend on these external conditions reveals why and how the two children will experience different levels of environmental protection from the same standard of pollution control for ground-level ozone.

The current standard for the allowable amount of ground-level ozone in the ambient air is .075 ppm, although it is a level frequently exceeded in various areas around the United States.[70] If two children with varying conditions of external well-being live in an area where poor air quality hovers around the .075 ppm standard but nonetheless frequently triggers asthma attacks, the child whose family has the financial resources and professional mobility to move away from the polluted area may do so, thus improving the child's *bodily health* capability.[71] Specifically, for an asthmatic child with wealth and

[70] Ground-level ozone is a gas formed when nitrogen oxide (e.g. from automobile emissions) reacts with oxygen in the presence of sunlight. The "ppm" designation refers to the allowable level or concentration of ozone—parts per million—in a specified amount (or unit) of air.

[71] See Bernard Williams's (1987:99–100) brief exchange with Amartya Sen, discussing the importance of one's ability to migrate away from an area with polluted air as influencing one's capability to function.

mobility, the .075 ppm standard may ultimately initiate a series of parental actions that increase the child's *bodily health* capability, and this child would experience a decline in asthmatic illness due to his new location in a geographic area that has cleaner air. This example demonstrates that for two children facing the same internal traits (having asthma) and different external conditions (unequal wealth and mobility), a given pollution control standard may result in more benefits for the child with external conditions that enable him to move away from the polluted area.

However, whereas the asthmatic child with wealth and mobility may benefit more from a .075 ppm ozone standard, a decision by the Environmental Protection Agency (EPA) to decrease the allowable level of ground-level ozone from .075 ppm to .060 ppm would produce a greater improvement in *bodily health* for the child who lacks the financial resources and professional mobility to migrate away from an area with poor air quality. This is because the new standard will presumably initiate some efforts to reduce emissions, so that even if the new standard is still sometimes violated, the less wealthy and less mobile child will now experience air quality (at least with respect to ground-level ozone) closer to that available to the asthmatic child whose family had the resources and mobility to move to an area with cleaner air. The child who moved, in contrast, may not benefit from the improved air quality standard, because the area where he lives already has cleaner air and therefore will not adopt less polluting practices due to new pollution control standards. Therefore, whereas the .075 ppm standard would produce greater capability improvements for the child with wealth and mobility, the .060 standard would provide greater capability improvements for the child whose family lacks those financial and professional resources.

In comparing the impact of pollution control policy on these two children, however, it is important to notice that the changes it produces in the *bodily health* of each child do not suggest the two standards, when taken together, will equalize the benefits that flow to each child from policies controlling air pollution. The child that lacks wealth and mobility may never experience an equivalent level of *bodily health* capability if his exposure to pollution at the .075 ppm standard has permanently compromised his respiratory system.[72] Likewise, this child may have lost irreplaceable recreational and educational opportunities during his exposure to air quality that met the .075 ppm standard.

An account of well-being that recognizes the importance of how variation in the conditions that define a person's capabilities will produce different

[72] For example, children who face repeated short-term exposure to high levels of ozone will experience reduced lung function as children, but because their lungs are developing, this exposure may also lead to reduced lung function in adulthood. This is because cells repeatedly damaged by ozone will eventually lead to permanent scarring of lung tissue. See EPA (2009:6).

and unequal levels of environmental protection can improve contemporary evaluation of environmental policy. With respect to air pollution control, the advantages of assessing people's capabilities in policy evaluation extend beyond merely avoiding the inaccuracies in valuation that a WTP approach entails.[73] Evaluating people's capabilities could indeed avoid such inaccuracies; however, this advantage is less pertinent to air pollution control policy because the US Congress has specifically directed EPA to set air pollution control standards according to what is necessary for protecting the nation's "public health and welfare."[74] More importantly, as the examples of exposure to fine particulate and ground-level ozone show, even in a policy area in which congressional intent is understood to explicitly prioritize public health over economic analysis, a capabilities approach can enhance policy outcomes by illuminating the varying impact a policy has on different people, due to the different circumstances they face.

In particular, assessing a policy impact on people's capabilities involves accounting for multiple internal and external conditions that determine whether people are actually able to make choices that will improve their lives. These conditions define well-being in a way that is broad enough to capture a policy's impact on one's bodily health, as well as the dimensions of one's overall health and welfare that tend to vary with changes in bodily health, such as one's recreational and educational activities. Likewise, the capabilities-based account of well-being is also nuanced enough to capture how these conditions situate people differently with respect to the stated goals of clean air policy, which are to provide citizens with protection from environmental harms caused by air pollution. In short, assessing a policy's impact on people's capabilities can guide policy evaluation toward producing information about *how* and *how much* environmental protection improves well-being, and *for whom*.

Understanding whom a policy benefits and the relative level of protection it confers is important for assessing a policy's contribution to non-economic legal and political goals, such as public health, equal opportunity, and equal protection of the law. While Chapter 5 develops an environmentally informed account of social justice that adopts this capabilities-based

[73] Kahn's (2001) economic analysis of clean air policy, for example, shows that the poor have benefitted more than the rich from air quality improvements, but he fails to account for the costs borne by the poor due to bad air quality prior to the improvements he discusses; these costs may offset any meaningful gains to the poor over the rich. Likewise, this analysis does not account for any individual variation among the poor that might result from different capabilities to move away from polluted areas.

[74] Despite legal challenge, the courts have continued to uphold the priority of public health in CAA regulation. See *Whitman et al.* vs. *American Trucking Association et al.* 121 S.Ct. 903. While EPA can consider economic costs determining the primary and secondary air quality standards, public health, not economic costs, is given priority as the relevant social goal. See 42 U.S.C. § 7409 (b) (1994).

conception of well-being, my present purpose has been to emphasize the conceptual advantages that capabilities theory offers to current thinking and reasoning about the value and distribution of environmental protection. Assessing the impact of environmental protection on human capabilities not only makes it possible to consider how environmental policies bear on non-economic social goals, it also requires gathering information that will be necessary for crafting environmental policies that provide equal protection to citizens facing vastly different life circumstances. Understanding the differential impacts a policy produces is crucial to identifying whose capabilities a policy supports and whose capabilities a policy constrains or undermines. By revealing instances in which a policy improving one person's capabilities may undermine another person's capabilities, a capabilities approach to policy evaluation can provide information necessary for resolving "capability conflicts." As I define them in Chapter 5, capability conflicts occur when policies protecting one person's capabilities at a threshold level function to undermine achieving a threshold level of protection for another person's capabilities. Identifying and resolving such conflicts are central to justifying policies in terms of social justice rather than economic efficiency. As a prelude to addressing these tradeoffs, I have endeavored to show how a capabilities-based conception of well-being bears on questions of environmental valuation and the justification of policies having differential impacts. Before taking up these topics of valuation and justification in more detail, let us consider the role a capabilities approach to policy evaluation can play in eliminating environmental relationships that produce "corrosive disadvantages" and supporting environmental relationships that produce "fertile functionings."

3.3.2 Corrosive disadvantages, fertile functionings, and environmental protection

An important feature of the capabilities approach to policy evaluation that I advance in the remaining chapters of this manuscript is that it can help to decluster disadvantage; specifically, by identifying the extent to which environmental policies will help to eliminate "corrosive disadvantages" and secure "fertile functionings." As defined by Wolff and de-Shalit, a "corrosive disadvantage" refers to a disadvantage in one category or dimension of well-being that has negative effects on another category or dimension of well-being.[75] For example, a person living in constant fear of arbitrary assault experiences a low level of *bodily integrity* capability, but may consequently also experience a low level of capabilities for *affiliation* and *control*

[75] Wolff and de-Shalit (2007:121).

over one's environment.[76] This is because fear of assault may lead the person to stay indoors after dark, limiting her ability to develop relationships with people in her community, which would have a negative affect on her social affiliations, as well as her effective participation in the political decisions that shape the community in which she lives.[77]

In contrast, "fertile functioning" refers to an achievement in one category of well-being that has positive effects on other categories of well-being, either by benefitting other categories of well-being directly, or indirectly (e.g. by reducing threats to them).[78] For example, as Wolff and de-Shalit explain, achievement in the area of affiliation is "a sort of immunization in the sense that people who experience a high sense of affiliation are better equipped to cope with threats and risks to their functionings." In part this is because one's affiliations are the basis for one's sense of community, and the real security that informal social networks in one's community can provide.[79] For instance, a high level of the *affiliation* capability enables one to take advantage of social connections and resources that produce and sustain the capability for *control over one's environment* and thus for high levels of the *body health* capability (i.e. such as those that result from employment and the opportunities to attain shelter that having control over one's environment makes possible).

Wolff and de-Shalit argue that because of these causal connections between subcategories of well-being, public policies that seek to decluster disadvantage should target the elimination of corrosive disadvantages while seeking to secure fertile functioning. As a goal of environmental policy, this would mean prioritizing environmental protections that do the most to eliminate corrosive disadvantages and to secure fertile functionings. Thus, a pollution control standard protecting children from exposure to a level of air pollution that triggers asthma should not only be understood to benefit one's *bodily health* capability, it should also be understood to prevent the corrosive effect of a low level of bodily health on one's capability for *senses, imagination and thought*, as well as on one's capability for *play*. Likewise, a water pollution

[76] Wolff and de-Shalit (2007:134). Young (1990:62) treats such bodily threats as one of five central "faces of oppression" that create injustice, in this instance, because daily knowledge of the threat to oneself, or to one's family or friends deprives one of freedom, dignity, and energy that could otherwise be directed toward meaningful forms of self-development.

[77] For example, if municipal-level decisions by a local city council are made in public meetings that occur after 7:00 p.m., then a person who stays indoors after dark due to fear of assault cannot effectively participate in local political decision-making.

[78] Wolff and de-Shalit (2007:121–122).

[79] See Wolff and de-Shalit (2007:139–140). If these informal social networks break down, then various forms of anti-social behavior (e.g. drug dealing and burglary) can rapidly escalate, producing a loss of control over one's environment. Such losses, in turn, may be the cause of further losses in opportunities for employment and shelter (and hence one's *bodily health* capability) that often appear in communities when their social fabric collapses.

control policy that protects water quality at a level that allows for fishing, as well as for swimming and other aquatic activities that members of a community value, should not only be understood to protect one's *bodily health* capability, it should also be understood to secure the proliferation of one's capability for *affiliation, play,* and *control over one's environment.* In this way, evaluating the extent to which environmental policies undermine capabilities that produce corrosive disadvantages (or that secure the capabilities that promote fertile functionings), will make it possible to identify and design policies that do the most to prevent the systematic persistence of disadvantage among particular groups of people.

The empirical challenges of gathering the kind of information that can inform such assessments may seem daunting. For instance, policy evaluation that reveals the impact of corrosive disadvantages and fertile functionings would need to verify whether there are causal connections between the subcategories of people's well-being, and between environmental protections and any given subcategory for which those protections operate as a precondition.[80] However, in practice, these challenges are far from insurmountable. For example, with respect to the example of water pollution control policy, a capabilities approach to evaluation might involve interviewing citizens about the relative importance of affiliation and play activities that are made possible by water of a certain quality.[81] This would mean gathering qualitative information about the subjective perspectives that current valuation seeks to measure quantitatively. However, scientific and observational information would also be a key component of this kind of policy evaluation. For example, the extent to which (a) bodily health enables these capabilities, (b) a certain standard of water quality threatens human health or otherwise makes *affiliation* and *play* capabilities unavailable, and (c) aquatic ecosystems must function in order to enable all of these capabilities, is more a matter of scientific and observational analysis than an matter of assessing people's subjective views regarding the relative importance of affiliation and play activities.[82] Information about individual WTP for protection of water quality may help illuminate the extent to which a group of people agree that the affiliation and play activities made possible by good water quality are of great importance. However, assessing the extent to which such protection serves more egalitarian social goals because of its relationship to corrosive disadvantages and fertile functions will involve further scientific,

[80] Wolff and de-Shalit (2007:138).

[81] These issues are explored in Gillroy and Holland (2008:279–332).

[82] Wolff and de-Shalit (2007:138–149) identify and discuss the literature claiming these causal effects on high-weight functionings.

objective, and observational analysis involving both qualitative and quantitative work.[83]

3.4 Conclusion

This chapter has introduced the capabilities theory of Amartya Sen and Martha Nussbaum as providing both a theory of well-being and a theory of social justice. A primary benefit of both theories is that they define well-being in terms of the conditions of enablement that are the basis of self-defined choice. Whereas current policy analysis conceives of individual well-being as a relationship between people's expressed preferences and their satisfaction, the capabilities theory that Sen and Nussbaum develop understands individual well-being as a relationship between people's capabilities and the variety of activities and achievements—or functionings—these capabilities enable people to pursue and achieve. Different views of individual well-being will produce different views of the natural environment's instrumental value. Specifically, when well-being is treated in terms of the satisfaction of preferences expressed in markets, then the environment is treated as an object of consumer choice. In contrast, when well-being is viewed as a relationship between human capabilities and the functionings they enable, the environment is viewed as a condition or state that enables people to pursue the functionings they choose to value. In this respect, the capabilities-based view of well-being treats the environment as a basis of individual choice. Although capability theorists have not yet systematically addressed how and why we should treat the natural environment as a central dimension of human capabilities, this chapter has offered two basic arguments for the merits of such a project.

First, conceiving of the environment as instrumental to people's capabilities to function broadens the dimensions of human well-being to which the benefits of environmental protection can be made relevant. A person's functionings can characterize a broad range of activities and achievements involving the natural environment besides the expression of a person's preferences in settings of consumer choice. When conceived of as the object of one's expressed preferences, the environment's value is only partially understood. This is because one's subjective preferences can only convey the value of things about which one has knowledge and understanding. However, even in considering the valuation of something as simple as a living tree,

[83] As Robeyns (2009:115) explains, capabilities provide a multidimensional metric for assessing inequalities, so that the assessment "does not only focus on either subjective assessments or material inequalities".

it becomes apparent that there are many ways in which the environment contributes to well-being that people do not know about or understand, and which cannot be accurately understood as valuable to satisfying a subjective preference. In contrast to subjective preferences, human functionings—as a category of well-being—are plural and incommensurable. Thus, they allow for (and will sometimes require) distinguishing the plural character of the environment's instrumental value. Specifically, I have argued that the loss of a tree that is involved in one kind of functioning activity cannot always be compensated for with the protection or use of a tree that is involved in another functioning activity. An accurate approach to valuing the environment will therefore require characterizing the relationship between people and environmental resources in the form these relationships actually take.

More important to accuracy in environmental valuation, conceiving of the environment's instrumental value in relation to people's capabilities permits valuing many distinct ways in which the natural environment makes people capable. Although the capability to satisfy one's preferences is something that does make a person's life go well, there are many additional capabilities that make up a decent human life to which the natural environment also makes instrumental contributions. In this respect, a capabilities-based conception of individual well-being broadens recognition of the vital links between the humans and their environment. It promises a more accurate account of the benefits that follow from environmental protection and consequently makes it possible to expand the scope and justification of environmental policy.

Second and related, I have also argued that conceiving of well-being in terms of people's capabilities to function can reveal the multiple channels through which environmental protection has disproportionate impacts on different people. This is primarily because the capabilities-based conception of well-being accounts for the personal, material, and social conditions of one's life, which is where variation in external conditions or internal powers and traits among different people translates into different levels of environmental protection for people subject to the same standards of environmental protection. I have explored the combined importance of the internal powers and traits and the external conditions that a person's capabilities refer to or depend on in the context of air pollution policies controlling fine particulate matter and ground-level ozone. Because people will vary with respect to their internal powers and traits and their external conditions, an established air quality standard will provide different levels of protection for different people. Specifically, viewing the impact of air pollution control in relation to people's capabilities to function reveals that people will be able to do different things and thus achieve different levels of protection when exposed to the same level of pollution. For this reason, assessing people's capabilities to function can help to account for the distributional impacts of a policy, and, thus, can help to provide information about the extent to which public policies can be justified with respect to goals such as equity and social justice.

Toward this end, I have proposed that policy evaluation should consider the extent to which environmental policies eliminate corrosive disadvantages and secure fertile functionings. Such a task is not without operational obstacles. Those obstacles are not insurmountable, however, and the outcome would open up the possibility of taking immediate steps toward addressing the distributional inequities that environmental policies produce without seeking to justify a wholesale and politically impossible reallocation of material resources. Far from defining the conditions of a fully egalitarian society, policies that eliminate corrosive disadvantages and secure fertile functionings would help to decluster disadvantage. Inequalities would inevitably persist, but no single person or group of people would be the worst off with respect to multiple dimensions of well-being.

Based on these advantages of conceiving of well-being in terms of people's capabilities to function, we can now answer the questions raised at the start of this chapter concerning how we should value the natural environment and how we should assess the distributional implications of its protection. I have argued that conceiving of human well-being in terms of people's capabilities to function will produce an account of the environment's instrumental value that is more accurate than the account that current economic valuation provides. Capabilities can further provide information about the extent to which environmental protection might have disproportionate impacts on different people. While the problem of inaccuracy bears on how we value the environment, the problem of disproportionate impact bears on how we justify policies that protect the environment. With respect to these questions, this chapter offers two preliminary conclusions: First, we should value the benefits of environmental protection in terms of the environment's contribution to human capabilities. Second, we should determine a policy's distributional implications by assessing its impact on the various capabilities that make up different people's overall capability to function.

The following two chapters develop an approach to valuing resources and assessing their relationship to non-economic social goals by beginning with the premise that capabilities are an illuminating and accurate way to conceptualize individual well-being. Because capability theorists have not yet systematically considered how and why the natural environment bears on human capabilities, I take up this task in Chapter 4. Chapter 5 then builds on the relationship between the natural environment and human capabilities that Chapter 4 conceptualizes, to propose an account of social and environmental justice that strengthens the political legitimacy of policies that will protect the environmental preconditions of human capabilities.

4

A Capabilities Approach to Environmental Valuation

4.1 Introduction

Environmental valuation, as I conceptualize it here, refers to the process by which we assess the environment's value for the purpose of determining whether a proposed environmental policy or management decision is good or bad for society. For instance, when administrative agencies change standards of regulatory protection for particular environmental mediums, such as air, land, or water, they must provide an account of why those changes are worth adopting. This means that, one way or another, agencies will have to document the value of the change in environmental quality that the proposed standard will produce. Broadly speaking, the account of value presented by those who assess this change will depend on *what* environmental changes are assessed, *how* they are assessed, and the criterion used to define *why* those changes have positive or negative impacts. In other words, the value of a change in environmental quality will depend on the theory of environmental value that underlies and gives structure to formal efforts to evaluate the importance of policy decisions. The purpose of this chapter is to sketch the theoretical features of an approach to assessing environmental value that is grounded in the capabilities approach to justice.

The capabilities approach implies a particular theory of environmental value. Most basically, it seeks to evaluate changes in environmental quality from the perspective of justice, rather than from, for example, the perspective of economic efficiency or of what our moral obligations to the environment require. In establishing criteria for environmental valuation, I build on the theory of justice that Martha Nussbaum advances, which requires protecting ten central human capabilities at a threshold level, for each person. As I argue in Chapter 3, Nussbaum's capabilities approach to justice is an especially good place to start in developing an approach to environmental valuation because it adopts a multidimensional view of human well-being and therefore provides the basis for assessing policy impacts on the multiple dimensions of environmental value that are relevant to human life. However, Nussbaum's capabilities approach does not consider the environment's instrumental role in making people capable in the ways that she proposes. For this reason, I propose ways in which we can extend her approach to justice to account for the environment's instrumental value. This extension is crucial for capturing the ecological context that all of human life is situated in and dependent upon. More important to assessing the distributional implications of environmental policy, accounting for the ecological context of human life allows for analysis of the ways in which humans are connected to each other through natural processes that determine who benefits from and who is burdened by changes in environmental quality. Accounting for the impacts of these changes is something that neither economic nor deliberative approaches to environmental valuation can accomplish; both of these contemporary methods for valuing the environment relativize environmental value to a process that is the subject of either individual or collective choice. In contrast, the capabilities approach to environmental valuation that I propose treats the environment as a basis of individual choice, and it therefore assesses the environment's contribution to some dimensions of well-being independent of what people know, what they can pay for, or what they agree to collectively. This entails disaggregating the impacts of changes in environmental quality and making them comparable along—but not commensurable across—the distinct dimensions of well-being that people specify as valuable capabilities.

The chapter begins (in Section 4.2) by highlighting two important trends shaping contemporary efforts to improve environmental valuation. One of these trends involves incorporating information from the science of ecology into assessments of environmental value. The other trend involves making the process of environmental valuation more democratic by creating a place for public participation, dialogue, learning, and reflection in the methods for determining the social value of environmental resources. Despite the potential of both efforts to overcome some problems with standard forms of economic valuation, I argue that they are insufficient for addressing the distributional implications of changes in environmental quality. In Section 4.3 I highlight the advantages of Nussbaum's capabilities approach to justice as an account of what to value when we assess changes in environmental quality. A capabilities approach retains both the ecological sophistication of the former trend and the democratic features of the latter while providing a framework to identify and redress distributional inequity. The approach to environmental valuation I suggest here, establishes the environment's role in determining the content and extent of human capabilities. It further entails recognizing the nature of human interdependence that ecosystems and broader ecological interactions create, and the implications of this for distributional outcomes. In Section 4.4 I propose a process of environmental valuation that can capture the implications of changes in environmental quality to who we are as individuals intimately connected through ecological relationships that determine the distribution of advantages and disadvantages resulting from environmental policies. Finally, in Section 4.5 I propose a process of environmental valuation that separates the task of value identification from the task of value measurement, privileging the views of citizens and experts respectively. Here I propose an authoritative role for citizens in specifying the capabilities that are relevant to environmental valuation, while experts do the work of characterizing how changes in environmental quality impact these capabilities. I argue that this process for evaluating the impact of changes in environmental quality can deal with preference adaptation, the pathologies of democratic processes, and the incommensurability of environmental values that arise in economic and deliberative approaches to contemporary environmental valuation.

4.2 Contextualizing Current Practice: Ecology and Democracy in Environmental Valuation

As explained in Chapter 2, the currently dominant economic approach to environmental valuation is insufficient in two important respects: (1) it does not accurately convey the full impact of changes in environmental quality on people's lives, and (2) it fails to address how changes in environmental quality bear on non-quantifiable and non-economic values and goals, such as spiritual realization and social justice. Over the last two decades, efforts to address these (and other) problems have manifested in two important contributions to the practice of environmental valuation. First, there has been a significant effort among both economists and ecologists to bring information about the role of ecosystems and their interactions with broader physical cycles and processes to bear on assessments of the environment's economic value to people. Second, political rather than economic approaches to valuation have emerged in the practice of "deliberative monetary valuation" (DMV), which is an approach to environmental valuation modeled on a process of communicative democratic interaction rather than the economic interactions that define market exchange.[1] DMV seeks to improve both the democratic legitimacy and empirical accuracy of standard

[1] See Vatn (2009) for a discussion of these distinct models of environmental valuation.

economic assessments of environmental value by creating space for citizens to articulate and learn from each other through discussion and reflection about their environmental values.[2]

To begin with the former trend, many important areas of contemporary environmental law have been shaped by the field of ecology.[3] However, as a science, the holistic study of ecosystems—which is concerned with structure and function of relatively large systems of plants, animals, and their physical environment—is relatively new. Ecosystems are the interactive systems making up our biological environment; they are composed of living things and components of the non-living physical environment in which they live. Because of the crucial role these systems play in creating the conditions for human life, accounting for ecosystems and the services they provide should be central to any contemporary approach to assessing the consequences of environmental policy for people. Toward this end, in the present context I treat ecosystems as important because of the multiple and significant ways in which they are connected to human living. I am not, for instance, treating ecosystems as entities that have inherent worth, or integrity, independent of their role in human life.[4] I am treating them as central to environmental valuation because, as many modern scientists have noted, they provide the fundamental life support services for humans and other forms of organic life. For instance, in carrying out activities such as groundwater recharge, soil fertilization, and regulation of the chemical composition of the atmosphere, ecosystems perform very basic life-giving services for human beings. They are also important in more particular ways, due to their provision of goods vital to the quality of human living, such as the basic materials for food, fuel, shelter, and medicines.[5]

The practice of environmental management has yet to fully appreciate the nature and extent of humans' dependence on ecosystems.[6] Many environmental policies, for instance, focus on protecting particular environmental mediums, such as air, land, or water, which are overseen by different "program offices" within the US Environmental Protection Agency (EPA).[7] These offices work independently, without addressing how ecological interactions connect pollution across the distinct domains they are charged with managing.[8] Consequently, regulatory activities that improve the quality of one environmental medium, such as air, can come at the cost of reducing the quality of another environmental medium, such as water. Even entire

[2] See Ward (1999) and Sagoff (1998b). [3] See Brooks et al. (2002:8).

[4] See Schlosberg (2007) for an effort to expand capabilities theory in a way that treats whole ecosystems as having a kind of integrity that is of intrinsic value.

[5] See Millennium Ecosystem Assessment (2003:43–60) for an overview of several different categories of ecosystem goods and services.

[6] See Liu et al. (2010:73). [7] See Rosenbaum (2008:88–90). [8] See Rabe (1986).

policies created to protect particular ecosystems, such as watersheds, often fail to achieve their preservation goals because components of the relevant ecosystem expand beyond the jurisdiction of the governing authority that seeks to protect it. In these and many other ways contemporary environmental policies remain insufficiently ecological; they often treat environmental problems as if they are confined to a single feature of the environment, and they treat the ecosystems as though they are disconnected from many of the people who contribute to their degradation. An empirically accurate assessment of how policies that change environmental quality will impact people must situate particular environmental resource and specific environmental mediums in the broader ecological context that connects those who degrade the environment and those who suffer the consequences.

To elaborate this point, accounting for a policy's ecological implications is especially important to assessing a policy's distributional implications. Most basically, this is because ecosystems are not discrete entities; rather they are organized by a set of interconnected processes that connect the activities of different people in ways that have significant implications for human well-being. As Arild Vatn explains, "If I destroy a habitat, you cannot at the same time have it with its original species and capacities. If you drain a marsh to build a road through it, we cannot at the same time enjoy its cleaning capacities, its species richness etc."[9] The point here is that, due to the interdependence of ecological processes, one person's use of a particular component of the environment can easily influence the kind and quality of the environment left for others. In this way ecological processes force interconnectedness upon us—our dependence on them makes humans unavoidably interdependent with each other.[10] Attaining a fully disaggregated view of a policy's impacts will, therefore, require conceptualizing the environment as partly composed of the interconnected ecological processes in which people are situated, for it is through these processes that one person's use of a particular resource impacts many different people.

Traditional economic valuation of the environment has not been unreceptive to the growing prominence of ecological science that has emerged since the 1960s. As I discussed in Chapter 2, in recent years standard economic approaches to valuing the environment have made significant progress in accounting for the broader set of "ecosystem services" that the environment provides. By using economic methods to impute the price of ecosystem services for which there are no markets—such as hedonic price indexes, replacement costs approaches, and contingent valuation—economists have done a great deal to improve the accuracy of efforts to assess the full economic

[9] Vatn (2009:2210). [10] See Vatn (2009:2210).

value of changes in environmental quality.[11] And yet, as Geoffrey Heal concludes after reviewing the various methods for imputing the value of unmarketed ecosystem services into standard economic assessment, "It is important to remember always that the [monetary] values that result are likely to be underestimates of the total value provided to society by the system under review."[12] By this Heal means that even when the goal of environmental valuation is only to assess the economic value of goods and services flowing from an ecosystem, the assessment is unlikely to account for the economic value of everything the ecosystem does.[13] To draw on a previous example, the total economic value of a watershed ecosystem may include the watershed's contribution to water purification, carbon sequestration, soil stabilization, recreation, and so on; however, economic valuation of a watershed's services does not generally include an assessment of all these economic benefits. For this and other reasons, such assessments will not reflect the extent of losses people would suffer if the relevant ecosystem services were removed.[14]

The bigger problem, perhaps, is that the total social value of the many instrumental benefits that healthy ecosystems provide includes more than their economic value. There are two reasons for this. First, ecosystem services provide more than economic value to individual people who benefit from them. Many of these other values emerge in the context of non-economic interactions surrounding family, culture, and spiritual tradition, and many of these values lose their meaning when they are quantified in economic terms. Second, ecosystems are relevant to non-economic political commitments, such as equal protection and political opportunity. For instance, as David Schlosberg argues, genuine political participation by people whose identities are closely connected to particular ecological communities may require decision-making procedures in which all the participants recognize these ecological values as such.[15] Likewise, ecosystems can function with more or less capacity, and in ways that are quite relevant to human well-being. For example, some thriving ecosystems may do better at purifying air or water, and therefore may produce better overall environmental quality from a given standard of environmental protection for people that live within them. In these ways the environment determines how people stand in relation to each other—it is part of what shapes whether people stand as equals with each other in relation to their political opportunities and legal protections.

It is important to emphasize that the second trend in environmental valuation—DMV—has emerged in the last two decades as a method for valuing environmental resources that addresses these and other limitations that challenge traditional economic valuation. As I have discussed in Chapter 2, DMV

[11] See Liu et al. (2010).
[12] Heal (2000:29).
[13] See Heal (2000:27).
[14] See Heal (2000:28).
[15] See Schlosberg (2007:26) and Schlosberg and Carruthers.

avoids some of the problems of validity associated with cost–benefit analysis (CBA) by using participatory, inclusive, and deliberative processes to expand democratic practice and therefore increase the political legitimacy of policy decisions based on environmental valuation.[16] These deliberative approaches to valuing the environment can take several different forms depending on whether the objective is to arrive at an individual or social account of environmental value, and according to whether that value is based on an individual or group choice. For instance, the "charitable contribution" model of DMV determines the social value of an environmental good or service by aggregating the monetized value of the good or service that each participant arrives at after engaging in a process of group discussion, learning, and reflection.[17] In contrast, the "group arbitrated social" model of DMV assesses an environmental good through group processes in which a representative group of participants achieve consensus about what the good is worth to society, as (for example) might be implemented through an income tax payment scheme.[18] Thus, in this latter model of DMV, a group of individuals that is representative of citizens collectively agrees on what a policy's provision of an environmental good at a particular level is worth to society as a whole.

Compared to standard economic valuation, in which individuals making isolated choices in the context of real or hypothetical markets determine environmental value, DMV has been advocated as having many advantages. For instance, from the perspective of economists carrying out CBA, the time DMV allots for group discussion and reflection allows participants to gain knowledge about features of the environmental good that are relevant to valuation, making participants' preferences better informed and therefore increasing the validity of their expressed willingness to pay for the good.[19] For critics of CBA who see economic valuation as requiring a form of undemocratic technocratic expertise and as potentially subject to manipulation by powerful special interests, DMV brings citizens into the process of valuation in a way that provides a stronger democratic basis for the policies these value estimates ultimately inform. Furthermore, in treating participants as citizens engaged in political processes (rather than as consumers engaged in market processes), DMV may evoke (or produce through preference transformation) less self-interested valuations, such as those associated with collective experience, identities, and values.[20] In the deliberative context, it is also possible

[16] For an overview of the theoretical and empirical literature proposing and applying DMV, see Spash (2008). For an account of the pre-1990s roots of this method, see Ward (1999:76–77).

[17] See Spash (2008:473–477) for this characterization of the charitable contribution model of DMV.

[18] See James and Blamey (2005) and the discussion in Spash (2008:480).

[19] See Kaplowitz and Hoehn (2001) and Spash (2008:471).

[20] Spash (2008:472), Ward (1999:86–87).

to directly address distributional issues, such as who does and does not benefit from environmental protection policies. For instance, in deliberating about the individual or collective value of an environmental good, deliberators could also discuss how the benefits of the good ought to be distributed among different people, generations, or even species.[21] In other words, DMV entails a process of environmental valuation that can produce more statistically valid and democratically legitimate results that are also more likely to account for non-economic individual and social values.

Although the actual practice of DMV has taken a form that undermines many of these claimed advantages, I wish to critique it on subtly different grounds.[22] To begin with, DMV should be understood as improving economic valuation only in a particular way: what it offers is a process for quantifying the monetary value of changes in environmental quality through a deliberative rather than economic (or market) process. This provides an answer to the question of "*How* should we value the environment?" that is different from the answer economic valuation provides. The nature of this process is indeed one in which participants may come to articulate distributional concerns and change their preferences in light of new information. It may ultimately facilitate an expression of environmental value that supports a more equitable distribution of environmental benefits and burdens. However, there is nothing inherent in DMV that guarantees this outcome or anything close to it. A process in which citizens can engage in deliberation about the distributional inequities that will result from changes in environmental quality does not even ensure that the distributional implications of a policy will be empirically assessed. Thus, a major limitation of DMV is that it does not systematically assess who benefits or suffers from environmental protection. Consequently, it provides little verifiable evidence for making decisions that are fair, or for revealing when decisions are unfair. In this sense, even on democratic grounds, we might say that DMV lacks an important epistemic dimension.[23]

The second and related problem with DMV is that it abdicates too much responsibility to deliberative politics. While it relies on a process of environmental valuation that is deliberative rather than economic, it is similar to economic valuation in relying on a highly subjective conception of environmental value. By this I mean that DMV ultimately seeks to base the

[21] See Ward (1999:88–89).

[22] See Spash (2008) for a discussion of the ways in which the practice of DMV has not allowed for attaining the advantages its advocates claim.

[23] See Estlund's (2008) argument that at least some of democracy's authority should come from its epistemic value, by which he means its tendency to produce outcomes that are correct by independent standards, as opposed to authority grounded in the fairness of democratic procedures.

environment's value on people's subjective preferences, albeit preferences that are informed and collectively transformed. As Sagoff explains this later aspect of DMV, individuals "state opinions about what *we* ought to do as a society rather than report preferences about what *I* want as a utility maximizer."[24] Presumably this predisposes DMV to produce valuations that are "principle based" in reflecting what society ought to do, as opposed to valuations that are "preference based" in reflecting what consumers want. However, it is also true that this may produce principle-based valuations that are entirely compatible with what consumers want, and therefore no different from what current economic valuations prescribe.

My point here is not that Sagoff's distinction is in some way meaningless, for there is certainly independent value in the deliberative process. Rather, I contend that substantive environmental outcomes are at least, if not more, important than the process through which people express their opinions. A political process undertaken by collectively concerned citizens has a number of advantages over a market process with respect to the breadth of criteria by which people might value the environment and recognize the impact of its use, but the environment's value should not be something that is entirely defined by the outcome of a democratic process. In part this is because the fairness of any process is only as good as the fairness of its initial conditions. For example, if people are being asked to deliberate about the value of losing an environmental good or service that is central to their health and political identity, then they are already on unequal terms with those who have much less to lose. More generally, making the environment's value relative to a political process does not ensure its protection as a basic condition of people's freedom to choose and express their subjectively or collectively determined environmental values. In order to protect the environment as a condition of human choice and expression, political processes must be understood as something that is subsumed within a broader set of ecological relationships that determine both what the process can produce and the extent to which its outcomes can persist without producing systemic failures.

The importance of extending an ecological worldview to include political as well as economic processes is perhaps most apparent when we admit the extent to which ecological systems and interactions connect the actions of different people. The self-governing actions of autonomous individuals can operate through these interactions in ways that go far beyond impeding citizens' democratic participation. Environmental impacts that impede democratic participation do provide a strong basis for defending substantive environmental protections as a condition of genuine democratic functioning.

[24] Sagoff (1998b:213).

However, as Tim Hayward has argued, substantive environmental protections also can be justified "on the *same* grounds that democracy itself is justified."[25] To put it simply, this is because environmental degradation does harm to individuals—the kind of harm to personal or bodily integrity that is unacceptable because it interferes with the basic rights of autonomy or self-governance that justify democracy as a form of government that respects these rights.[26] On these grounds, Hayward argues that respect for individual autonomy and self-determination imply "a presumptive right of individuals to be free of any interference that is not justified on the grounds of being necessary for the functioning of democracy." This is true with respect to the environment as much as any other system through which severe personal and bodily harms threaten individuals.[27] The harms occurring through ecological processes are not all so severe as to breach the boundaries of individual autonomy or self-governance, but some of them, such as exposure to toxic pollutants or the onslaught of severe flooding brought on by climate change, are certainly significant enough to justify actions that go beyond protecting whatever citizens happen to agree is valuable (by consensus or majority voting) in processes of democratic deliberation.

Thus, while DMV can incorporate and foster dialogue about whatever policy consequences participants introduce into the deliberative process, and while it may yield an agreement reflecting the importance of impacts raised in that process as relevant, unfortunately that is all DMV can do. Epistemic value notwithstanding, there are some consequences of environmental policy that environmental valuation should document and treat as relevant, even if deliberators do not agree or conclude these consequences matter. Of course, absent a process that entails empirically assessing how changes in environmental quality impact the dimensions of well-being that matter to people, it is unlikely that even the most ideal deliberative processes can give due weight to distributional concerns. This is why, even if one follows advocates of DMV in assuming that policy should always be based on what deliberators agree to, the task of environmental valuation should still provide a substantive and empirical account of a policy's implications for people's lives. While I stake out the stronger position for substantive environmental protections in Chapter 6, in the remainder of this chapter I wish to merely sketch the features of a capabilities approach to environmental valuation that can provide such an account of a policy's implications.

The approach to valuation I propose does not ignore people's subjective perspectives. The things that matter to people are relevant to any form of government that is in some way committed to the democratic ideal of popular

[25] Hayward (2005:157). [26] Hayward (2005:157–158). [27] Hayward (2005:158).

sovereignty. However, there is a difference between registering what people care about and providing an empirical account of how changes in environmental quality impact different people. Citizens may be a reliable and therefore appropriate authority on the former, while also being ill-equipped to be an authority on the latter. It is for this reason that the capabilities approach to environmental valuation that I develop in the following sections incorporates a role for citizens in defining the impacts that matter to them, but assesses the distributional impact of changes in environmental quality independent of deliberative processes, and of the preferences that end up carrying weight in those processes.

To summarize before proceeding, economic evaluation, even if ecologically informed, does not try to see a policy's impact on and through the non-economic commitments a society may value. By incorporating the value of ecosystem services, ecological economists have been successful in broadening the scope of what we value about policies that protect the environment. Most significantly, their work reveals that the environment is composed of goods that are embedded in and interrelated through ecological processes that subsume both individuals and the economy. However, how we value the environment is still confined to the monetary terms of market valuation. While Chapter 2 has elaborated these problems, my point in the present context is to emphasize the fact that, despite the more holistic and interrelated view of environmental value that ecological science has revealed, it has not fundamentally altered the paradigm by which we continue to measure the environment's value to people.

The capabilities approach to valuation that I develop in the following sections of this chapter seeks to push the discussion of environmental value toward a new paradigm. I do this by relating the importance of ecological conditions—ecosystems and the broader ecological processes that connect them—to the multidimensional and irreducibly plural view of human well-being that the capabilities approach to justice adopts. This provides the basis for evaluating the distributional implications of changes in environmental quality based on a comparison of how those changes impact the distinct capabilities of different people. In this way, the capabilities approach to environmental valuation seeks to provide a fuller account of environmental value and to make it relevant to distributional analysis; but importantly, as I will explain in Section 4.4.2 of this chapter, it does this without being subject to problems of value incommensurability.

Several implications follow from these points about the place of ecology and democracy in contemporary environmental valuation. First, accounting for the distributional implications of changes in environmental quality that environmental policies produce requires a conception of environmental value that takes ecology seriously. This is because people are dependent on ecological conditions but in highly variable ways. Thus, it is through these conditions that activities degrading the environment will have different impacts on different people. Second, assessing the instrumental value of changes in environmental quality that environmental policies produce must do more than assess people's subjective perspectives (even if reflective and informed) regarding what they want as individuals or citizens. Because defining what is valuable is different from assessing the extent to which changes in environmental quality make those valued things more or less possible for differently situated people, it is not sufficient to answer the question "What to value?" with whatever emerges from people's subjective preferences, whether expressed in a market processes, or informed and transformed through a deliberative process. With this in mind, I now turn to developing an account of what to value that is more appropriate for assessing the value of changes in environmental quality that operate through ecological systems to distribute some of the relevant benefits and burdens.

4.3 What to Value

Environmental valuation, as I have defined it in Section 4.2, refers to the process of assessing the environment's value for the purpose of making decisions about whether government should pursue a policy action that will change environmental quality. If we think about this process of assessment in a broadly theoretical way, then it is not difficult to see that different social goals will imply different views of the environment, as well as different views of people and the relevant relationship between people and the environment. For instance, the goal of the currently dominant economic approach to environmental valuation is to assess a policy's economic impact, and specifically, whether a policy meets conditions of economic efficiency. In this context, particular components of the environment are treated as economic commodities to which a price reflecting their value to individual consumers can be attached. People, therefore, are treated as consumers seeking the satisfaction of their rational and self-interested preferences.[28] The relevant relationship is one of environmentally provided preference satisfaction. In contrast, DMV seeks to base policy decisions on the values that emerge from a process of democratic deliberation, in which participants have time to gather information about the environmental benefits that are at stake, to reflect on what they have learned in talking about the relevant issues with each other, and to work toward a consensus on the policy's value as something to which

[28] See Sagoff (1988b) for a frequently cited characterization of people as consumers in the context of economic valuation of the environment.

all can agree. Here the environment is treated as a good or object of collective choice; proper specification of its value is the subject of a democratic decision. People are treated as citizens, interested in arriving at or otherwise accepting a collective decision. The relevant relationship is environmentally focused political deliberation that determines what is collectively valued, if not by consensus, then ultimately by a majority voting rule.[29]

A capabilities approach to environmental valuation is distinct from these approaches, most basically, because it prioritizes protecting the environmental conditions of human freedom and opportunity rather than economic efficiency or democratic deliberation. To be clear, although the explicit goal of democratic deliberation that DMV adopts can be understood as instantiating a certain kind of political fairness or freedom, a capabilities approach to environmental valuation instantiates something that is more substantive than procedural. Specifically, its goal is to ensure each person has a threshold level of the ten central human capabilities that are necessary for living a minimally decent human life. For Nussbaum, the capabilities (protected at a threshold level) are a bare minimum of what makes it possible for people to live a life that is worthy of human dignity; that is, they make it possible for people to develop their unique human faculties and forms of living. The capabilities are: *Life; Bodily Health; Bodily Integrity; Senses, Imagination, and Thought; Emotions; Practical Reason; Affiliation; Other Species; Play; (Political and Material) Control over One's Environment.*[30] An approach to environmental valuation that prioritizes the protection of these ten capabilities will require assessing how they are impacted by changes in environmental quality. An account of a policy's distributional impact will therefore consist in an assessment of a policy's varying impact on the capabilities of the different people for whom it has consequences. In this context, the environment is treated as instrumental to the capabilities that make it possible for people to do and achieve different things.

It is important to note that some of the capabilities relevant to this form of environmental valuation will entail being able to purchase consumer goods through markets. For instance, Nussbaum's tenth capability, which entails *material control over one's environment*, requires that people be able to hold property in land and moveable goods and that they have a purchasable right to these goods on an equal basis with others.[31] Likewise, some things the list of capabilities enables people to do will entail being able to engage in forms of political participation that are central to DMV. For instance, Nussbaum's

[29] See Spash (2008) for a discussion of DMV and when the different models of DMV resort to majority rule.

[30] See Nussbaum (2000a:78–80) and the Appendix for the full definition of each of these capabilities.

[31] See Nussbaum (2000a:80).

tenth capability also entails *political control over one's environment*, which she defines as including being able to participate effectively in political choices that govern one's life.[32] In these ways, a capabilities approach to environmental valuation admits the importance of both economic and political processes as enabling people to do and achieve things that are crucial to a good human life. However, while sharing these commitments with current approaches to environmental valuation, the capabilities approach seeks to protect the actual conditions that make it possible for people to make genuine choices about what they value within these processes. Likewise, the approach to valuation I am proposing does not limit other crucial dimensions of living to what emerges as valuable from these economic and political interactions. Instead people are treated as multidimensional—or irreducibly plural—beings, capable of flourishing in a variety of activities, each of which may be central to living a fully human life. Therefore, just as market-based consumption and political participation may be crucial to people's lives, so too are social and familial activities, physical and mental accomplishments, as well as personal, emotional, creative, and spiritual development. A capabilities approach to environmental valuation seeks to assess the environment's value in relation to each of these dimensions of well-being even if they are not expressible in economic terms or convincing as the subject of collective agreement regarding their importance to society.

While these features of a capabilities approach to environmental valuation follow from the multidimensional view of well-being that capabilities theory adopts, and its specific characterization in Nussbaum's capabilities approach to justice, very little work has been done in theorizing the central role of the natural environment in making people capable. For instance, Nussbaum's theory of justice does recognize the central importance some people find in having personally meaningful relationships to plants, animals, and the world of nature, by treating the opportunity to have these relationships as a central capability of humans—the *other species* capability.[33] Nussbaum even alludes to the environment's instrumental value to this capability when she explains that, despite the controversy surrounding her inclusion of this capability as a basic entitlement, "Government can do quite a lot about this capability, through its choices of policy regarding endangered species, the health and life of animals, and the ecology."[34] When later defending this capability, she explicitly states that while there are widely divergent preferences about the importance of the relationships that this *other species* capability protects, "we can at least get agreement about the instrumental importance of environmental factors."[35] But she does not theorize how we should conceptualize

[32] Nussbaum (2000a:80).
[33] See Nussbaum (2000a:80).
[34] Nussbaum (2000a:80).
[35] Nussbaum (2000a:158).

the environment's instrumental value in relation to the various capabilities she defines as central to human life, nor, as I discuss in Chapter 5, what implications follow for her theory of justice.

Given this incomplete account of environmental value in Nussbaum's theory of justice, for the present task of developing a capabilities approach to environmental valuation that can account for the distributive implications of changes in environmental quality, the pioneering work of Anantha Duraiappah is especially helpful.[36] Duraiappah draws on a capabilities-based conception of human well-being in order to establish the connection between environmental resources, ecosystem services, and human poverty, which he defines as a pronounced deprivation of well-being. Specifically, Duraiappah identifies ten primary constituents and determinants of well-being that are closely related to ecosystems. Some of these are quite similar to the capabilities on Nussbaum's list, such "being able to be adequately nourished" and "being able to be free from avoidable disease." Others are more specific to the environmental conditions that are instrumental to Nussbaum's capabilities, such as "being able to continue using natural elements found in ecosystems for traditional cultural and spiritual practices," which, for example, could be a way of specifying her *senses, imagination, and thought* capability or her *affiliation* capability. Likewise, given the dramatic emotional turmoil brought on by weather-related disasters, Duraiappah's reference to "being able to cope with extreme natural events including floods, tropical storms and landslides" could be a way of specifying Nussbaum's *emotions* capability.[37]

In explaining how ecosystems shape each of these dimensions of well-being, Duraiappah characterizes the relationship between capabilities and the environment in a way that is explicitly ecological.[38] For example, he explains that when human activities result in excessive removal of flora within ecosystems, the naturally cleansing properties of ecosystems will degrade, potentially producing an increase in pollution concentrations that negatively impact people's capability to be free from diseases closely associated with air pollution, such as asthma and chronic lung disease.[39] Likewise, in certain poorer and rural communities, people are dependent on wild plants for their fat intake. Damage to ecosystems that sustain those plants, therefore, can prevent people from being able to be adequately nourished. As these examples demonstrate, human capabilities depend on ecosystems, their processes, and the species that constitute them. People rely on specific features of their environments to sustain and fulfill their lives. As I discuss in Chapter 2, ecological conditions not only provide crucial life support "services" such as soil formation and renewal, they also regulate climate, purify water and air,

[36] Duraiappah (2004). [37] See Holland (2012). [38] Duraiappah (2004:11).
[39] Duraiappah (2004:15).

and provide food and a variety of other material and non-material benefits to humans.[40]

In order to sufficiently account for the extent to which human capabilities are both dependent on ecosystems and made interdependent with each other through their impact on them, a capabilities approach to environmental valuation must follow Duraiappah in treating the natural environment's ecological functioning as a central dimension of human well-being. Elsewhere I have argued that we can think about this kind of instrumental value as an "ecological meta-capability" that underlies all the capabilities on Nussbaum's list of central human capabilities.[41] The environment's ecological functioning is a meta-capability in the sense that it is a precondition of all the capabilities that Nussbaum defines as necessary for living a good human life. In this respect, an ecologically functioning natural environment can be understood as a condition that makes it possible for people to live and to chose to live the kind of life they value: it consists in being able to live one's life in the context of ecological conditions that enable the protection of one's central human capabilities at a threshold level.[42] When the environment is understood in this way, the relationship that is relevant to environmental valuation is capability protection; and specifically, protecting people's central human capabilities at a threshold level. Therefore, assessing the value of changes in environmental quality that result from environmental policy decisions requires assessing how those changes support or undermine a threshold level of capability protection for each person that is treated as relevant to the policy's impact.

Before elaborating this last point, let us first consider whether the environment warrants this status as a capability of any sort, and as a meta-capability in particular. In many ways, an ecologically functioning natural environment is a component of individual capabilities in the same way that other non-human components of the material world are a component of capabilities. For instance, Nussbaum's *bodily health* capability partly consists in being able to have adequate nourishment and shelter. Likewise, her capability for *material control over one's environment* partly consists in being able to have landed and moveable property.[43] In these instances, nourishment, shelter, and property are inseparable from the exercise of capabilities—they constitute the opportunities that people have for *bodily health* and m*aterial control over one's environment*. An ecologically functioning natural environment is similarly inseparable from the exercise of capabilities. For instance, it may provide and maintain the particular environmental resources that make it possible for people to experience religious expression in the way that choose,

[40] See Millennium Ecosystem Assessment (2003:57). [41] See Holland (2008a).
[42] See Holland (2008a:324). [43] See Nussbaum (2000a:78–80).

as the *senses, imagination, and thought* capability requires; it can determine whether one experiences the kind of stable background context that makes it possible to form a conception of the good and engage in the planning of one's life, as the *practical reason* capability requires.[44]

But an ecologically functioning natural environment does not just provide particular environmental resources that are inseparable from particular capabilities, it also provides the broader ecological context necessary for all of the capabilities. In this way it is unlike other material goods, such as property and shelter. Consider, for instance, a person who lacks property. Bina Agarwal has argued that this may be the single most important contributor to inequalities of economic well-being, social status, and empowerment between men and women in South Asia. For this reason, a person who lacks property may lack a threshold level of her capability for *material control over one's environment*. However, this does not necessarily mean the person lacks a threshold level of protection of other capabilities.[45] For instance, one may lack property and still have the protection of one's *play* and *emotions* capabilities at a threshold level. An ecologically functioning natural environment is unique from this and other material dimensions of human capabilities because any and all human capabilities are dependent on it. Thus, while its causal role in making people more or less capable with respect to any individual capability makes it similar to other material components of capabilities, its systemic relation to all of the capabilities gives it a more distinct status as part of the opportunity set that defines human well-being.

Understood as a capability of humans, an ecologically functioning natural environment is also distinct from other highly pervasive conditions and processes that play a central role in making people capable. For instance, consider the conditions and processes that make up economic, political, and social systems that also play a crucial causal role in enabling people to do and achieve different things. Most of us get many of the basic ingredients of our *bodily health* capability through economic processes, and it is through political processes that we ensure the protection of our *bodily integrity* capability. Likewise, various social institutions such as family, love, culture, and community are central to the protection of our *affiliation* capability. But these are human-created processes, in which humans construct and reconstruct what is exchanged or achieved within them. The environment's provision of ecological functions that are most crucial to human life is not something that humans do or can produce and construct in this way. We know enough about our impact on natural systems to hypothesize ways of minimizing the

[44] For a more detailed discussion of the relationship between a functioning natural environment and the *practical reason* capability, see Holland (2012).

[45] See Agarwal (1994:1455) for this characterization of property and gender inequality.

environmental damage we do, but we have no idea how to create or reproduce them in a way that ensures the continued provision of the goods and services they currently provide.[46] Thus, while many economists argue that interventions in a far less complicated "free" market will be dangerously damaging, interventions in the environment's ecological functioning are far more perilously so.

The fact that an ecologically functioning natural environment is something that humans can destroy—but not create—has significant implications for the freedom of choice that the capabilities approach seeks to preserve. In making it possible for people to do and accomplish things they value, capabilities allow for human choice, and this is indeed the central reason why Nussbaum emphasizes that public policy should seek to protect people's capabilities and not push them into particular actions or achievements.[47] A capability refers to an opportunity that is actually within a person's reach: having it does not require engaging in the things it makes possible. Put differently, having a capability to do something means having the capability to not do something. For instance, having the capability to be well nourished means being able to avoid starvation, but also being able to fast, and hence, to choose to be undernourished. A capability to be well nourished allows someone to choose otherwise—that is, to opt out of being well nourished. This relationship between capability and choice, however, is more complicated when we are talking about the ecological meta-capability. For instance, what would it mean to opt out of the ecological meta-capability? How does one choose not to live one's life in the context of ecological conditions that enable the protection of one's central human capabilities at a threshold level? Can we choose not to interact with the environment in ways that make us capable?

With respect to some particular resources, it is certainly possible to avoid such interactions. For instance, we can have the capability to *play* in nature, or to celebrate a particular natural place as part of our culture, and choose to do neither. Likewise, we can have access to clean fresh water and choose to drink dirty water instead. However, with respect to the broader ecological conditions that provide these particular resources, the presumed option is more questionable. This is because how we opt out of choosing to realize the ecological meta-capability can turn an individual choice into a collective choice. Specifically, to choose not to live one's life in the context of ecological conditions that enable the protection of one's central human capabilities at a threshold level, is to choose to live one's life in the context of ecological

[46] See Daily et al. (1997).

[47] More technically, the capabilities approach seeks to avoid pushing people into what Sen and Nussbaum have referred to as human "functionings."

conditions that do not enable this basic threshold level of protection for the other central human capabilities. It is to choose to live one's life in the context of a natural environment that is not functioning at some minimal ecological level; that is, to live in the context of a natural environment that is ecologically degraded. A person who selects such an option is a person that makes informed choices to produce this kind of intentionally degraded environment. This is a person that disregards her ecological impact because she does not choose to live in the context of ecological conditions that enable her capabilities. For instance, she may engage in especially unconscious environmental behavior, driving as much as possible, regardless of the implications for the chemical composition of the atmosphere; she may dump the remnants of her lead-filled paint in pristine ecosystems; she may consume as many plastic containers as possible, and throw them all in a landfill that leaches dangerous chemicals into streams that filter into drinking water wells. The crucial point about these examples is that they demonstrate that in opting out of her own ecological functioning, this person is making herself and others ecologically uncapable.

The ecological meta-capability is not the only condition through which an individual choice can obviate a collective choice. For instance, a person who has the capability for *bodily health* may choose to fast (as is often noted), but she may also choose to live with a highly contagious disease without protecting others from it. Likewise, a person who has the capability for *life* may choose to commit suicide, causing significant damage to members of her family, potentially undermining their capability for *emotions*; for example, by making them less capable of having attachments to things outside themselves. In these instances, the exercise of individual choices that a person's capabilities make possible have collective consequences that influence the capabilities of other people. However, there are differences between these latter cases, which concern the implications of choosing not to exercise the capabilities on Nussbaum's list of capabilities, and the former case, which concerns the implications of choosing not to exercise the ecological meta-capability. These differences concern (1) the number or amount of people that choose non-functioning, and consequently (2) the nature and scale of the consequences.

Generally speaking, while the quantity of people who contract, choose not to treat, and risk transmitting a communicable disease is relatively small, the number of people that recognize and disregard their ecological impact is relatively large. Likewise, whereas the aggregate impact of those who commit suicide is most consequential to friends and family, the aggregate impact of those who disregard their ecological impact is highly uncontained, due to the global nature of interactions among ecosystems and broader ecological cycles and processes. My suggestion here is that the ecological meta-capability allows for individual choices that have collective impacts of a magnitude much greater than other capabilities. But, more importantly, the ecological meta-capability also allows for individual choices that pose unique threats to other people. For instance, one person's choice to commit suicide can have a dramatic influence on the *emotions* capability of other people. It may make people less capable of attaching *emotions* to things outside themselves as I have suggested, but it may also lead people to expand their range of emotional attachments. In the latter case, one person's choice to opt out of her capability for *life* can have collective impacts that expand other people's capabilities. Furthermore, even if the former case prevails—in which a suicide has collective impacts that diminish people's emotional attachments—the collective implications are of a different order than those that result from opting out of the ecological meta-capability. Specifically, while all the capabilities are central to a good human life, individual choices that operate through ecological conditions to remove a person's access to clean water, threaten climate stability, or otherwise expose people to environmental hazards that threaten their lives, limit individual actions in ways that are quite severe. This is why the ecological meta-capability should be understood as allowing for individual choices that have collective impacts of a distinct kind.

Thus, to summarize, there are three reasons why being able to live one's life in the context of ecological conditions that enable the protection of one's central human capabilities at a threshold level should be understood as a human capability with a special "meta" status. First, while particular components of the natural environment are inseparable from human capabilities in the way that other material things are inseparable from these capabilities, the natural systems and processes that the ecological meta-capability would protect have a systemic relation to all the other capabilities that these material things (e.g. food and shelter) lack. Any and all of the human capabilities are dependent on ecological conditions. Second, unlike social, economic, and political institutions and processes, which also play a crucial role as preconditions for human capabilities, the ecological conditions that enable human capabilities are not something that humans can create. Because failures of protection therefore are not necessarily correctable or compensable, the loss of ecological functioning has distinct importance to society. Third, while all the capabilities preserve an individual's option to choose not to exercise the relevant functioning, the choice of ecological non-functioning that the ecological meta-capability makes available has implications of a nature and scale that are unmatched by other capabilities.

In distinguishing the ecological meta-capability, my aim is not to provide a full defense of its status as a distinct capability of humans. Rather, my point is to emphasize the relevance of its unique relationship to other capabilities in the context of valuing the distributional implications of environmental protection. In giving priority to the goal of social justice, the capabilities approach to valuation that I am proposing seeks to assess the distributional implications of changes in environmental quality that environmental policies produce. This entails assessing how changes in environmental quality cause changes in people's capabilities, and particularly, in supporting or undermining the threshold levels of capability protection that justice requires. The point, therefore, is not merely to assess whether environmental inequity exists, but rather to assess how changes in environmental quality bear on people's capabilities in ways that either increase or decrease those inequities. If we understand the ecological meta-capability—being able to live in the context of ecological conditions that enable the ten central capabilities that Nussbaum defines as central to a truly human life—as a distinct capability of humans that is relevant to this assessment, then we can answer the question of "What to value?" in the following way: we should value changes in environmental quality based on the extent to which they impact resources, services, and broader ecological conditions that are necessary for protecting people's ten central human capabilities at a threshold level.

Thus, expanding Nussbaum's account of well-being to include the crucial role the natural environment plays in making people capable of living good and decent human lives can make it more applicable to the question of what to value when we assess the importance of policies that change environmental quality. In particular, this account of *what* to value has specific implications for *how* we value the environment. Generally speaking, how we value changes in environmental quality will entail assessing whether it is possible for a person to live in the context of relations to the environment that support her central human capabilities. While this is an abstract point, I make it here in order to distinguish the process of valuation I propose in Section 4.4 from current practice. The question of how to value changes in environmental quality is not about determining *how much* one wants to adopt or maintain certain relations with nature or the environment, as we might understand economic analysis to determine. Likewise, how to value changes in environmental quality is not about whether the impacted individuals arrive at an agreement that living in a certain relation to nature or the environment is valuable, as we might understand DMV to determine. Instead, how to value changes in environmental quality is about whether the environment is making people capable of doing and achieving a range of different things. For the purpose of assessing how changes in environmental quality make people more or less capable in this respect, the capabilities approach to valuation will require a distinct approach to the process of environmental valuation, to which I turn now.

4.4 How to Value

If a capabilities approach to environmental valuation treats the natural environment as instrumentally valuable to people's capabilities, then how should we go about assessing the impact of changes in environmental quality that result from public policies? This question concerns the process of environmental valuation, by which I mean the process that determines a policy's worth or contribution to a given social goal. In the economic approach to environmental valuation, the process entails asking citizens how much they are "willing to pay" (WTP) for provision or protection of an environmental resource at a particular level. For instance, a sample of citizens might be asked, "How much would you pay to preserve X?" These individual responses regarding a resource's monetary worth to individuals are then aggregated, averaged, and multiplied by the relevant population count to determine the overall social value of a policy ensuring the resource's protection or provision. By contrast, in the deliberative approach to environmental valuation, individuals would deliberate about the value of an environmental good at a particular level of protection or provision, and then collectively agree or vote on the monetary worth of that good to society.

Economic valuation has been criticized for preventing citizens from accurately defining and expressing environmental values, but in theory the advantage of the market model is its capacity to establish value from the bottom up; that is, based on what citizens' value. Both approaches claim to give citizens a central role in the valuation process. Specifically, citizens play a central role in both *identifying* the values that are relevant to the provision of an environmental good (at a particular level), and in *quantifying* those values. For instance, in economic valuation, the choices citizens make with respect to their willingness to pay are taken to reflect the economic value of the resource for the ends or purposes people value. Although certain kinds of environmental value are difficult or impossible to express in monetary terms, open-ended WTP questions do allow citizens to assign a quantitative value to a resource, based on its relation to any value they personally identify as relevant. Likewise, a central advantage claimed by advocates of DMV is that the process of value articulation is even less constrained because monetizing an environmental resource does not happen until all the relevant values have been articulated in a process of public dialogue.[48] Participants need not monetize these values in the initial stage of the valuation process, and therefore, a broader range of values can presumably be brought to bear on collective judgments about the appropriate price that emerges from the deliberative

[48] See Sagoff (1998b:224).

setting. Thus, in theory, both economic and deliberative approaches to environmental valuation seek to ensure that the policy assessment is grounded in the preferences and voices of actual citizens, lending the results of this assessment a certain kind of democratic legitimacy.

Unfortunately, practical problems with both economic and deliberative approaches to environmental valuation bring this legitimacy into question. As I discuss in Chapter 2, the subjective preferences citizens reveal in WTP study are subject to distortion, adaptation, and limited information; consequently, economic valuation may disregard certain kinds of environmental value and it may inaccurately represent environmental values that citizens do understand as relevant. By contrast, the process of reasoned and informed debate that DMV employs does solve some of these problems, but only by placing too much responsibility on deliberative politics. The subjective perspective of those who manage to strategically shape these deliberative settings can exert an excessive influence on the outcome. Consequently, the values that become compelling as a basis for collective agreement may reflect what only a small (but influential) group of deliberative participants subjectively value.[49] Furthermore, the eventual need to express these values in terms of a social (or total) WTP reproduces the problem of inaccurately representing non-quantifiable values that troubles assessments based on individual WTP.[50]

In seeking to assess a policy's impact with respect to the goal of social justice rather than economic efficiency or democratic deliberation, the capabilities approach to environmental valuation is not constrained by these economic and deliberative methods of determining environmental value. In particular, for the purpose of assessing how environmental policies will impact people's capabilities, the process of valuation must provide more and different information than people's subjective preferences reveal. Likewise, an account of whose capabilities a change in environmental quality will support or undermine, and by how much, must be consistent in how it assesses the policy's disaggregated impacts.

Crucial to delivering policy assessments with these features is separating the task of "value identification" from the task of "value measurement." In a capabilities approach to environmental valuation, the former component of the valuation process—*value identification*—concerns identifying the capabilities of people to which a change in environmental quality is relevant. While Nussbaum's list of capabilities and the ecological meta-capability that I have defended in Section 4.3 provide a good starting point for identifying the relevance of changes in environmental quality, these capabilities are

[49] See Dryzek (1987:202). [50] See Spash (2008).

intentionally vague and abstract and will therefore need to be specified in a way that can reflect the importance of changes in environmental quality to specific people. With respect to the latter component of environmental valuation, which I have referred to as *value measurement*, the purpose is to assess the extent to which a policy supports or undermines the environment's instrumental value to the capabilities of these people. This component of the capabilities approach to environmental valuation aims to quantify or otherwise make comparable (but not commensurable) how much changes in environmental quality support or undermine the capabilities that define well-being and the activities people choose to pursue. I will explain these components of the capabilities-based valuation process in turn.

4.4.1 Value identification

The crucial feature of the value identification component of the valuation process is that while it initially relies on Nussbaum's list of ten central human capabilities to define the dimensions of well-being to which changes in environmental quality are relevant, it proceeds by enlisting citizens to specify the capabilities that the expected changes in environmental quality will impact. Specifically, in order to identify the values relevant to policy assessment, citizens must work with experts to understand the changes in environmental quality that will result from a given policy, and to identify the specific dimensions of their life on which these changes will have a meaningful impact. Here, citizens exchange information with experts who understand the physical changes that an environmental policy will produce in order to identify the ways in which anticipated changes bear on the activities and achievements that characterize people's daily lives. In carving out a space for this communicative learning and dialogue, the process of value identification in the capabilities approach to environmental valuation should be understood to incorporate an important democratic commitment to understanding what matters to people.

Whereas the deliberative process in DMV is subject to the strategic abuse of those that have power to shape deliberation, the process of value identification in the capabilities approach to environmental valuation is structured in ways that prevent this kind of manipulation by the powerful or compelling. First, the goal of this component of the valuation process is not to arrive at agreement regarding the social value of environmental resource, rather it is to specify the value of that resource in terms of particular capabilities that matter to people. Thus, the purpose of dialogue among the participants is not to transform preferences, but rather to specify abstract capabilities in a way that can reveal the environment's instrumental role in contributing to them.

Second, by considering how changes in environmental quality will bear on ten abstractly defined central human capabilities, the process of environmental valuation ensures that changes in environmental quality are always assessed with respect to some meaningful set of core human interests—that is, the dimensions of well-being that are central to living a life worthy of human dignity. In this context, participants that seek to dominate the discussion about relevant impacts have no ultimate authority over what capabilities other participants define as relevant to the change in environmental quality. Powerful and compelling participants can only identify capabilities they think *ought* to matter to others and put those forward for others to learn from and accept or reject on their own terms as relevant or irrelevant to their lives.

Third and most important to debates about political agency in capabilities theory, although the list of capabilities represents a benchmark set of human interests with respect to which changes in environmental quality can be assessed, the process of specifying the capabilities to which changes in environmental quality are relevant allows the relevant capabilities to be defined and expanded in a contextually sensitive way.[51] Specifically, the process of value identification entails specifying, and therefore further defining, the central human capabilities in ways that are relevant to the values of distinct individuals and communities. As I have explained the process, this produces a list of capabilities, to which environmental change is relevant, that is context specific and variable. It reflects the different and distinct needs, culture, history, and practices of specific communities. However, it also creates the opportunity for people to identify additional capabilities that cannot be derived from the list Nussbaum has proposed. Locally determined capabilities can then be added to the list of capabilities to which changes in environmental quality are relevant.[52] In this respect, the list of relevant capabilities can be the subject of self-defined values that are sure to go beyond abstract theorizing to engage the conditions and states of enablement that matter to specific people.[53]

In these ways the process of value identification I am proposing seeks to base a policy's relevance on an account of environmental value that is more empirically informed and less subject to problems of preference adaptation and strategic abuse that arise in economic and deliberative methods

[51] See Chapter 3, Section 3.2.2.

[52] See, for instance, Wolff and de-Shalit (2007:62), who develop a framework for assessing disadvantage that starts with Nussbaum's list of central capabilities and then adds several capabilities to the list after interviewing people to determine if there are additional dimensions of well-being that are central to their characterization of advantage.

[53] See Crocker (2008:185) for the view that Nussbaum's "capabilities approach" relies too heavily on philosophic theorizing.

of environmental valuation. It does this by integrating expert knowledge of physical changes in the environment with citizens' characterization of the things in their lives that matter to them. This produces a specified list of central human capabilities to which a particular change in environmental quality is relevant. Before further elaborating the advantages of this approach in identifying the values to which a change in environmental quality is relevant, let me first explain the second component of the valuation process: the process of *value measurement.*

4.4.2 Value measurement

A capabilities approach to environmental valuation entails two steps, one of value identification and another of value measurement. Value identification involves specifying the capabilities to which changes in environmental quality are relevant, but we also need to know the extent to which a change in environmental quality makes a person more or less capable of exercising one of these capabilities by choosing to pursue a specific activity or achievement. The latter concerns the process of value measurement. This component of the valuation process entails quantifying or otherwise rendering comparable (but not commensurable) the degree to which changes in environmental quality support or undermine the threshold level of people's central capabilities. Rather than assessing the value of changes in environmental quality by asking people how much they would be willing to pay for them, the process of value measurement in a capabilities approach to environmental valuation relates empirical information about the relevant change in environmental quality directly to the capabilities identified as relevant to those impacts. For example, in many areas of the United States, people would probably identify a policy changing the allowable level of fine particulate matter (PM2.5) per unit of air as relevant to their capabilities for being in good respiratory health (which would therefore be a defined as a specification of the *bodily health* capability). Or, to use a different example, a proposal for a new hazardous waste storage facility in a given community would be related to citizens' capability to control the environmental hazards affecting their well-being (which could defined as a specification of the *material control over one's environment* capability).

Whereas citizens have a crucial role to play in the component of the valuation process that entails value identification, the process of value measurement is more squarely in the domain of experts because they have the skills necessary to bring information about physical changes in environmental quality to bear on changes in the capabilities that citizens have worked with them to identify as relevant. In Chapter 6 I propose some constraints for keeping experts accountable to citizens in the administrative rulemaking process, and these constraints are equally relevant to keeping experts accountable to citizens in the process of environmental valuation that I am proposing here. However, for present purposes, I set the topic of expert accountability aside in order to continue sketching a capabilities approach to environmental valuation suitable for assessing the distributional implications of environmental policies.

In the process of environmental valuation that I am proposing, value measurement entails assessing how changes in environmental quality precipitated by environmental policies will impact the distinct capabilities of different people. The goal is to measure and compare the distributional impacts of a policy that changes environmental quality. For this purpose, the impact of a change in environmental quality on a particular capability of different people can be measured in the same way. For instance, the impact of an increase in air quality on the capability for respiratory health for two different people, John and Jane, can be measured by the number of asthma attacks that will be triggered or avoided. If John has asthma but already lives in a relatively unpolluted area, then a relatively small increase in air quality may be effective in eliminating his asthma attacks. If Jane, on the other hand, also has asthma but lives in a relatively polluted area, then a small increase in air quality may not be effective in reducing the asthma attacks she suffers. Thus, while a policy improving air quality will increase John's capability for respiratory health, given Jane's circumstances it may do little to improve her respiratory health capability. Consequently, with respect to the respiratory health capability, we can say that John gets more benefits than Jane from the proposed change in air quality. If both John and Jane live in a society where the existing level of air quality already protects their respiratory health capability above the threshold level of what justice requires, then the policy change can claim to be just. However, if the respiratory health capability is not protected at a threshold level, then this is a policy that might push John above the level of health capability that justice requires, while failing to do the same for Jane. In the latter case, the policy change could not claim to be just because it would not protect Jane's respiratory health capability at the level justice requires.

This example demonstrates an important feature of the capabilities approach to environmental valuation: the value of changes in environmental quality are measured in a way that makes it possible to compare expansions and contractions of the same capability across differently situated people. Toward this end, it is important to emphasize that a change in one's respiratory health capability is only one way in which an increase in air quality may impact people. Specifically, for a given change in environmental quality, a different form or dimension of environmental value might emerge along each dimension of individual well-being that the capabilities articulate. For instance, the environment's aesthetic value may emerge when a policy improving air quality brings a beautiful mountainous setting into view, making John capable of enjoying a beautiful view (which he may have defined as a specification of the *senses, imagination, and thought* capability). Or, the environment's recreational value may emerge when a policy improving air quality makes John more capable of playing outside with other children on high temperature days (which he may have defined as a specification of the *play* capability). In a capabilities approach to valuation these distinct capabilities need not be made commensurate with each other, so that John's overall level of capability improvement can be measured and then aggregated with the capability improvements that benefit others. Likewise, they need not be made commensurate so that different capabilities of different people can be compared in terms of aggregate capability improvements accruing to each person. Instead, a capabilities approach to environmental valuation need only compare how a change in environmental quality impacts the same capability (e.g. for respiratory health or enjoying a beautiful view) of different people (e.g. John and Jane), with respect to the threshold level of capability protection that justice requires. For this purpose, the method for measuring the value of changes in environmental quality must be the same with respect to particular capabilities, but not across capabilities.

Thus, when the multidimensional approach to value identification is combined with this empirical approach to value measurement, the capabilities approach to environmental valuation is able to deal with the plural nature of environmental values in a unique way. It assesses a policy's consequences for different people by comparing people within rather than across different dimensions of environmental value. Jane's capability for respiratory health is compared to John's capability for respiratory health, but not to John's capability for enjoying a beautiful view. Since justice requires protection of each capability at a threshold level, the extent to which it is achieved for John and Jane, therefore, can be determined with respect to each capability, revealing the ways and extent to which a policy advantages some people and disadvantages others. To reiterate these points, if justice requires a threshold level of capability protection for each person, the capabilities approach to environment valuation makes the environmental impacts experienced by different people comparable along the same dimension of well-being with respect to that threshold level of capability protection. Because different forms of empirical measurement can be used to assess the environment's impact on different capabilities, this approach to valuation promises to deliver an empirically rich and accurate account of the distributional implications resulting from an environmental policy or management decision.

4.5 Conclusion

In this chapter I have sketched the basic features of a capabilities approach to environmental valuation. This approach treats the environment as a precondition of Nussbaum's list of central human capabilities and evaluates changes in environmental quality with respect to their implications for the threshold level of capability protection that justice requires for each person. For this purpose, I argued that human capabilities should be understood in the context of ecosystems and broader ecological interactions on which they are dependent. This ecological dependence reveals the nature of human interdependence, and therefore illuminates the reason why changes in environmental quality necessarily distribute environmental advantage and disadvantage differently among different people.

When environmental value is understood as a relationship between broad ecological conditions and human capabilities, the value of changes in environmental quality can be defined by how those changes impact the irreducibly plural ways in which the environment makes humans capable. Assessing these changes in environmental quality with respect to goals of social justice should entail a process of environmental valuation that separates the task of identifying what people value from the task of assessing the extent to which policy will therefore make people's lives better or worse. This allows citizens to specify an abstract list of valuable capabilities in terms of the opportunities for doing and achieving the things that matter most to them. However, it also allows for empirically assessing capability changes that environmental policies produce in a way that is systematic and empirically verifiable, revealing who a policy impacts, in what way, and by how much. While environmental valuation of this kind would demand a rich array of information, this does not diminish the normative case for assessing substantive environmental impacts in a way that is undistorted by the malleability of human preferences, the pathologies of democratic processes, or the incommensurability of environmental values. Before considering how this approach to environmental valuation can operate within the administrative rulemaking process that structures environmental management, let us first consider a capabilities approach to justifying environmental policy that complements the approach to environmental valuation I have advanced in this chapter.

5

A Capabilities Approach to Policy Justification

5.1 Introduction

Who benefits from environmental protection? This question is crucial to assessing environmental policies in terms of their contribution to social justice rather than economic efficiency. In Chapter 3 I argued that, for the purpose of answering this question, a capabilities-based conception of individual well-being has a distinct advantage over economic metrics: it can reveal the channels through which environmental protection has different and unequal impacts on different people. Having elaborated how we should understand the natural environment's value to individual well-being in Chapter 4, I now develop a broader normative framework for justifying policies that protect the environment. Building on Martha Nussbaum's theory of social justice, I propose an approach to justifying policies that considers whether they protect people's central capabilities at a threshold level. Nussbaum's theory provides an appealing basis for policy justification because it can help to recast environmental protection as a condition of justice and choice, rather than an aggregation of the preferences people express in market interactions. Furthermore, when her approach to justice is informed by an understanding of the environment's role in creating and maintaining human capabilities that I developed in Chapter 4, it also can be used to resolve tradeoffs among conflicting policy goals.

As a theoretical ideal for policy analysis, protecting each person's capabilities at a threshold level contrasts significantly with the cost–benefit approach to policy analysis, which is commonly employed in assessing the impact of contemporary environmental laws and policies. Cost–benefit analysis (CBA)

Sections 5.2 and 5.3 of this chapter incorporate ideas from "Ecology and the Limits of Justice: Establishing Capability Ceilings in Nussbaum's Capabilities Approach" by Breena Holland, published in the Journal of Human Development, copyright © United Nations Development Programme, and reprinted here by permission of Taylor & Francis Ltd, (http://www.tandfonline.com) on behalf of United Nations Development Programme.

advances policies that maximize net social benefits, defined in monetary terms. This ideal finds its most common justification in the achievement of a Pareto efficient outcome, which refers to a condition in which it is not possible to improve any one person's situation without worsening that of another person. In Chapter 2 I explained that, because of this requirement, a government implementing Pareto efficient policies can claim to avoid at least some of the most morally contestable outcomes, such as those that improve the aggregate condition of society by burdening those who are already least well off. The ideal of Pareto efficiency demonstrates an important commitment to fairness and equality because it requires correcting policies that bring gains to some at the cost of losses to others.

In practice, however, CBA is not constrained by a Pareto efficient standard. In the real world of regulatory politics, policies that depart from the Pareto efficient condition can still pass a cost–benefit test, and thus be justified as economically efficient. Due to the problems that arise in distributing a policy's benefits so that no person is in fact worse off after the policy's implementation, the actual application of CBA jettisons Pareto efficiency in favor of Kaldor–Hicks efficiency. Kaldor–Hicks efficiency imposes the much lower standard that a policy's benefits merely outweigh its costs.[1] Those who favor the use of quantitative CBA argue that if the Kaldor–Hicks condition is met, the beneficiaries of policy (the winners) *could* compensate those whom the policy burdens (the losers), *potentially* meeting the condition that Pareto efficiency requires. From this perspective, the possibility of compensation is sufficient for policy justification; actual compensation is not required. Thus, although the possibility of retroactive compensation of those who lose under policies meeting the standard of Kaldor–Hicks efficiency appears to maintain the distributive goals of Pareto efficiency while overcoming the practical challenges to implementing the higher standard, there is no mechanism to guarantee redistribution of the benefits after the policy is implemented. Failure to actually compensate people for the negative impacts of a policy renders the more normatively compelling justification of CBA in Pareto efficiency purely hypothetical.[2]

Significant distributional problems arise from relying on Kaldor–Hicks efficiency as the central criterion for evaluating policies. For example, a CBA might approve a policy allowing coal-fired power plants to trade pollution permits because this produces an overall reduction of mercury pollution with positive net benefits.[3] However, a policy might achieve this overall

[1] See Boardman et al. (2001:29–30).

[2] For a discussion of this criticism of CBA, see Gillroy and Wade (1992:6–13) and Ackerman and Heinzerling (2004:31–35). See Boardman et al. (2001:30) for the standard justification of non-compensation through CBA.

[3] Indeed, the Environmental Protection Agency's benefits analysis of the rule regulating mercury emissions through a pollution trading scheme found the benefits to be in excess of costs by billions of dollars. See US EPA (Jan. 2004:2–49).

reduction by allowing plants for which those reductions are least expensive to produce reductions at cost, while allowing plants for which reductions are most expensive to simply buy up enough permits to continue emitting the same or higher levels of pollution. In this scenario, although the policy achieves an overall reduction in mercury emissions, residents living downwind of plants that avoid high reduction costs by purchasing permits will be exposed to continued or even elevated levels of air pollution.[4]

From the perspective of justice, these distributional outcomes matter. Justice, at least among contemporary liberal theorists, is concerned with the interests of distinct individual people, even if ignoring the interests of any particular person will produce a greater overall good.[5] As John Rawls describes this commitment, "Each person possesses an inviolability founded on justice that even the welfare of society as a whole cannot override."[6] Viewed in comparison to this ideal, the policy analyst that aggregates a policy's costs and benefits is like the utilitarian that calculates the overall amount of pleasure or happiness in society. Each errs in denying the separateness of individual people; each fails to approach the task of designing and evaluating institutions that order collective life in a way that treats individual people with equal concern and respect.[7]

Where environmental relationships are concerned, the question of what it means to treat people with equal concern and respect remains unaddressed by many political theorists engaging in the liberal democratic tradition.[8] One reason for this is that environmental ethicists have, for many decades, responded to the narrowly economic and instrumental treatment of the environment in law and public policy by arguing that nature should be treated as having "intrinsic" value. For intrinsic value theorists, nature has value as an end in itself, independent of its contribution to human life and therefore to justice among people.[9] These theorists have sought to establish nature (and/

[4] The failure of such a policy to meet the "Good Neighbor Provision" of the Clean Air Act (CAA) (see Section 7410(a)(2)(D)) was the primary reason why a DC court vacated the George W. Bush administration's policy—the "Clean Air Interstate Rule" (CAIR)—creating this kind of pollution trading program among power plants that emit mercury into the air. (See *North Carolina v. EPA* 531 F.3d 907–908 (D.C. Cir. 2008).) The Good Neighbor Provision of the CAA requires that states implementing the National Ambient Air Quality Standards established under the CAA must prevent any type of emissions activity from making a significant contribution to another (downwind) state's non-attainment of those standards. Thus, in vacating the Mercury Rule, the court found that the cap-and-trade scheme the Bush administration's EPA intended to promulgate threatened to allow upwind states housing power plants (that were allowed to increase their emissions under the rule) to push downwind states out of compliance with existing standards; i.e. as a consequence of those increased emissions crossing the border into downwind states. (See *North Carolina v. EPA* 531 F.3d 908–911 (D.C. Cir. 2008).)

[5] See Schlosberg (2007:11–41) for a concise overview of distributive (and other) conceptions of justice in contemporary political theory that are relevant to matters of environmental justice.

[6] Rawls (1971:3). [7] See Rawls (1975) and Sen and Williams (1982:1–21).

[8] See Miller (1999:151–153) and Bell (2004:289).

[9] For example, see Taylor (1981) making this argument from a biocentric perspective and Jamison (2002) for a more contemporary elaboration.

or its components) as worthy of respect in its own right, not simply because it has instrumental value to people. Viewed in this light, although contemporary liberal political theorists have made important strides in focusing on the interests of each individual person rather than aggregate outcomes, they have also perpetuated a highly anthropocentric view of the environment, giving insufficient attention to theorizing and challenging accepted views about the place of humans in a broader natural order.

A second reason why the relationship between nature and social justice has been undertheorized is that the most prominent theorists of justice, who are concerned with human life, have not systematically addressed how the natural environment bears on whatever basic conditions they argue government should protect when it allocates social advantages and disadvantages.[10] John Rawls's early work, for example, treats environmental problems as something that society can solve by merely internalizing externalities that market prices do not take into account. Rawls assumes environmental problems can be managed if the government simply applies taxes and subsidies to force polluters to pay the (true) cost of public goods they use, such as the sinks of air and water that absorb pollutants they emit.[11] While limited, Rawls's original framing of the environment in narrowly economic terms is not surprising. In 1971, when he was first advancing social justice as an ideal for evaluating what social institutions (rather than individuals) do, society's scientific understanding of environmental problems was far less sophisticated than it is today. For instance, at that time environmental thinkers had only just started to popularize the idea that the earth is a closed system with limited natural resources and a limited capacity to absorb the wastes that humans produce.[12] Rawls's contribution to the study of politics was in bringing social and political institutions under the lens of justice, not in theorizing the natural environment's role as essential to both.

In seeking to develop an approach to justice that remains true to Rawls's basic liberal political commitments, Martha Nussbaum's "capabilities approach" to justice does overcome several important limitations in Rawls's theory.[13] However, like Rawls, Nussbaum does not theorize the environment's instrumental role as a basic condition of justice for humans.[14] By theorizing

[10] See Miller (1999:151–153) and Bell (2004:289).

[11] See Rawls (1971:268); see Holland (2008b), for a discussion of why this characterization of the environment puts Rawls's two principles of justice in tension with each other.

[12] For example, see Matthews (1970); for a related contemporary argument see Jackson (2009).

[13] See Nussbaum (2006) where she takes up three unresolved problems for Rawlsian justice as well as problems that confront traditional social contract theories.

[14] See Holland (2008b) for a discussion of the differences between Rawls's and Nussbaum's theories of justice and Holland (2008a) for a discussion of this problem in Nussbaum's theory of justice. Also see Nussbaum (2011:163–166) endorsing Holland's approach to addressing the relationship between the natural environment and social justice.

the relationship between the natural environment and the substantive view of justice Nussbaum develops in her capabilities approach, my aim in this chapter is to provide a stronger and more effective basis for evaluating and determining the distributive implications of environmental policies.

The chapter will proceed as follows. I first contrast the approach to policy justification that I am proposing with the cost–benefit approach to policy justification, discussed earlier in this chapter and in Chapter 2. Second, I take up the central challenge that non-economic approaches to policy evaluation must confront, which is how to resolve the conflicts that arise among the positive and negative impacts that public policies produce. Third, I develop the idea of "capability ceilings" as a conceptual tool for resolving these conflicts, and then explore the relevance of this idea to resolving conflicts among the capabilities of people impacted by air pollution policies. Fourth, I address how the "ecological meta-capability" introduced Chapter 4 can be brought to bear on an approach to policy justification that incorporates the use of both capability thresholds and ceilings. What emerges from this discussion is a "capabilities approach to social and environmental justice," which I advance as distinct theory of justice that can be used to guide the evaluation of environmental policies and justify environmental protection.

5.2 Justice as Capabilities: A Goal for Environmental Policy

In appealing to justice as a criterion for assessing a public policy's value to society, a capabilities approach to policy justification holds the position that justice is a normative ideal or goal at which a liberal democratic society should aim. For example, one might maintain that the normal "regulatory review" of proposed public policies should involve assessing the extent to which policies further a fair or substantively just allocation of resources, rather than (or in addition to) an economically efficient allocation.[15] Alternatively, one might think that justice is an ideal a democratic society should systematically consider or reason about in its normal deliberations about policy choices. In either case, valuing substantive justice as a policy ideal entails treating a policy's impact on the conditions that define justice as worthy of comprehensive and consistent assessment. To do this in practice involves assessing a policy's actual or expected consequences with respect to that ideal, in the same way that CBA assesses a policy's consequences with respect to the costs and benefits that define the ideal of economic efficiency.

[15] By "regulatory review" I refer to the process originally established in Executive Order 12,291, which requires the president's Office of Management and Budget (OMB) to evaluate all major federal rules and regulations according to their economic costs and benefits.

Just as a policy analysis that appeals to the criterion of Pareto efficiency will yield different results than one appealing to Kaldor–Hicks efficiency, a policy analysis that appeals to one account of justice will yield different results than one appealing to other accounts of justice.[16] For instance, if justice requires protecting people's civil and political freedoms, then a policy that degrades the natural environment might appear to have a minimal impact on justice because the connections that link environmental degradation to people's civil and political freedoms can be difficult to identify, document, or otherwise establish as a matter of scientific "certainty." Alternatively, if justice is defined to also require the protection of social and economic freedoms that are highly resource dependent, then the ways in which a policy that degrades the natural environment undermines justice will be far more obvious.[17] To put this point differently, because different theories of justice provide different accounts of *what* justice consists in and *why* a society should pursue that understanding of justice as a social goal, assessments of the extent to which environmental protection is meeting goals of social justice will vary depending on what a given account of justice requires. Likewise, as David Schlosberg has shown, these different requirements of justice are also reflected in the evolving politics of the environmental justice movement; for example, as the environmental justice movement evolved and expanded, it shifted from articulating claims of justice primarily in terms of equity, to articulating claims of justice in terms of individual and community capabilities, with a corresponding shift in the policy expectations that the movement demanded.[18]

As explained earlier in this chapter, the account of justice that I develop for evaluating and justifying environmental policies builds on the ideal of justice that Martha Nussbaum advances. Nussbaum's theory of justice offers a substantive ideal in that she defines justice as consisting in specific conditions or states of human enablement; specifically, justice requires protecting the capabilities that are central to a good or decent human life at a threshold level for each person.[19] Although Nussbaum's primary focus has been on justifying substantive political protections for these capabilities she is also concerned with procedural fairness as a capability in itself and as a function of other capabilities. Her tenth capability, the capability for *political control over one's environment,* makes an explicit commitment to fairness in democratic decision-making procedures. This capability requires that people be able to participate effectively in political choices that bear on their lives, and that

[16] See Wenz (1988).

[17] As Chapter 4 has shown, the natural environment is instrumental to a variety of social and economic interactions. Also see, Hayward (2005:5).

[18] See Schlosberg (2004:522–529, 2007) and Fraser (2000:107–108).

[19] Nussbaum (2000a:6, 2006:71).

they have the basic right to political participation.[20] However, Nussbaum does not specify what participation means in practice, nor does she treat it as something that must be central to her project of establishing the background constitutional commitments of a democracy that will be effective in making political decisions in a way that is procedurally just.

Clearly, capabilities theory, as developed and applied by various people, can inform both procedural and substantive accounts of justice. For instance, in his account of the evolution of the environmental justice movement, Schlosberg argues that equalizing political capabilities among participants in environmental decision-making processes requires sufficient recognition or respect for different kinds of relationships to the environment that are central to individual identity.[21] In Chapter 6 I address some related concerns about the structure of decision-making processes and procedures. However, for the present purpose of developing a capabilities approach to evaluating and justifying the substantive impacts of policies that protect the environment, I treat Nussbaum's theory of justice as an attainable ideal in societies committed to the coexistence of people with diverse views about what a good human life involves and to protecting the freedom of people to pursue a way of life that they personally value.[22] By operating within the boundaries of these basic "liberal" political commitments, the governmental interventions necessary for protecting people's capabilities can be more convincingly justified as legitimate political goals. Let us consider, then, how this approach to justice can inform the theory and practice of policy evaluation.

5.3 The Capabilities Approach as a Theory of Justice for Policy Evaluation

A central advantage of a capabilities approach to justice with respect to environmental policy is its illumination of individual-level impacts that get masked in CBA's practice of aggregating the benefits of environmental policies.[23] As I have previously discussed, CBA judges policies based on whether the total benefits they produce outweigh their total costs. This permits policy evaluation to disregard the losses that accrue to individual people as long as a policy's overall benefits are large enough to outweigh its overall costs.

[20] Nussbaum (2000a:80).

[21] See Schlosberg (2007:45–78); more generally, see Young (1990, 2002) and Fraser (2000).

[22] See Rawls (1993:19) explaining the view that Nussbaum adopts, which is that in a politically "liberal" society each person should be able to pursue "a more or less determinate scheme of final ends, that is, ends that we want to realize for their own sake, as well as attachments to other persons and loyalties to various groups and associations."

[23] See Shrader-Frechette (2002:13, 1991).

A capabilities approach to policy justification starkly contrasts with this because it judges polices based on whether they ensure that *each person* has access to environmental goods—or experiences the environmental conditions—necessary for protecting his or her central human capabilities at a threshold level. In a capabilities approach to justice, each person must be treated as valuable and worthy of respect. People are each ends in themselves, and never a mere means to the ends of others.[24] Judging policies according to this commitment requires assessing the extent to which they protect a threshold level of each person's capabilities, because beneath this threshold level a life that is truly human—or worthy of human dignity—is not available to citizens.[25] As Nussbaum explains, "the social goal should be understood in terms of getting citizens above this capability threshold."[26] Thus, not only does a policy's impact on each individual person matter, the extent of its impact in relation to some minimum standard of well-being is also important.

In Chapter 3 I explained why human capabilities offer a conception of individual well-being that is helpful in revealing how environmental policies actually impact people and therefore can result in different levels of protection from environmental harms.[27] The crucial point is that a person's capabilities reflect whether her personal traits and circumstances make it possible for her to translate her environmental assets and conditions into valuable outcomes or achievements. For the purpose of considering issues of equity and distribution that pertain to environmental impacts, I argued that the conceptual focus on people's capabilities is especially important because assessing how a policy impacts people's capabilities can reveal why seemingly uniform pollution control standards will inevitably provide variable levels of protection to different people.

To apply and build on this point, consider, for instance, how protection provided by a regulatory standard that limits the emission of pollutants harming the atmosphere's ozone layer will play out across geographical space. The ozone layer, which is located many miles from the earth's surface, filters out harmful ultra-violet radiation from the sun. However, the ozone layer's thickness, and therefore its success in filtering out these harmful rays, varies according to season and geographical location. People that live close to the earth's northern or southern poles, where the ozone layer is thinnest, will face bigger threats from ultra-violet radiation than those who live closer to the earth's equator. People living near the earth's poles, consequently, will be

[24] Nussbaum (2000a:56). Nussbaum (2000a:5) refers to this as the *principle of each person's capability*.

[25] See Nussbaum (2000a:72).

[26] Nussbaum (2000a:6).

[27] Also see Chapters 2 and 4.

less able to translate a given level of pollution control into the achievement of avoiding cancer, due to where they live. In this sense, a regulation limiting pollutants that damage this layer of atmospheric protection does not provide equal protection to all people. People living near the earth's poles will be less capable of achieving good health. Because the capabilities approach conceives of a person's well-being in terms of a person's conditions and abilities, it provides a perspective for observing how these and other variations in one's geographical circumstance pose barriers to providing people with equal protection from environmental harms.

The irreducible value of capabilities that are central to a good human life in this approach to justice is also a key component of policy justification. Capabilities have irreducible value in the sense that they each require a minimal level of protection. A policy's impact on a given person does not meet the conditions of justice if it pushes one of the person's capabilities above the threshold of what justice requires while pushing another one of the person's capabilities below the threshold of what justice requires. As Nussbaum has argued "If people are below the threshold on any one of the capabilities, that is a failure of basic justice, no matter how high up they are on all the others."[28] This demand to provide absolute protections for each of a person's central human capabilities is also helpful for evaluating environmental policies, and distinguishes the capabilities approach from other liberal theories of justice. In particular, the list of fundamentally important capabilities that Nussbaum proposes encompasses social and economic protections, not just people's civil and political freedoms.[29] Although the former are more directly related to environmental conditions and therefore are helpful in establishing an account of the environment's actual value to human life, these protections are less commonly accepted (than civil and political freedoms) as justifiable political goals.

More specifically, because the capabilities approach recognizes that certain social and economic protections are preconditions of people's civil and political freedoms, it views these social and economic goods as central to any view of justice that seeks to secure civil and political freedoms. One's bodily health, for instance, is central to participating in politics and various forms of religious and cultural freedom. In treating a person's capability for *bodily health* (among other capabilities) as a basic condition of justice, the capabilities approach provides a substantive ideal that can be used as a criterion for assessing and comparing how environmental policies impact a wide variety of conditions connected to the natural environment that significantly impact what people are able to do. Thus, for the purpose of evaluating a policy's

[28] Nussbaum (2006:167). [29] See Nussbaum (2006:289).

distributional consequences, the capabilities approach has the advantage of defining justice in a way that can better observe the environment's role in maintaining the conditions necessary for living the kinds of lives people do and want to live. It does not assume that people face background conditions of social and economic justice, and therefore ignore the relevance of such conditions to genuine protection of people's civil and political freedoms.

Although Nussbaum has not proposed treating the environmental conditions of human capabilities as a central component of justice, if her account of justice is extended to include the ecological meta-capability as I have proposed in Chapter 4, then it can provide a basic criterion for evaluating the relative distribution of benefits and burdens that result from environmental policies.[30] Such a criterion would require evaluating how environmental policies impact the ecological conditions necessary for protecting people's central human capabilities at a threshold level. Since these ecological conditions define the systemic interactions through which degradation of particular environmental goods or ecosystems services in one place end up undermining the environmental goods or services that support people's capabilities in another place, an approach to policy evaluation that treats the ecological meta-capability as a basic component of justice will entail assessing the distributional and procedural implications of changes in environmental quality resulting from environmental policies. In this context, a policy that is socially and environmentally just is one that secures the environmental conditions supporting each person's capabilities, including the capability for *political control over one's environment*. In order to evaluate and justify policies with respect to this criterion, policy evaluation must account for *what* capabilities a policy supports or undermines, as well as for *whose*.

Thus, to draw out these points, rather than aggregating a policy's impacts into an overall sum of total monetary benefits, a capabilities approach to policy evaluation remains focused on the distribution of those benefits and any associated burdens. Furthermore, because it relies on capabilities as its metric of well-being, it can illuminate the individual impacts that economic analysis conceals, and with a level of breadth and nuance that monetary valuation cannot provide. As Sen's original work criticizing standard economic accounts of poverty emphasized, monetary measures do not provide sufficient information for determining how well off people really are. By addressing the non-economic conditions that are necessary for humans to thrive and flourish, capabilities theory broadens the account of what it is that makes

[30] In Chapter 6 I explain how this account of justice can also provide the basis for a procedurally just approach to designing and evaluating processes for making and implementing environmental decisions at the administrative level. See Nussbaum (2011:164–165) for a discussion of the advantages of treating the natural environment as instrumental to human capabilities in the way that I am proposing in the present chapter.

people able to lead good lives, and provides a metric of well-being that can refer to what that might entail. I have proposed that we further specify this account of well-being to include the environmental conditions under which people can in fact be capable of leading good lives.[31] This will ensure it is possible to use the capabilities approach as a basis for making either generalized or specific comparisons of a policy's real impacts on different people so that it is possible to determine *who* the policy is benefitting and burdening.[32]

While this approach to reasoning about and justifying environmental policies has both normative appeal and evaluative clarity, as currently theorized it lacks a method for resolving the conflicts among capabilities that public policies often produce. Specifically, when it is impossible for a proposed policy to push the capabilities of one person above the threshold level of protection that justice requires without simultaneously pushing the capabilities of another person below the threshold level of protection that justice requires, a "tragic question" arises: What or whose capabilities will be sacrificed? Nussbaum considers such situations—of "capability conflict"—as tragic because none of the available political or policy choices are morally acceptable.[33] Nonetheless, recognizing such conflicts for what they are can have the positive impact of pushing society toward justice, not least because it acknowledges the moral commitments a policy may deny, and, consequently, the kinds of policy outcomes that ought to be avoided in the future.[34]

Applied to the environmental context, when policy evaluation is grounded in a capabilities approach to justice, environmental policies producing capability conflicts would be characterized as failing to meet basic conditions of justice. Just as policies for which net economic costs outweigh net economic benefits fail to meet standards of economic efficiency, we could then say that policies producing capabilities conflicts fail to meet standards of justice. But the capabilities approach can provide more than a basis for identifying and therefore helping to name an injustice. As I argue in the following sections, it can also be used to resolve capability conflicts in a way that does not violate the basic conditions of justice to which it is committed. Protecting these basic conditions of justice will also prevent an unequal imposition of harms to which the ideal of Pareto efficiency appeals.

[31] See Chapter 4.

[32] As Wolff and de-Shalit show (207:87–107), evaluating policy impacts along the plural dimensions of well-being that define the functionings enabled by a person's capabilities need not result in a complete ordering of disadvantage. For instance, the less challenging task of determining whether policies tend to cluster disadvantage among particular groups would significantly improve on current forms of distributional analysis.

[33] See Nussbaum (2000b:1007).

[34] Nussbaum (2000b:1009–1016, 2011:37–39).

To briefly summarize before turning to this argument: a capabilities approach to justice that treats the natural environment as a meta-capability of human beings can be an effective basis for an approach to policy evaluation that has distinct advantages over CBA. A capabilities framework enables policy analysts to assess the full extent to which changes in environmental quality impact individual people. Such an approach can reveal the conflicts among the environmental preconditions required for protecting and providing a threshold level of capabilities for each person, illuminating the extent to which a policy supports or undermines the capabilities people need to live minimally decent lives, in which their flourishing is a real possibility. Although I have argued that this framework is valuable in diagnosing inequities that policies produce, and therefore for determining whether policies meet conditions of justice, this approach does not tell us how to produce a more just policy. It is one thing to illuminate the ways in which a policy undermines people's capabilities and yet another to create a policy that produces a more just outcome. Let us consider, then, how a capabilities approach to policy justification might inform the design of policies that overcome capability conflicts to achieve the goals of social and environmental justice.

5.3.1 The problem of capability conflicts

As currently theorized, Nussbaum's account of justice provides little guidance on how to address capability conflicts resulting from environmental policies. This is due in part to the role she envisions for democratic deliberation in both resolving such conflicts and establishing capability thresholds. Nussbaum has suggested that remedies to capabilities conflicts should be determined through a deliberative process involving the public as well as legislative and judicial actors.[35] Some argue that this solution is an insufficient actualization of the deliberative democratic ideal because it limits citizens' involvement to specifying the requirements of pre-established commitments to the list of central human capabilities.[36] Others, such as David Schlosberg, persuasively argue that certain personal, social, and cultural relationships to the natural environment are, for some people, a precondition of their capability to deliberate and otherwise participate in politics in a meaningful way.[37] For Schlosberg, depriving people of the very environmental conditions

[35] Nussbaum (2000b:1007); also see Holland (2008b) for a longer discussion of the features and limitations of Nussbaum's discussion of capability conflicts.

[36] See Crocker (2008:162–163).

[37] Although Schlosberg (2007:58–75) has a populist and highly participatory ideal of deliberative democracy in mind, presumably the importance of the natural environment to individual identity would be relevant to the more institutional forms of deliberation that Nussbaum

that define their individual and community identities fundamentally undermines the norms of fair participation and recognition for all participants that underpin the deliberative ideal and are the basis of institutional legitimacy in a democratic context. Thus, a crucial implication of Schlosberg's argument is that certain environmental protections should be understood as preconditions of political processes that give people an equal opportunity to influence political decisions.

But even if such preconditions of people's political capabilities are established as a basis for democratic reasoning and deliberation about capability conflicts and the capability thresholds that should define basic conditions of justice, a capabilities approach to policy evaluation need not only appeal to procedural ideals of democratic deliberation to reveal and then resolve the tragic tradeoffs that policy decisions entail. Indeed, as a general approach to evaluating national policies that are intended to cross the borders of many communities and geographical contexts, deliberative and participatory approaches to policy formation and evaluation are highly impracticable, at least in the context of present models for achieving genuine deliberation.[38] As I discuss in Chapter 6, even for the purpose of designing environmental policies on a more local or regional scale, efforts to democratize decision-making suffer from numerous barriers that prevent the conditions of genuine deliberation and participatory decision-making being established. These problems should not deter such efforts, but neither should they lead us to assume such approaches will result in better outcomes simply because they are purportedly more democratic than technocratic.

Rather than appealing to the procedural ideals implicit in arguments that favor increasing democratic reasoning and deliberation in policy decisions, the capabilities approach to policy evaluation I am proposing can reveal and resolve capability conflicts by appealing to the substantive ideals of justice it embraces. This is a worthwhile goal because although the environmental justice movement has made some important progress in the area of decision-making processes—by opening up administrative agencies' decision-making procedures to greater public scrutiny and community participation—significant and troubling substantive environmental inequities remain.[39] To take one example, in its analysis of the implementation of President Clinton's (1994) executive order on Environmental Justice (E.O. 12,898), a 2004 report by the EPA's Office of Inspector General documented that "The Agency [EPA] has not provided a clear vision on environmental

imagines as going on among legislative and judicial actors, for these actors are still held accountable to a system of democratic representation.

[38] Although see Crocker (2008:392–397) for a discussion of three strategies for "humanizing" and "democratizing" globalization.

[39] See Faber (2008:133–162).

justice integration, or objectives that are clear, precise, and focused on environmental results."[40] Appealing to substantive ideals of justice when evaluating federal policies that have allowed for significant inequalities in environmental benefits and burdens would create a space for policy responses that go beyond changing decision-making procedures to actually ensure substantive goals of environmental protection are achieved. This would not deny the importance of inclusive and transparent decision-making processes, which can do much to influence policy decisions, and for the reasons Schlosberg proposes this may even be required as a component of protecting people's capability for *political control over one's environment*. However, a capabilities approach to policy evaluation can also address substantive inequities arising from environmental policy by appealing directly to the substantive protections implicit in a capabilities approach to justice.

For this purpose, as well as for the purpose of theorizing how to positively construct policies that reduce or eliminate tragic tradeoffs among conflicting capabilities, let us assume that a socially accepted threshold level of capabilities has already been established. These levels of protection might be the result of deliberative reasoning along the lines of what Schlosberg proposes or of some other form of reasoning, such as expert analysis of public health requirements like those already implicit in current law.[41] I will return to this topic of how to establish the relevant specifications for capability provision and protection in Chapter 6. At present my purpose is to consider a general approach to evaluating and designing policies that can resolve tragic tradeoffs among conflicting capabilities that policies do or will eventually produce. Resolving such tradeoffs is necessary if a capabilities approach to policy justification is going to do more than provide the conceptual basis for identifying injustice.

Resolving such conflicts in environmental policy is especially complex because the biogeochemical interactions through which these conflicts arise often span different and vast geographical distances. The case of ozone depletion discussed earlier in Section 5.3 is a prime example of a problem in which the activities of people who live in one place (say, near the earth's equator) have cumulative effects on people who live in quite distant places (near the earth's northern and southern poles). Climate change is similarly complicated because those who emit the majority of greenhouse gases will suffer less from the consequences these gases have on earth's climate than those who have emitted relatively less. In both instances, the processes through which activities of people in one place impact the capabilities of

[40] See EPA Office of Inspector General (2004:13).

[41] For example, we might follow the CAA in defining adequate protection of bodily health as including exposure to less than 75 parts per billion (ppb) of ozone in the ambient air.

people living in distant places are global in scale, making it difficult to link causes and consequences in any clear and reliable way.

Complicated cases of capability conflict in environmental policy can also emerge at the local or regional level. For instance, in the state of Pennsylvania, many residents fear that the application of new "hydro-fracking" technologies allowing natural gas to be extracted from shale rocks deep beneath the earth's surface will create air channels through which this gas and related pollutants can damage water supplies that are relatively close to the earth's surface. While some of the benefits and burdens of gas extraction are clearly visible, others remain undocumented and unstudied.[42] In either instance, my point for present purposes is that complicated biogeochemical processes connect people's actions in ways that can both support and weaken their capabilities, determining the extent to which people are genuinely free to live the lives they choose.

Economic analysis has a particular way of understanding these kinds of problems. In the classic case of "environmental externalities," a manufacturing facility located adjacent to a river releases pollution that has negative effects on down-river users who are not party to the exchange in which the manufactured product is sold. Because the market price for the manufactured product does not include these "externalized" costs suffered by those exposed to the resulting pollution, government intervention is necessary to make the market operate in a way that ensures no party is worse off than they were prior to the transaction. Ideally, if government puts an appropriate monetary cost on the pollution (e.g. established by some kind of pollution fee paid for by the manufacturer), then the manufacturer will find ways to limit the amount of pollution produced, ensuring that third parties do not suffer such harms; or, alternatively, revenues from the fee can go toward compensating down-river users for their losses. In this way, government intervention can achieve the admirable goal of offsetting negative "third-party effects" so that no person is in fact worse off than they were prior to the exchange of the manufactured good.

At a theoretical level, the goal of making no person worse off demonstrates an important commitment to ideals of fairness and equality, providing an important justification for the role of markets in society. The problem, however, is that what fairness and equality requires often is not what monetary penalties and/or compensation do and can achieve. For instance, economic methods for determining the appropriate pollution fee may price pollution at costs that do not reflect the actual and/or unknown negative health impacts accruing to exposed populations.[43] These methods may also establish fees

[42] Swartz (2012).

[43] See Vatn and Bromley (1994) for a discussion of informational deficiencies that limit the success of efforts to price environmental resources.

that are insufficient for ensuring that environmental conditions are protected at a level that promises to ensure all people are able to live lives that involve environmental relationships they define as meaningful. Likewise, compensating for some pollution damages with money, as the ideal of Pareto efficiency would require, cannot promise to ensure no one is worse off, especially when the environmental damage is significant, because there are some environmental impacts for which no amount of money can compensate. Thus, although standard economic analysis admits that government regulation may be necessary in such circumstances, its method for resolving the conflict between those who benefit and those who suffer from changes in environmental quality is insufficient for ensuring goals of fairness and equality. It is for this reason that goals of fairness and equality are often treated as requiring a distinct form of policy evaluation.[44]

Nussbaum's capabilities approach to justice offers a new way of thinking about what it means to treat people equally in a socially just society. Human capabilities, as conditions and states of enablement that make it possible for people to choose and to pursue the activities and achievements they value, provide a concrete way to think about and define the conditions of human freedom and flourishing. In the liberal democratic society Nussbaum envisions, freedom does not just consist of the absence of interference with one's political speech, it requires the positive conditions that make one able to formulate, reason about, and articulate political speech in public spaces. In this sense, capabilities make abstract goals of freedom concrete, prioritizing the material and social components of people's basic civil and political freedoms to live self-defined lives of meaning and value. Applied within the context of economic analysis, the goal of protecting people's capabilities at a threshold level might effectively be used to define what dimensions of well-being should be protected when an allocation of resources promises to make no person worse off. For instance, a capabilities approach to economic valuation of the environment might specify that externalized costs should be internalized by pricing goods high enough to ensure a level of pollution that does in fact leave no person worse off with respect to the provision and protection of a threshold level of their central human capabilities. Although improving economic analysis is not my primary aim here, I raise this as one way of applying the capabilities approach to reestablish a more effective commitment to the ideals of Pareto efficiency.

To return to my present purpose of developing a capabilities approach to policy evaluation, a list of central human capabilities can provide a specifiable account of well-being that helps to define and characterize environmental

[44] See Liu et al. (2010:55) for an approach to evaluation that goes beyond assessing individual preferences in an effort to achieve utility maximization.

degradation as a real threat to human freedom. Policy evaluation that accurately accounts for the factors that limit people's freedoms is necessary for resolving conflicts that arise due to harms occurring through environmental processes. Given the global nature of many contemporary environmental problems, such as climate change and ocean acidification, these harms are increasingly prevalent as a new kind of threat to human freedom. Resolving or correcting the injustices these harms produce requires establishing a role for "capability ceilings" in the context of the general capabilities approach to social and environmental justice I am advancing here. A capabilities approach to policy evaluation can then help resolve capability conflicts in a way that protects basic conditions of justice in society.

5.3.2 Establishing capability ceilings to resolve capability conflicts

In environmental policy, when government policies protecting some people's capabilities permit actions that operate, through environmental processes, to push other people's capabilities below the threshold level of capability protection and provision that justice requires, then the conditions of justice are not met, and a situation of capability conflict arises. In such situations, the conflict should be resolved by establishing *capability ceilings*. As I conceive them, "capability ceilings" establish maximum levels on the protection and provision of capabilities that can cause harm to others. In contrast to capability thresholds, which secure minimum levels of capability provision and protection, capability ceilings establish limits on what people are able to do and achieve, for the specific purpose of securing threshold levels of capability protection for everyone. Thus, whereas capability thresholds make people able to do certain things, capability ceilings make people unable to do certain things.[45]

Establishing capability ceilings as a feature of a capabilities approach to justice has two general implications. First, capability ceilings refer to limitations on the choice to pursue certain individual actions that are justifiable when those actions can have or significantly contribute to the effect of undermining another person's minimum threshold of capability provision and protection. To use a simple example, in a just society citizens should be capable of free expression. But this capability is not without limit. People should not be capable of expressing themselves in ways that physically injure others, for example, in ways that incite or cause a clear and present danger of

[45] See Holland (2008b). As Peeters, Dirix, and Sterck (2013), have noted, a capability ceiling implies a "functioning constraint". However, I prefer to use the language of capability ceilings in discussing the appropriateness of limits on human freedom because this conveys the emphasis on individual choice that distinguishes capabilities from functionings as the political goal in a capabilities approach to justice.

imminent violence. Thus, legally, I should be capable of passionately swinging my arms around to fully express my views, but not capable of using my arms to express my views in ways that happen to smack other people in the face, which would violate their capability to be free from bodily harm. In this sense, capability ceilings imply constraints on the opportunity to choose individual actions that can cause harms; they do this by limiting the ways in which people can choose to realize their capabilities as an actual action or achievement. Put differently, a capability ceiling limits the ways in which a capability can be achieved as a functioning. Because ceilings imply a limit on individual action, they express the basic conviction that people should be made capable up to the point that they have the potential to cause harm to others, where harm is defined as what results from an action that pushes another person's capability below the threshold level of capability provision and protection that is required as a matter of justice.

Second, as proposed here, the fundamental reason for limiting a person's potential actions is to resolve capability conflicts by securing the central human capabilities at a threshold level for everyone. For instance, if government policy directs resources toward protecting the capabilities of some people far above the threshold level of protection that justice requires, then establishing a capability ceiling would mean redirecting resources in a way that will achieve capability thresholds for people whose capabilities are below the threshold level that justice requires. Therefore, when grounded in a capabilities approach to justice that incorporates a role for capability ceilings, policy evaluation will require spelling out conflicts arising within single policies that have different impacts on different people, as well as among policies that use societal resources to protect capabilities above the level of what justice requires. More specifically, when policies are found to provide and protect (above-threshold) levels of central capabilities that actually or potentially permit actions harming others, then the policy should be recrafted to resolve the conflict in the following way: by limiting the capabilities of those with above-threshold levels of capability provision and protection that can cause these harms. Thus, a capabilities approach to policy evaluation and design that incorporates a role for capability ceilings can establish and justify *whose* capabilities a policy should limit and *why*. This approach would seek to establish policies that put ceilings on the capabilities of those whose actions can function to push the level of capability protection and provision of others below a minimum threshold, and it would do this in order to secure everyone's capabilities at that minimum threshold level.

Thus, at a basic level, the kind of policy evaluation I am proposing requires balancing the advantages of some against the advantages of others. In theory, economic analysis seeks to avoid such comparisons when it assesses a policy's impact on different people by making sure that the policy outcome is something that at least one person prefers, and that no person prefers the pre-policy situation. At the level of theory, economic analysis need not assess how much different people gain from the policy, it need only ensure that one person gains and no one is worse off as a consequence of it. As long as there is at least one winner and no loser(s) the policy meets the standards of Pareto efficiency.[46] Even though CBA ultimately adopts the Kaldor–Hicks efficiency standard rather than the Pareto efficiency standard, it can still avoid comparing people with respect to the advantages they receive from a policy because it simply seeks to identify policies that produce positive (or the highest) aggregate gains over losses. However, as I have previously discussed, a central problem with the Kaldor–Hicks efficiency standard is that it disregards how the gains and losses are distributed among people and therefore fails to instantiate the goals of equity and fairness that the Pareto efficiency standard embraces.

One reason liberal theories of justice provide a better theoretical basis for instantiating a commitment to these goals is that these theories take balancing the freedoms of some against the freedoms of others as central to their political project. For instance, John Rawls's theory prioritizes a principle of justice that requires protecting a set of basic civil and political freedoms for each person. As originally given in *A Theory of Justice*, Rawls's principle states that "each person is to have an equal right to the most extensive basic liberty compatible with a similar liberty for others."[47] By basic liberty, Rawls is primarily referring to commonly accepted civil and political freedoms, such as the right to vote and to serve in public office, as well as rights to speech, assembly, religion, property, and so on. In stating that the extent of these liberties should be compatible with a "similar liberty for others," Rawls is making it explicit that these liberties can be circumscribed only when they come to "interfere with one another."[48] While Rawls did not extend the sphere of absolute individual protections to include the social and economic preconditions of people's basic liberties, Nussbaum's list of central human capabilities does include these social and economic protections as equally worthy of the status of constitutional entitlements that are to be protected and provided to all.[49] Extending the list of basic entitlements to include the preconditions on which people's civil and political freedoms are dependent is one way that Nussbaum extends Rawls's account of justice so that it is able to address an emergent set of political interests concerning disabled people, non-citizens, and non-human forms of life, for which Rawls's theory provides insufficient

[46] See O'Neill, Holland, and Light (2008:28–29).
[47] Rawls (1971:60).
[48] Rawls (1971:64).
[49] See Holland (2008b) discussing the difference between the theories of justice advanced by Rawls and Nussbaum in further detail.

protection.[50] However, to realize the limits on individual protections that Rawls's commitment to protecting a "similar liberty for others" embraces, Nussbaum's theory of justice needs to incorporate capability ceilings as a feature or implication of her principle that each person must have a threshold level of each central capability.[51]

The importance of balancing and establishing limits on individual freedom is taken up by other thinkers in the liberal political tradition who, like Nussbaum, adopt an Aristotelian ideal of humans as developmental beings with the potential to develop in many different and uniquely human ways.[52] For instance, the capability ceilings I have proposed earlier in this chapter as a means for resolving capability conflict might be most closely associated with John Stuart Mill's "harm principle." While Mill is often invoked as a defender of individual liberty against the threat of government encroachment, he clearly defends the position that government has a right to limit the actions of individuals causing harm. As Mill states in the introductory chapter of *On Liberty*, "the purpose for which [government] power can be rightfully exercised over any member of a civilized community, against his will, is to prevent harm to others."[53] Like Rawls after him, Mill envisioned a society in which the extent of individual liberty was as extensive as possible, yet limited by the negative consequences emerging from interconnectedness of actions among people that share a society. For Mill, "The only freedom which deserves the name is that of pursuing our own good in our own way, so long as we do not attempt to deprive others of theirs or impede their efforts to obtain it."[54] Thus, it is when the individual makes himself a "nuisance to other people" that his actions must be limited.[55]

Although neither Mill nor Rawls offers a conception of individual well-being that captures the extent to which people are materially and physically embedded in environmental processes, Nussbaum's capabilities approach to justice does provide an account of well-being that can capture the extent to which one's environmental circumstance determines one's potential for human freedom. However, for the purpose of advancing Nussbaum's theory in the way I am proposing, we might conceive of the task as building on and following the basic effort by Rawls and Mill to establish limits on individual freedom, but in a way that responds to those relationships that pose the biggest threats to individual freedom today. For instance, Rawls's "first principle of justice" emerged partly from his recognition that the utilitarian goal of maximizing an aggregate good posed

[50] For example, see Thero (1995) discussing the limitations of Rawls's theory of justice for application to issues arising in environmental ethics.
[51] Nussbaum (2006:71). [52] See Mill (1959:67–90). [53] Mill (1959:13).
[54] Mill (1959:16–17). [55] See Mill (1959:68).

a significant threat to individual liberty because of its potential to justify sacrificing the individual. In this context the first principle of justice provides justification for establishing a set of basic freedoms for each person outside the domain of political choices that might otherwise promote a greater overall good. Likewise, Mill, while also skeptical of utilitarian principles, articulates his harm principle as a constraint on liberty emerging from his fear about the potential dangers of popular rule in highly democratic forms of government. No longer consumed with the threats to liberty posed by monarchical power, Mill came to recognize tyranny of a majority of the "common people" under popular rule as the threat against which precautions preventing the abuse of power were needed.[56] The threat of policy choices that serve a utilitarian goal of maximizing aggregate gains, as CBA requires, or that emerge from the influence of a powerful majority exercising control over democratic debate, as may emerge in deliberative and collaborative approaches to environmental decision-making, remain highly relevant to environmental policy today. However, neither Rawls nor Mill provide the best conceptual resources for an approach to making policy decisions that can fully reveal these potential threats, and successfully establish barriers to them.

The role I am proposing for capability ceilings should be understood in this broader historical context, as the natural progression of a capabilities approach to justice that seeks to guide a society toward the ideal of ensuring each person has what is necessary for protecting their central capabilities at a threshold level. Providing the environmental conditions of people's capabilities requires establishing these protections as something that is beyond the reach of political choices that subject environmental decisions to (1) maximizing aggregate gains, defined in monetary terms, or (2) democratic discussion and debate that can privilege the views of a few who have the resources and power to dominate the dialogue or otherwise suppress the views of participants who disagree. While these utilitarian and democratic forms of policy decision-making may have advantages, neither establishes a substantive commitment to equal protection or equal opportunity. A capabilities approach to social and environmental justice can establish these commitments by defining a justifiable policy as that which secures the environmental conditions necessary for protecting and providing people's central capabilities at a threshold level. Furthermore, it can also resolve tradeoffs by establishing capability ceilings that limit the protection of capabilities that can cause harm to others. Let us consider, then, how such ceilings, might play out in the context of policy choices.

[56] Mill (1959:6).

5.3.3 Policy reasoning in a threshold-ceiling framework

A capabilities approach to justice that establishes capability ceilings would not only involve establishing what people should be able to do; it would also require establishing the limits of those capabilities, but only to the degree that they threaten other people's capability thresholds. As presently conceived, the capabilities approach to justice involves protecting every person's central capabilities at a threshold level. By treating the environmental conditions of these capabilities as a meta-capability of humans, as I have proposed, this approach to justice also requires protecting the environmental conditions that ensure each person has this threshold level of capability protection. Establishing capability ceilings in addition to these thresholds is necessary if government policies are going to ensure every person's capabilities are secured at a threshold level. Currently such protections are not in place. Instead, some people's capabilities are protected far above a reasonable threshold level of what justice requires while other people do not get these capabilities protected at even a minimum level.

For instance, in the United States, many people drive sports utility vehicles (SUVs), which burn relatively larger amounts of gasoline per vehicle mile traveled than smaller, more fuel-efficient vehicles. We can understand this use of SUVs as a currently protected dimension of one's capability for *bodily integrity*, because this capability entails "being able to move freely from place to place." By allowing vehicles meeting one set of standards (i.e. low fuel-efficiency standards) to be bought and sold, government is protecting people's capability to move freely from place to place in those vehicles (e.g. in SUVs) as one dimension of people's capability for *bodily integrity*. However, government is not ensuring that everyone has this level of capability provision and protection, it is only a protection provided to those who can afford to purchase an SUV. Specifically, the threshold level of protection given to this mobility component of people's *bodily integrity* capability is actually lower. The government does support some forms of transportation for people who cannot afford SUVs. For example, it subsidizes many forms of public transportation for all people. Therefore, we might think of the establishment of a threshold for the mobility component of one's *bodily integrity* capability as something set at the cost of reasonably accessible public transportation. While the resources government spends to provide and protect this threshold level of the mobility component of people's *bodily integrity* capability makes public transportation available to many as a way of moving freely from place to place, people who have access to personally owned SUVs actually have greater capability to move freely from place to place. SUV owners are capable of taking public transportation as a means of mobility, but they are also capable of moving freely from place to place by other means. In this sense,

SUV owners have a higher level of capability protection for the mobility component of the *bodily integrity* capability.

As this example reveals, we can understand government as providing and protecting people's capabilities in many different ways. Sometimes it subsidizes services necessary for protecting threshold levels of people's capabilities, and sometimes it subsidizes infrastructure and establishes regulatory standards that protect higher levels of these same capabilities. When government policy protects the capabilities of some people far above the threshold level of protection that justice requires, then establishing a capability ceiling would provide the basis for redirecting resources in a way that will secure threshold levels of capabilities for people who experience mobility conditions that are below the threshold level that justice requires. For instance, establishing a ceiling could entail making some people less capable of driving freely from place to place in SUVs so that other people can be made capable of moving freely from place to place in reasonably accessible public transportation. Government might achieve this reprioritizing of policy goals by establishing a registration tax on SUVs, the revenues of which would go toward improving the availability of public transportation for those who currently lack access to basic means of mobility. Here, government would be providing less support for people with high levels of capability provision and protection so that it could provide more support for people with lower levels of capability provision and protection.

The case for establishing such ceilings arises most prominently when the capabilities that are secured for one person or group of people have the direct or indirect effect of pushing the level of capability protection and provision offered to other persons or groups of people below the threshold level that is required as a matter of basic justice. As I have argued earlier in this chapter, in such situations—of capability conflict—capability ceilings establish a limit on the capabilities of some people, but only to the degree that their capabilities threaten other people's capability thresholds. When incorporated into a capabilities approach to designing or evaluating environmental policies, determining the justifiable capability ceilings requires determining whose capabilities a policy should limit and why. In practice, therefore, designing or evaluating an environmental policy will require identifying whose capabilities to which the policy allows direct or indirect harm, and it requires mechanisms for limiting people's capabilities to cause these harms.

Establishing the constraints (or ceilings) on potential actions is necessary for translating ideals of justice into actual policy prescriptions. Consider, for instance, Henry Shue's argument that we should slow the pace of global climate change by limiting the "luxury" emissions of citizens in developed societies who have emitted more than their fair share of the gases producing global climate change.[57] For Shue, emissions reductions strategies that will prevent climate changes causing severe harm to people who lack the resources to cope with the relevant environmental harms must account for the differential impact of emissions reductions on people's quality of life. He argues that reducing carbon emissions is a challenge that should be borne by those who are already relatively well off, not by limiting the emissions of people who burn fossil fuels for mere subsistence purposes.[58] In other words, for Shue, policies addressing climate change should impose limits on the emissions of affluent people that arise from consumption levels and activities that are far above what is needed for mere subsistence.[59] In practice, this will require establishing limits or ceilings on affluent people's capabilities. To return to the previous example, it may require limiting the mobility component of affluent people's *bodily integrity* capability, so that these people are less capable of moving freely from place to place in luxury vehicles that (in aggregate) have harmful effects.

In a capabilities approach to designing or evaluating environmental policies, capability ceilings can be applied to justify policies that put limits on the luxury emissions of the rich. Consider, for example, if the capability ceiling were first implemented by placing a tax on registering luxury vehicles, such as SUVs. The tax can be understood as imposing a capability ceiling because it makes people less able to drive in high-emitting vehicles, and it therefore limits the way in which people can move freely from place to place. At present, this mobility component of people's *bodily integrity* capability has some limits, but they are set quite high. For example, existing laws allow people to move freely from place to place in any functioning passenger vehicle that passes a vehicle emissions test (i.e. a "smog test"). However, if people are permitted this extent of mobility freedom, then they can carelessly and perhaps unknowingly contribute to global climate change, undermining the provision and protection of fundamental capabilities (such as *life and bodily health*) for others.[60] This is precisely why a capability ceiling is needed. In the absence of a ceiling on the mobility component of one's *bodily integrity* capability, moving freely from place to place in an SUV, regardless of the purpose and lower impact alternatives, is being treated as equivalent to securing a threshold level of *life* and *bodily health* capabilities for those who lack them as a matter of basic justice. In this context, the capabilities approach would justify policies constraining the ways in which some people who already have above-threshold levels of capability provision and protection are able

[57] See Shue (1993). [58] See Shue (2001).

[59] See Vanderheiden (2008) for an extension of Shue's argument.

[60] The choice to purchase and drive SUVs will also promote competitive tendencies that artificially inflate how others value SUVs.

to realize their capabilities in order to get other people's capabilities up to a minimum threshold level.

Capability ceilings imply similar constraints if we treat driving SUVs as a component of one's capability for *material control over one's environment.* This capability enables people to hold property in both land and moveable goods, not just formally but in terms of real opportunity.[61] If driving an SUV is understood as a specification of one's real opportunity to do what one wants with one's property, then preventing people from driving SUVs limits the ways in which people can pursue the opportunities that holding property currently makes available. But in this case, even if the threshold level of the *material control over one's environment* capability is not set so high as to include being able to put one's property (i.e. an SUV) to whatever uses one chooses, a capability ceiling can justify freeing up the resources involved in driving SUVs so that these resources can be put toward achieving protection of each person's central capabilities.

As I have proposed, a registration tax on luxury vehicles such as SUVs is justifiable within a capabilities approach to justice that establishes capability ceilings as a way to resolve capability conflicts. Specifically, the tax is the instantiation of an initial ceiling on the mobility component of one's *bodily integrity* capability or on the property ownership component of the capability for *material control over one's environment.*[62] On one hand, the tax would discourage the use of vehicles emitting climate-damaging gases that cause harm to especially vulnerable people who lack the resources to cope with climate change. On the other hand, the tax would also generate revenue that can be used to directly mitigate the impact of climate change on vulnerable people's capabilities. For instance, if money from a tax on registering SUVs were to be set aside in an emergency fund to protect the *bodily integrity* capability of all citizens in times of climate-related need, then some of the problems caused by climate-related natural disasters, such as floods, would not result in such extreme forms of capability failure. If this kind of tax had been used to protect the *bodily integrity* capability of vehicle-less people to move freely from place to place in the wake of Hurricane Katrina, many lives would have been saved.[63] Thus, as a central feature of a capabilities approach to social and environmental justice, capability ceilings instantiated through taxes are justifiable as a limitation on capabilities that can cause harm to

[61] Nussbaum (2000a:80).

[62] Increases in fuel efficiency standards or outright bans on fuel inefficient vehicles are different mechanisms for establishing the same kind of ceiling or limit on the mobility component of a person's *bodily integrity* capability.

[63] This is not to say that people would not still suffer with respect to other capabilities, and in ways that a redirection of monetary resources cannot solve, as I discuss in Holland (2012).

others, and for the purpose of reallocating resources in a way that more effectively protects everyone's capabilities at a threshold level.

These examples of capability ceilings demonstrate their usefulness in defining what public policies should aim to do: *when combined with capability thresholds, capability ceilings can define the extent to which a society ought to limit the harmful effects of capability protections.* In order to determine and justify the *extent* to which a policy should limit these non-fundamental dimensions of people's capabilities (such as the ability to pollute with excess), it is necessary, first, to identify the more fundamental source of a given capability's justification; and second, to clarify why the limitation on capability protection—the ceiling—is necessary for protecting something equally fundamental. In the context of a capabilities approach to policy evaluation, harmful effects should be defined as those that push a person's capabilities below the minimum threshold required for living a decent or dignified life, as a matter of basic justice.[64] Resolving capability conflicts will then entail limiting some above-threshold levels of capability protection so that the negative effects of those protections diminishes, and so that resources can otherwise be put to shoring up a threshold level of capabilities for those who lack them. In this way, a capabilities approach to justice that establishes a role for capability ceilings in addition to capability thresholds can provide a basic framework for evaluating the relative effects of environmental benefits and burdens and for resolving the tragic tradeoffs to which these benefits and burdens sometimes give rise.

Consider these points in further detail. When applying the threshold-ceiling framework I am proposing to policy evaluation and design, we can understand the vehicular pollution that a person produces as a component of a person's capability for *material control over one's environment.* Perhaps each of us should be assured *some* freedom to pollute as a component of being able to have this kind of control over our material environment. However, to provide and protect this capability far above a threshold level allows for polluting activities that undermine equally fundamental basic entitlements, such as the *life* and *bodily health capabilities* of those who are exposed to that pollution. When we evaluate policies in the context of a threshold-ceiling framework, we can determine and justify the extent to which a policy ought to limit freedoms protected by the capability to have *material control over one's environment* by specifying the impact of

[64] For present purposes, we can assume that this threshold is already established in existing environmental laws (some of which are routinely violated), or we can assume that the level ought to be set at a higher level. While I realize that the method for establishing acceptable threshold levels of capabilities protection is an important issue, I address this issue more directly in Chapter 6, and here remain focused on the basic justification for establishing capability ceilings and the general implications for policy.

protecting those capabilities at various levels on other fundamental entitlements. A capabilities approach to policy evaluation allows for and requires this kind of assessment in part because it is based on a theory of justice that gives the protections required by the *life* and *bodily health* capabilities the same status as broadly accepted constitutional protections such as free expression and political participation, for which a person's life and health are preconditions. By treating these preconditions as equal to the civil and political protections they put within a person's reach, the approach points toward an assessment that can reveal why extensive protection for the capabilities of some people may function to limit the capabilities of other people that are equally fundamental.

A threshold-ceiling framework also opens up a conceptual space for determining what, whether, and when capabilities require ceilings. As conceived in the preceding text (Section 5.3.2), ceilings are only necessary to limit people's capabilities to do things that threaten securing a threshold level of other people's capabilities. For instance, some ways of realizing the mobility component of a person's *bodily integrity* capability may justifiably be protected far above what the threshold level of the *bodily integrity* capability requires. In the framework I am proposing, policies that allow wide latitude for moving freely from place to place with low- or non-polluting forms of transportation (e.g. bicycles and low-emissions vehicles) would be justifiable. However, this latitude would end when it comes to protecting and providing opportunities for people to freely joyride in highly polluting forms of transportation, such as Hummer trucks. However, if technologies were to evolve in ways that turned Hummer trucks into zero-emissions vehicles, then such a ceiling would be removed. Thus, although establishing a ceiling on the capability to move freely from place to place in highly polluting forms of transportation does deny some kinds of individual choice, it does so in order to protect an equal range of choices among functioning possibilities for those who would otherwise be harmed.

The point of this example is to illustrate that evaluating policies within a threshold-ceiling framework allows for levels of capability provision and protection that can vary along the different components of a single central human capability; for example, by expanding and creating choices along some dimensions of a capability (such as carbon-free forms of mobility) and contracting and constraining choices along other dimensions of a capability (such as carbon-intense forms of mobility). This framework treats capability thresholds as distinct from capability ceilings and in doing so opens up a space for reasoning about the possible tradeoffs that can be made among the different thresholds and ceilings of different people's capabilities. As a general rule, a capabilities approach to social and environmental justice would allow for protecting and expanding a single person's capabilities up to the point at which doing so allows a person to pursue activities that directly or indirectly undermine threshold-level protections for other people's basic freedoms.

To summarize: environmentally just policies require determining whose capabilities a given policy will secure and whose capabilities it will undermine. A socially and environmentally just policy will be one that reallocates above-threshold levels of capability provision and protection in ways that allow everyone's capabilities to be brought up to a minimum threshold. If policy outcomes are held to this standard, those who wish to pursue activities that might undermine people's capabilities will need to come up with the data demonstrating that their favored activities do not and will not have these negative effects. In this context, protecting and expanding people's capabilities is only just if doing so does not undermine or threaten other people's capabilities in ways that push them below the threshold level that is required as a matter of basic justice. In this way, the threshold-ceiling framework provides an approach to defining and reasoning about the conditions under which policies should limit capabilities having harmful effects, making it possible to evaluate policies with respect to goals of environmental and social justice, and to design policies that push society toward these goals. Let us now consider how this threshold-ceiling framework might be applied at the domestic level, to evaluate and improve air quality policies that have already been established through federal laws.

5.3.4 Applying a threshold-ceiling framework to domestic air quality policy

As is well known, air pollution results from various economically productive industrial activities, such as the production and transport of goods and services that drive the economy. These activities produce income and wealth for the employees and owners of profiting companies, as well as valuable consumer goods for the larger society. In these ways activities creating air pollution contribute to or improve various human capabilities, such as people's capabilities for *life, bodily health,* and *play.* Equally important to understanding the relationship between air quality and human capabilities is that the polluting activities contributing to people's capabilities are already enabled by some existing capability provisions and protections, such as *material control over one's environment, practical reason, life,* and *bodily integrity.* This is because at least some of these capabilities must precede securing employment, entrepreneurial activity, and the selection of consumer goods that one values. Thus, the activities producing air pollution both enable and are enabled by capabilities, corresponding to the simultaneous evolution of industrialization and human development.

On the other hand, it is also well known that polluting activities produce capability decline—most notably in some people's capabilities for *life* and *bodily health*. The impact of pollution on life and bodily health also negatively affects various other capabilities such as *political control over one's environment, play*, and *senses, imagination and thought*, because living and a certain level of bodily health are prerequisites of these latter capabilities. Furthermore, in addition to limiting a person's internal or physical capacity to engage in politics, play, and the educational development activities that define these latter capabilities, air pollution might alter external environmental conditions in ways that put certain activities beyond people's reach. For example, children who suffer from asthma as a consequence of exposure to air pollution may be unable to play outdoors in highly polluted areas, undermining their capabilities for *affiliation* and for having relationships with *other species*.[65] Likewise, if air pollution degrades the ecological systems that sustain certain species, then those species may no longer be available as the basis for relations that some people find especially meaningful. Exposure to more dangerous air pollutants, such as lead and mercury, can produce or lead to cognitive and neurological impairments that leave children with fewer opportunities, and contribute to larger social problems such as crime and costly forms of health care.[66] Thus, just as air pollution results from activities that improve capabilities, it can also produce capability decline.

Viewed side by side, the various positive and negative consequences of polluting activities demonstrate a conflict of basic capabilities that rests at the center of policies regulating air pollution. Given the extent to which the current transportation sector is dependent on fossil fuel energy that emits locally and globally harmful air pollutants, protecting the environment by limiting allowable emissions of these pollutants will involve supporting some people's capabilities while undermining the capabilities of others. An approach to policy evaluation that is structured on the threshold-ceiling framework proposed in Section 5.3.3 can help to resolve this capability conflict in a way that pushes society toward justice.

The capabilities approach to social and environmental justice requires, first and foremost, that a threshold level of each capability be guaranteed for each person. As an application of this theory, a capabilities approach to evaluating existing and proposed environmental protection policies would require assessing whether a given policy provides this threshold level of protection for each person whose capabilities are threatened by air pollution. Even if we assume air quality standards established by the USA's current Clean Air Act

[65] See Nocon and Booth (1989–1990) for a discussion of the social impacts of asthma.

[66] For example, see Needleman (2004), Nevin (2009), Carpenter and Nevin (2010), and Mazumdar et al. (2011).

(CAA) are adequate for protecting people's bodily health (which some people would contest[67]), we would still find that the current air pollution control policy fails to meet this threshold requirement for all people. This is because there are hundreds of counties around the country that do not comply with at least one regulatory standard for a "criteria pollutant" that the CAA regulates.[68] In this respect, current air pollution control policy fails to secure a threshold level of the *bodily health* capability because it allows some people's bodily health (i.e. people living in areas not compliant with CAA standards) to fall below an already established legal threshold of what protection of public health requires.[69] In this instance, a capabilities approach to policy evaluation would find that current air pollution control policy is not producing just outcomes, and therefore that it lacks sufficient legal and political justification.[70]

Unfortunately, responding to this injustice by simply halting the various polluting activities that are pushing counties out of compliance with CAA standards would violate the various capability protections enabling these activities and forgo the various capability improvements resulting from them.[71] How then would a capabilities approach to environmental policy evaluation propose resolving this tragic tradeoff? It would resolve the tradeoff by establishing capability ceilings, which, as I have argued, define the extent to which a policy ought to limit capabilities that are in conflict with each other. Specifically, the appropriate capability ceiling established for those who are benefitting from polluting activities should be based on assessment of the extent of capability protection a policy can realistically promise while simultaneously protecting a threshold level of central capabilities for each person. Since capability ceilings establish maximum levels of capability

[67] I say the assumption is contested because some of the standards set by the EPA during the presidency of George W. Bush were weaker than what the EPA's own scientists recommended, based on the evidence of human health impacts. See *American Farm Bureau Federation v. EPA*, 559 F.3d 512 (D.C. Cir. 2009).

[68] See <http://www.epa.gov/air/oaqps/greenbk/> (accessed April 24, 2014).

[69] Here I am assuming for the sake of argument that existing regulatory standards, if met, are sufficient for protecting the air quality component of a person's *bodily health* capability.

[70] Even if all counties were found to be compliant with the air quality standards that the CAA establishes, a capabilities approach to evaluating environmental policy might still find that current air pollution control policy fails to provide an adequate threshold level of protection for each person's *bodily health* capability. For example, one might find that an existing standard conflicts with scientific assessments of what is necessary to protect human health, especially for vulnerable populations. Alternatively, one might find that an existing standard fails to provide adequate protection for citizens facing cumulative exposures to multiple pollutants; see Morello-Frosch (2001) for a discussion of the importance of addressing cumulative exposures in communities facing environmental threats.

[71] As I have discussed earlier in this chapter, the capabilities that polluting activities improve include capabilities for *life, bodily health*, and *play*, which financial resources and consumer goods enable; the capability protections that enable the pursuit of these polluting include *material control over one's environment, practical reason, life*, and *bodily integrity*.

protection, the goal of this assessment should be to establish the ceilings for people who already experience a level of capability protection that is above the threshold required to meet basic conditions of justice—that is, to meet the conditions of what Nussbaum defines as a life worthy of the dignity of a human being, or what others might characterize as basic human needs.

For example, regulating the polluting activities that lead to a decline in asthmatic children's capabilities for *bodily health, affiliation, play*, and *senses, imagination and thought*, should involve constraining (or putting ceilings on) the capabilities of the beneficiaries of polluting activities who already experience a level of capability protection that is above this threshold level. This may mean establishing ceilings on the capabilities of those who amass large financial profits from polluting activities; profits that make them capable of achieving far more than the minimum threshold of what a decent and dignified life requires.[72] To return to an earlier point, perhaps an air pollution control policy should limit (or put ceilings on) people's capabilities to move freely from place to place in vehicles (such as SUVs) that emit relatively higher quantities of criteria air pollutants per vehicle mile traveled (VMT). Or, perhaps a policy should put a tax on the registration of new and highly polluting luxury vehicles, which then could be used to secure the capabilities of those for whom the pollution has significant negative impacts. As this last proposal suggests, a variety of market-based instruments might reasonably be used to achieve the goals of fairness and equity that are implicit in protecting each person's capabilities.

Consider, for instance, Australia's carbon tax, which was approved by its parliament in November 2011. As a means of regulating stationary sources of carbon dioxide emissions, this tax puts a price on each ton of carbon that the biggest domestic air polluters release into the atmosphere.[73] Notably, half of the money raised from the tax is dedicated to providing tax cuts to households (who will presumably bear some of the costs that big polluters pass onto them as consumers) and payments (cash bonuses and pension increases) to low-income citizens who may need help coping with the rising cost of living in a more energy-expensive world.[74] In the Australian model, the remaining half of the money the carbon tax raises will go to supporting a transition to more sustainable sources of energy, such as the development of cleaner and renewable energy sources, and to helping farmers adopt technologies and practices that cut their carbon emissions. While this tax policy

[72] For the purpose of working through this example, I have assumed this threshold for the *bodily health* capability is met when one is exposed to the level of air quality that current law establishes as safe for public health.

[73] See <http://www.carbontax.net.au/> (accessed April 24, 2014).

[74] See Spash and Lo (2012) for a critique of various features of Australia's carbon tax, other than those discussed here.

is plagued with a number of substantial problems, such as questionable assumptions about the potential for market forces to stimulate innovation, the reallocation feature of the Australian model is especially innovative in its aspiration.[75] In particular, the policy intends to incorporate a mechanism for eventually eliminating the conflict between big domestic polluters who are contributing the most to climate change and members of society who will be least able to cope with the consequences of climate change (i.e. those who will suffer the most from environmental changes and the price increases that result from more aggressive regulation of carbon emissions).

Evaluating such environmental policies within a threshold-ceiling framework makes it possible to reason toward solutions to capability conflicts that are justified directly in terms of their implications for the provision and protection of capabilities that define the basic conditions of social and environmental justice. For instance, due to the carbon tax's focus on high-emissions polluters, executives in the coal mining industry may oppose the tax, fearing it will limit their companies' international competitiveness, and therefore their personal capabilities as executives to exert *control over one's environment*. However, in comparison to many others, industry executives already have this capability protected and provided at a relatively high level. The carbon tax may indeed limit their capability to control their political environment in ways that effectively allow them to avoid internalizing the cost of their companies' carbon emissions, but it does this because the extent of their current capability for *political control over one's environment* is so high that they are able to serve their companies' own financial interests at the cost of significant harm to others. Likewise, the carbon tax may reduce executives' control over their material environment by reducing company profits, and consequently executives' salaries, but not in ways that threaten threshold levels of protection for this or other capabilities. For instance, the tax won't even prevent executives from continuing to move from place to place in private luxury vehicles.[76]

Thus, even if the carbon tax has further secondary impacts on the capabilities of coal company executives, such as preventing them from making profits that allow for the extravagant forms of recreation or leisure characterizing the actual extent of their *play* capabilities, it does so by redirecting resources to protect and provide a threshold level of equally fundamental capabilities, such as *life* and *bodily health* of those who would otherwise be burdened with rising energy costs and the struggle to remain alive and safe in the context of

[75] See Spash and Lo (2011:71) for a discussion of why the technological dividend needs to incorporate issues of invention uncertainty and longer-term time frames.

[76] Although, as I have argued in the preceding text, a constraint of this form on executive's mobility might also be justifiable from the perspective of a capabilities approach to social and environmental justice.

a changing global climate. Furthermore, because the provision of assistance funded by the carbon tax is assessed based on factors such as income and the number of dependents in a household, the coal industry's efforts to pass the cost of the carbon tax on to employees in the industry by lowering wages will also be offset (at least to some extent) by a provision of greater assistance from the tax-created fund.

For these reasons, despite the failure of Australia's carbon tax to meet ambitious carbon emissions reduction targets, it incorporates some basic distributional features that a capabilities approach to policy evaluation would also suggest and justify. Within the regulatory context of the proposed carbon tax some people who benefit from polluting activities (e.g. owners and employees of polluting industries) may experience a level of provision and protection for capabilities that is far above the threshold level of protection that justice requires, while others may experience a level of capability protection and provision that is below the levels of what justice requires. Whereas Australia's carbon tax targets specific industries, a registration tax on highly inefficient luxury vehicles in the context of US domestic policy could serve similar purposes of capability provision and protection. Not only would the tax produce emissions reductions that help counties non-compliant with current air pollution standards reach air quality "attainment," but, additionally, the money generated from the tax could be used to recover the *bodily health* capabilities of citizens most burdened by poor air quality, such as asthmatic children. This way of putting a ceiling on the capabilities of those who benefit the most from actions having harmful effects makes it possible to redirect resources so that all members of society can attain a threshold level of capability provision and protection, as a feature of the equally fundamental capabilities they protect. Because a capabilities approach to policy evaluation is concerned with protecting each central capability for all citizens, the limits it establishes on above-threshold levels of capability protection are justified. This framing of the tragic tradeoff makes it easier to identify and implement strategies that resolve the tradeoffs in a way that achieves goals of individual protection, as well as goals of equity and fairness.

To return to the Kaldor–Hicks criterion discussed at the start of this chapter, the capabilities approach to policy evaluation that I have elaborated here rejects the premise that a greater overall good can make up for the burdens that are suffered by some subsets of citizens. The capabilities approach to social and environmental justice that underlies this approach to policy evaluation holds that every person deserves to have their capabilities provided and protected at a threshold level. Thus, a policy that pushes any individual below the threshold of what justice requires is not acceptable for the sake of a greater overall amount of capability protection. When the capabilities of different people come into conflict such that an existing or proposed policy undermines this goal, capability ceilings can define the extent to which the provision and protection of one person's capabilities above a minimum threshold of what justice requires should be limited, in order to ensure that another person receives a level of capability provision and protection that is the bare minimum of what justice requires. In this way, a threshold-ceiling framework can help to create policies that treat people with equal concern and respect, and justify policies that do this as a basic feature of what social justice requires.

5.4 Ecological Thresholds and the Limits of Justice

In the threshold-ceiling framework I am proposing for reasoning about the distributional implications of policies that change environmental quality, capability ceilings function to block actions that have certain kinds of harmful effects. I have argued that these ceilings should be set at a level that will prevent activities impacting ecological systems in ways that push some people's capabilities below the threshold level that defines the basic conditions necessary for living a life that is worthy of human dignity in a just society.[77] For the purpose of making this argument in the preceding sections, I have also assumed that existing environmental laws establish the levels of environmental protection that are necessary for protecting a threshold level of people's capabilities, or that these thresholds might be established through a fair and equitable form of democratic deliberation. Both assumptions can be brought into question. For instance, some may argue that the established level of environmental protection is insufficient for protecting people's capabilities, while others may argue that existing laws provide an excessive level of protection, ultimately placing cost-prohibitive constraints on industry in ways that stifle the capability improvements otherwise resulting from economic growth. This debate is one of many contentious areas of environmental policy that reveals how the interplay of environmental interests, industry, and technical expertise sometimes produces regulations that unduly burden industry or that fail to provide safe levels of environmental quality. Chapter 6 enters this debate by proposing a capabilities approach to administrative rulemaking that applies constraints on these various interests involved in administrative decision-making procedures.[78] For now I set aside

[77] See Holland (2008a, 2008b). In his friendly critique of the "development rights framework" as an approach to achieving climate justice, Schlosberg (2009, 2012) makes a similar argument for mitigating climate impacts that impede the multiple capabilities that make it possible for people to lead flourishing lives.

[78] Sec Section 6.5 of Chapter 6, especially.

this debate in order to continue developing a role for capability ceilings to play as a conceptual constraint that can inform our reasoning about the justness of policies producing changes in environmental quality.

Capability ceilings, as I have posited them here, function to connect questions about the range and level of capability protections with questions about the capacity of earth's ecological systems to continue providing the ecological conditions on which the possibility and quality of human life depends.[79] For instance, in the economic context, ecological economists have shown that there is only so much "throughput"—that is, material coming from the environment, going through the economy, and returning to the environment as waste—that the earth's ecological systems can sustain over time.[80] Consequently, many argue that ecological boundaries should be understood as posing justifiable limits to economic growth. Minimally this would entail limiting the form and extent of economic interactions through improved market signals, such as pricing ecosystem services and true cost accounting, which could ultimately be incorporated into a CBA that monetizes the benefits of policies protecting those services.[81]

Just as an ideal economic system that produces consumer goods must not transcend ecological limits necessary for sustaining the environmental conditions of economic production, an ideal political system that secures people's capabilities must not transcend ecological limits necessary for ensuring the material basis for people's politically protected freedoms. As a feature of this latter ideal, we should think of capability ceilings as something that is defined in relation to an ecological limit. The most basic reason for defining capability ceilings in relation to certain ecological limits is because there is not an unlimited amount of individual opportunity or freedom that earth's ecological systems can sustain over time. Some of these resources and conditions on which human capabilities depend are irreplaceable and non-substitutable.[82] Therefore, we should understand them as limited in supply, and we should understand their protection as crucial to protecting the human capabilities they support and constitute.

To make this point in a different way, there would be no need to put limits on the level of capability protection that governments secure if we were in fact living in a world of endless resources, infinite substitution possibilities, and unbounded waste absorption capacities. In such a world there would be no ecological limits on people's political protections; my capabilities to do what I want with my personal property or with collectively owned goods

[79] See Schlosberg (2007:136–151) for an argument that the capacity of whole ecological systems should be understood as something having the status of intrinsic value.
[80] Daly (1991).
[81] For example, see Costanza (1997) and Costanza and D'Arge (1997).
[82] See Sagoff (1998a) and Daly (1998).

would be constrained more by social rules and relationships than by ecological rules and relationships. However, in the ecological reality we actually inhabit, what we can do in relation to the environment is partly dependent on what other people do in relation to it, both individually and in aggregate. In this sense, our human capabilities are inevitably ecological.

The science of ecology continues to reveal the form and extent of ecological processes that tie humans together. Successfully designing and evaluating environmental policies therefore requires concepts and tools that can bring the full import of these findings to bear on the environmental protections that governments provide. In this context, the concept of a capability ceiling is helpful because identifying and resolving the capability conflicts these protections produce will require establishing the links between the actions of different people who are connected through ecological processes. Specifically, as I have proposed, capability ceilings imply limits on the capability provisions and protections government provides to some people, precisely because those protections sometimes allow for activities that operate through ecological processes to have harmful effects on others, pushing their capabilities below the threshold level of protection that justice requires. It is these effects that provide the rationale for defining capability ceilings in reference to ecological rules and relationships. While too much protection of ecological systems will require limiting some people's capabilities beyond what is necessary for protecting other people's capabilities at a threshold level, too little protection of ecological systems will fail to ensure that these systems can continue to sustain people's capabilities at a threshold level. This is why the ecological conditions that are instrumental to achieving a threshold level of capability protection—which I refer to as an ecological meta-capability in Chapter 4—also should be understood as having a limit, or a ceiling. Justice requires both floors and ceilings on people's capabilities, including the ecological meta-capability, which defines what it means for humans to be ecologically capable—that is, to live in the context of ecological conditions that can provide the physical preconditions of their other, central human capabilities.

As a conceptual tool, a ceiling is helpful for defining what humans can justifiably do to ecological systems, because a ceiling reminds us that when we go beyond it we are breaking something. For instance, allowing for levels of capability protection that go beyond a ceiling may offer advantages to a particular individual or group of individuals, but the ceiling reminds us that there will be consequences, some of which are beyond repair. A crucial goal for protecting the ecological conditions over time, therefore, is that we prevent ecological processes from falling into irreparable decline. Determining the level at which capability ceilings are set should, therefore, entail specific reference to these ecological conditions, and particularly to preventing an irreversible collapse in ecosystem functioning on which human capabilities depend.

With this in mind, the ceiling established for people's capabilities—as a limit on the extent of individual protection that a government should provide—will have to be defined in relation to an "ecological threshold." An ecological threshold is the point at which an abrupt change in some quality, property, or phenomenon in an ecosystem, or a small change in an environmental driver, produces a large response in the ecosystem. Such a response may be non-linear, caused by both human and natural impacts, and driven by and responded to by variables operating at different time scales.[83] There are two primary reasons why ecological thresholds should play a central role in defining the ceilings established for people's capabilities. First, the response, or shift, in an ecosystem that results from crossing a threshold can diminish its provision of an ecosystem service to people who may or may not play a role in pushing the system beyond its threshold; that is, crossing an ecological threshold may harm and benefit different groups of people, and, therefore, have distributive implications that are relevant to justice. Second, the threshold behavior ecosystems exhibit often mask a decline in their ability to produce services until a collapse in their functioning occurs.[84] This means that once a threshold is passed, it may not be possible to recover the services previously provided. A situation of non-recovery is not always the case; for example, an aquatic ecosystem that is pushed into a eutrophic, turbid water state due to excessive phosphorus or sewage inputs may return to a clear water state by reducing those inputs.[85] However, in some cases, ecosystems cannot recover from human impacts. For instance, reducing the acid rain inputs to the US's northeastern forests may not be enough to allow streams to recover their capacity to neutralize acid up to their pre-acid deposition levels.[86]

Thus, in defining the ceilings that should be put on human capabilities, it will be essential to assess the extent to which the human activities that policies make people capable of pursuing would threaten to push an impacted ecosystem toward or beyond an ecological threshold. One way to instantiate this kind of assessment in policy evaluation would be to define the threshold level of the ecological meta-capability in reference to the ecological thresholds of ecosystems that support the other human capabilities. Policies protecting this ecological meta-capability at a threshold level will be those that avoid crossing the ecological thresholds of ecosystems providing services that are crucial to humans' central capabilities. Policies that avoid crossing this threshold, but that have impacts which subtly inch ecosystems toward

[83] See Groffman et al. (2006:2–3).
[84] See Scheffer et al. (2001).
[85] See Carpenter et al. (1999).
[86] See Driscoll et al. (2001).

the threshold should be recognized as increasing ecological risk, and, therefore, as imposing a risk to human capabilities.

While defining the precise point at which ecosystems will fall into non-recoverable collapse in their functional capacity to provide ecosystem services may be informationally demanding, there are some general features and characteristics of ecosystems that can more easily be brought to bear in evaluating the extent to which environmental policies allow for excessive levels of capability protection for some people while failing to protect the capabilities of people dependent on those ecosystems for important ecosystem services. For instance, crucial to preventing irreparable damage in ecosystems is maintaining their "resilience," which is their capacity to absorb a disturbance without changing states. Ecosystem resilience helps ecosystems to avoid the threshold behavior that leads to a collapse in their functioning, and it emerges from the interactions of ecosystems' functional diversity, response diversity, and cross-scale diversity.[87] Specifically, ecosystems' functional diversity refers to different functional types of species within an ecosystem and to the number of functionally equivalent species (redundancy) and populations within those different functional types. Response diversity is the variability or diversity of responses to environmental change of species within these functional types of species and populations. Cross-scale diversity refers to the richness and distribution of functional groups across different scales of ecosystem processes.

Given these components of resilience, a great deal of a policy's negative distributional consequences can be prevented by first assessing a policy's impact on the forms of diversity within and across ecosystems.[88] Policies that promise to stay within the ecological limits of justice will, at a minimum, establish capability ceilings that protect the resilience of ecosystems they influence. For example, policies should not allow activities that inch ecosystems closer to their ecological thresholds by allowing for a gradual decline of diversity within and across these systems. To develop a more scientifically demanding and nuanced form of policy evaluation would entail establishing capability ceilings in more direct relation to ecological thresholds so as to ensure the capability protections a policy provides will prevent the activities that push an ecosystem beyond the point at which a collapse in its functioning occurs.

[87] See Lundberg and Moberg (2003) and Elmqvist et al. (2003).

[88] We might consider this proposal as somewhat similar to Wolff and de-Shalit's (2007:103–105) "pragmatic method" for assessing disadvantage among different groups of people. Rather than assess how the environmental degradation that a policy produces or allows will impact ecosystems services (one by one), the assessment can significantly reduce the empirical work needed by investigating if the policy permits human activities that will produce a convergence of threats to an ecosystem across all three forms of biodiversity. In such situations, we can more easily agree that these impacts will undermine capabilities, since they will be most likely to reduce the ecosystem resilience on which human capabilities depend.

Note, however, that even this more nuanced form of evaluation involves assessing the functional capacity of ecosystems, rather than relating particular policy impacts to particular services those ecosystems provide.

Used in these ways, capability ceilings can provide a conceptual mechanism for bringing information from ecological science to bear on evaluating policies from the perspective of justice. Because ecological interactions tie together the activities of different people, evaluating a policy's distributional impacts—and creating policies that protect the ecological conditions necessary for protecting a threshold level of human capabilities—must endeavor to link the human capabilities a policy protects to the resilience of ecosystems involved in these ecological interactions. Establishing capability ceilings is one way of institutionalizing assessments of these human–ecological relationships, and justifying policies in relation to them.

5.5 Conclusion

This chapter has advanced a capabilities-based framework for evaluating and designing environmental policies in terms of their contribution to social and environmental justice. Using the capabilities approach for this purpose appeals to an ideal of social justice as a justification for environmental protection.

Among capability theorists, Nussbaum offers the most fully developed theory of substantive justice, and she leaves open a route for incorporating a commitment to the environmental dimensions of procedural justice through the specification of the tenth capability on her list of central human capabilities, which I take up in Chapter 6. While there are many advantages in using the capabilities approach as a basis for evaluating the distributive implications of changes in environmental quality that public policies produce, I have argued that this account of justice should be extended to include capability *ceilings*, in addition to the capability *thresholds* that Nussbaum seeks to provide and protect as constitutional guarantees. Specifically, capability ceilings are necessary for making tradeoffs that arise when protecting one person's capabilities degrades the environmental conditions that are necessary for protecting a threshold level of another person's capabilities. The relevance of capability ceilings to social justice emerges once we admit the extent to which human activities are connected through ecological interactions that can span different and sometimes vast geographical distances. Determining the level at which capability ceilings are set should therefore entail specific reference to these ecological interactions, and particularly to the ecological thresholds that, when crossed, can produce an irreversible collapse in ecosystem functioning on which human capabilities depend. The relationship between capability ceilings and ecological thresholds must be informed on an ongoing basis by the science of ecology, which continues to reveal the form and extent of ecological processes that tie humans together.

While Nussbaum has already defended capability thresholds as constitutional guarantees, establishing capability ceilings creates a threshold-ceiling framework for reasoning about the justness of tradeoffs that environmental policies produce. In order to demonstrate the implications of this threshold-ceiling framework, I have used it to identify what a capabilities approach to social and environmental justice would require in the context of tradeoffs implicit in current air pollution control policy. Far from ignoring the distributional impacts of policies that maximize net economic benefits—and, hence, meet the currently prevalent evaluative standard of Kaldor–Hicks efficiency—a capabilities approach to evaluating and designing environmental policy would requiring disaggregating the impact of a policy on different people. It would also make it possible to identify policy options that meet the demand of treating each person with equal concern and respect by resolving conflicts in a way that promises to deliver for each person the threshold level of capability provision and protection necessary for meeting basic conditions of justice. While a capabilities approach to social and environmental justice can in this way provide a framework for evaluating and designing environmental policies that overcome problems challenging the current economic framework, in Chapter 6 I consider how it might also be used to improve administrative rulemaking processes that incorporate citizen collaboration and participation, rather than economic analysis.

6

A Capabilities Approach to Democratic Participation in Regulatory Rulemaking

6.1 Protecting Capabilities as Administrative Practice

In 2004, the Office of Inspector General within the US Environmental Protection Agency (EPA) issued a report evaluating the EPA's implementation of Executive Order 12,898. Issued by President Bill Clinton in 1994, this Executive Order was titled "Federal Action to Address Environmental Justice in Minority Populations and Low-income Populations." Among other goals, it intends to ensure that minority and low-income populations are not disproportionately subjected to high levels of environmental risk. The 2004 Office of Inspector General's report concludes that these goals have not been achieved. Specifically, it concludes that the "EPA has not fully implemented Executive Order 12,898 nor consistently integrated environmental justice into its day-to-day operations. EPA has not identified minority and low-income, nor identified populations addressed in the Executive Order, and has neither defined nor developed criteria for determining [what it means to be] disproportionately impacted."[1] These failures at the administrative level stand in contrast to many symbolic and substantive victories the environmental justice movement achieved during the ten years following President Clinton's effort to bring the attention of government agencies to issues of environmental inequity. However, as the Office of Inspector General report highlights, both the procedures through which environmental policies are designed and implemented and the relative distribution of benefits and burdens resulting from those policies remain highly inequitable.[2] The

[1] See Office of Inspector General (2004:i).

[2] For a discussion of the environmental justice movement's accomplishments, see Bullard et al. (2011) and the "Environmental Justice Timeline/Milestones," available at <http://www.ejrc.cau.edu/EJSUMMITwelcome.html> (accessed April 24, 2014). For a less optimistic account of the movement's accomplishments, see Faber (2008:133–162).

commitment to environmental justice stated in Executive Order 12,898 has yet to deeply penetrate the practices of government agencies charged with designing and implementing environmental policies.

This chapter addresses such persistent problems within administrative agencies by using the capabilities approach to social and environmental justice to develop a model for designing environmental policies that treats a certain level of environmental protection for each person as a basic political commitment. The model is evaluative because it involves assessing environmental management decisions with respect to whether they provide the level of environmental protection that justice requires *for each person*, and rejecting or revising those decisions when they do not. However, in contrast to the framework proposed in the preceding chapters, here I focus on using the capabilities approach to guide the decision-making *process* that shapes environmental policies at the administrative level. The capabilities approach to valuation and justification developed in Chapter 4 and Chapter 5, respectively, proposes what substantive protections environmental policies should establish. In this chapter I consider the role of democratic politics in policy articulation and implementation. The process I propose for specifying environmental protections aims to prevent both the inequalities of power and voice that characterize some democratic approaches to policymaking at the administrative level, as well as the kind of expert control over policy decisions that tends to put these decisions beyond the reach of ordinary citizens. Overall, my primary goal is to present a model of decision-making in which participatory processes and substantive ideals shape and constrain each other.

The chapter addresses two basic questions: First, how can the capabilities approach to social and environmental justice developed in the preceding chapters contribute to processes involved in designing (rather than merely evaluating) environmental policies that determine the distribution of environmental benefits and burdens? Second, why is using a capabilities approach to substantively shape the design of environmental policies consistent with the political goals of a liberal democratic society? Since my aim is to propose a model of decision-making suitable for the political system of the United States, I focus, in particular, on environmental policy decisions made in the context of administrative rulemaking in the United States. The administrative rulemaking context is important because rulemaking defines a crucial point within the policymaking process when government agencies translate laws into "regulatory rules" that specify environmental standards, such as permissible levels of pollution in different environmental media (e.g. air and water) or acceptable degrees of ecological disruption on publicly owned lands.[3] In proposing an approach to designing and evaluating these rules

[3] In the US context, the statutes creating administrative agencies grant them the authority to perform this legislative function. See Kubasek and Silverman (2008:90–91). As Richardson

with respect to their impact on people's capabilities, I illustrate how a capabilities approach to social and environmental justice can be part of a broader model of decision-making that aims to correct the substantive inequities environmental policies produce, without forsaking important democratic commitments.

In order to delineate administrative rulemaking as the context to which the model of decision-making I advance is relevant, I will refer to the model as a "capabilities approach to regulatory rulemaking" (CARR). The processes through which legislatively approved laws such as the federal Clean Air Act (CAA) are implemented exemplify this rulemaking context. The CAA requires that the federal EPA set standards for air quality that protect human health with an "adequate margin of safety."[4] In fulfillment of this responsibility the EPA drafts regulatory rules designating the relevant pollutants (e.g. fine particulate matter and sulfur dioxide) and specifying the concentration of those pollutants allowable in a given unit of air (e.g. a cubic meter). State-level regulatory agencies then use these designations in developing their own state implementation plans (SIPs), which establish allowable amounts of pollution in specific geographical regions, and therefore the quantity and kind of allowable polluting activities. In this way, the regulatory rulemaking process significantly shapes the scope and extent of environmental law.[5] By advancing a model of decision-making to guide activities and choices made within this rulemaking process, this chapter applies the CARR to decisions that have a significant impact on the direction and substance of current environmental law.

My overarching normative argument is that a CARR should be used to determine and justify substantive levels of environmental protection, even if these levels of environmental protection conflict with outcomes emerging from current procedural or process-based approaches to making environmental decisions at the implementation stage of policy. As I have summarized in Chapter 1, contemporary efforts to develop "deliberative" or "participatory" decision-making processes manifest in what is commonly referred to as "devolved," "negotiated," or "collaborative" rulemaking.[6] For present purposes I will refer to this general category of procedural or process-based

(2002:225) explains, agencies are "creatures of statutory law"; their political legitimacy stems from a one-time democratic decision to charge them with responsibility for the concerns addressed in their enabling statutes.

[4] See CAA 109(b)(1).

[5] See Richardson (2002), discussing how administrative responsibility to specify the ends of policy puts administrative agencies in a position to exercise power arbitrarily, potentially conflicting with democratic ideals, such as collective self-rule.

[6] See Klyza and Sousa (2008:195–246) for an overview of the context and form of these collaborative approaches to regulatory rulemaking.

approaches to policy decisions as *democratic rulemaking* or *democratized rulemaking*. Although these forms of rulemaking may not be genuinely deliberative, as a number of scholars contend, they can be understood as intentionally democratic for two reasons. First, in contrast to post-1970s forms of administrative rulemaking that many criticize for excluding the public while advantaging organized and private interests, they exemplify an effort to bring ordinary citizens back into the rulemaking process, primarily by creating a place for citizens to participate in dialogue and debate about regulatory decisions.[7] Second, with a compelling justification in democratic political theory, these forms of rulemaking appear to align well with the ideal of an inclusive and egalitarian form of deliberative democratic engagement, in which participants seek to persuade each other of their views through fair and rational discussion about collective values and purposes.[8] In theory, inclusive participation, in which all the relevant parties publicly express their interests in a language others can hear and understand, has the potential to transform stakeholders' preferences as they recognize and reflect on the perspectives of others involved.[9]

In the specific area of environmental policy, "ecosystem-based management" (EBM) has been an especially potent variant of this form of rulemaking.[10] EBM claims the democratic credential of incorporating citizens' views while also delivering policies that are sensitive to the ecological context and scale of the relevant environmental resource.[11] In particular, those with "place-based" expertise have the opportunity to engage in dialogue with citizens and regulated interests in order to arrive at environmental goals that are agreeable to all parties.[12] As discussed in Chapter 1, advocates of EBM claim this form of participation will produce policies that (1) correspond to the particular geographic features of resources a given policy is intended to

[7] See Lowi (1999:17–18, 1969) for a discussion of how the vagueness of statutory language characterizing New Deal era regulation has created opportunities for organized interests to dominate the processes in which administrative agencies determine what these regulations would mean in practice. See Weber (2003) for a discussion of how collaborative forms of rulemaking can bring the public back into environmental policy decisions.

[8] Shapiro (2003:21–34) provides a summary of recent theoretical literature on deliberative democracy as a model of political practice, which he contrasts with aggregative models of democracy. Also see Benhabib (1996:69, 1992:29), and Eckersley (2004:116).

[9] See Miller (1992) and Phillips (1995).

[10] Collaborative approaches to regulatory rulemaking in environmental policy are also referenced in relation to the following more specific areas: habitat conservation planning, negotiated regulation, and collaborative conservation.

[11] Layzer (2008:20). Somewhat ironically, the trend toward public involvement in agency implementation of environmental laws first emerged during Ronald Reagan's presidency. In that context collaboration was advanced as a way to temper conflicts of interest resulting from an aggressive response by the business community and conservative activists to the first wave of environmental laws passed by Congress in the 1970s. See Amy (1990).

[12] See Graham Smith (2003:61–66) for a summary of the reasons why democratic deliberation offers a model of political practice that is environmentally appealing.

protect, (2) are supported by the best scientific knowledge, and (3) will be implemented without challenge (i.e. due to pre-implementation agreement among interested parties, which will minimize post-decision adversarial relationships among stakeholders).[13] Thus, in addition to giving citizens access to the processes and decisions that determine how environmental policies are designed and enforced, these democratic forms of rulemaking presumably enable environmental protection to proceed in a more effective and less adversarial way.

The CARR I advance is distinct from this democratized model of administrative rulemaking because it establishes and prioritizes substantive standards as an independent check or constraint on participatory processes or procedures. It gives precedence to the ideal of justice implicit in decisions that protect the environmental conditions necessary for ensuring each citizen has a threshold level of central human capabilities.[14] A CARR gives precedence to this ideal in the sense that it blocks alternative policy goals from displacing the priority of justice. For instance, although the ideal of democratic deliberation is embodied in democratic forms of regulatory rulemaking that sometimes produce substantively unjust outcomes, in a CARR deliberation cannot displace or supersede substantive justice as a policy goal. Therefore, if a democratic form of regulatory rulemaking produces policy outcomes that fail to protect the environmental conditions of human capabilities, the CARR would require rejecting or amending the relevant rule.

While I will discuss some related goals of justice that are implicit in current environmental law, I emphasize that *genuine democratic participation requires protection of people's fundamental capabilities and their environmental preconditions*. The substantive standards I propose should be understood as a precondition of genuine democratic participation in environmental decisions. A CARR is distinct from democratic approaches to regulatory rulemaking that hold policy outcomes to lower substantive standards as a result of the priority they accord to an ideal of deliberative process, but it shares the political commitments that underwrite the latter's emphasis on deliberation. For these reasons, a CARR is ultimately more effective in securing both the material conditions of deliberative fairness and the substantive goals that justify democratic procedure.

In prioritizing substantive justice, the CARR is also distinct from common approaches to regulatory rulemaking that seek to maximize economic efficiency. As discussed in Chapter 2, the current use of cost–benefit analysis (CBA) within the regulatory rulemaking process allows the president's Office

[13] Layzer (2008:26–27); Beierle and Long (1999:10,402); Applegate (1998:921); Williams and Matheny (1995:190).

[14] See Chapter 4 and Chapter 5, where I develop this idea.

of Management and Budget (OMB) to reject or require the amendment of regulatory rules that fail to meet standards of economic efficiency, defined as a condition in which the overall economic benefits of a regulatory rule outweigh the overall economic costs.[15] Regulatory rules meeting this efficiency standard may also protect the environmental conditions necessary for ensuring people have a threshold level of human capabilities; however, in cases where this compatibility (i.e. between economic efficiency and justice) is lacking, the CARR does not allow economic efficiency to displace the goal of justice. Economically efficient rules that advantage some people's capabilities while pushing other people's capabilities below a threshold level will fail to meet the relevant standard. In such situations, a CARR would require agencies to amend or remake the regulatory rule. Thus, regardless of whether regulatory rules are justified with respect to public participation and deliberation, economic efficiency, or some other political goal, the distinguishing feature of a CARR is that it establishes a standard for rejecting policy decisions that fail to protect the environmental conditions necessary to ensure citizens a threshold level of their central human capabilities.

In developing and defending this approach to regulatory rulemaking, the chapter proceeds as follows. First, in Section 6.2 I elaborate the institutional context in which the need for a CARR emerges by problematizing what I have described as democratic or democratized approaches to regulatory rulemaking. Because I discuss the weaknesses of CBA in previous chapters, I focus here on how a CARR can solve problems within current efforts to decentralize and democratize policy implementation. Second, in Sections 6.3 and 6.4 I justify the proposed model of regulatory rulemaking by casting its legitimacy as a "substantive moment in democratic law." This involves connecting the ideal of justice implicit in the CARR to the variety of democratic institutions from which its democratic legitimacy emerges. On this basis, I present the CARR as fully justifiable within the existing framework of statutory law. Third, in Section 6.5 I further theorize the CARR sketched in preceding sections by demonstrating the significance of an approach to regulatory rulemaking that can navigate the tension in contemporary environmental policy between the need for administrative expertise and the threat this poses to democratic procedure. To resolve this tension I define a role for citizens and experts in the CARR that maintains an important place for citizen participation, while proposing how to focus and constrain the role of administrative expertise. Let us turn first to the institutional context that gives rise to problems the CARR is intended to resolve.

[15] See Executive Order 12,291.

6.2 The Institutional Context of Democratized Rulemaking

As a model for decision-making at the implementation stage of environmental policy, a CARR is distinct in appealing to substantive justice as criteria for evaluating the standards and guidelines that emerge from the regulatory rulemaking process. The primary purpose of the CARR is to ensure that regulatory rules necessary for implementing environmental laws will not undermine the threshold level of protection for citizens' central capabilities because these protections define what it means for society to provide basic conditions of justice. The contribution of this approach to agency rulemaking concerning environmental protection is best understood in the broader regulatory context in which recent efforts to institutionalize democratic forms of rulemaking such as EBM have emerged. In particular, two difficult problems define the contours of this regulatory setting.

First, while many indicators of environmental quality have improved since the 1970s, there is still a widespread lack of compliance with environmental laws. In many areas of the United States, current environmental standards (e.g. standards for air and water quality) are frequently violated, leaving vast numbers of people without the benefit of legally established protections.[16] From the perspective of polluters, it may be more cost-effective to pay the fines for violations than to invest in expensive capital improvements that would bring them into compliance with the law. From the perspective of the state-level environmental protection agencies charged with implementing federal laws, political control by state legislators can impede enforcement, significantly constraining their ability to do their jobs.[17] Furthermore, even in states with a political environment that supports strong environmental protection, population growth and changing economic activities may alter polluting practices in ways that offset expected gains in pollution reduction. Consequently, state regulators may end up permitting levels of pollution that

[16] For instance, in 2005, as many as a million people in the USA lived in counties that did not meet the Clean Air Act's standard for eight-hour ozone. More generally, in 2009, over 80 million people nationwide lived in counties with pollution levels above the primary *national ambient air quality standards* (NAAQS). See <http://www.epa.gov/airtrends/aqtrends.html>. Likewise, a recent report by the EPA on the status of water quality in individual states explains that among all the surface waters that have been assessed, water quality standards were met for only 61 percent of the river and stream miles, 54 percent of the lake acres, 49 percent of the estuarine square miles, and 22 percent of the Great Lakes shoreline miles. See US EPA Office of Water (2000:ES-3).

[17] For example, in Pennsylvania, Governor Corbett, who is strongly in favor of drilling for natural gas in the state's Marcellus Shale reserve, recently required that all punishment and enforcement actions (including simple notices of violation) brought against drill operators be approved by high-level officials in the state's Department of Environmental Protection. Critics claimed that "The idea that the secretary himself and the deputy secretary [of the Department of Environmental Protection] would presumably review, literally hundreds if not thousands of (notices of violation) before they were issued, when they were not on the site, they didn't do the inspection, is incredible." See Levy (2011).

exceed pollution control standards. A crucial factor in understanding the motivation behind creating a place for more public involvement in rulemaking is that these failures of compliance occur in the context of a highly polarized politics that poses apparently insurmountable barriers to political and legislative action at the national or subnational level.[18]

Environmental groups have often responded to this political "gridlock" by turning to the courts, bringing lawsuits against either the polluters themselves, or the state environmental protection agencies that fail to fully implement federal laws. At times, forcing compliance through the courts has been an effective strategy. However, while environmental groups may have been able to hold some polluters and regulators accountable to standards established by environmental laws, they have also helped to produce a regulatory rulemaking context that is highly adversarial and limited in its reach. The contentious relationship among polluters, regulators, environmental groups, and other interested citizens produces costly battles that drag on for long periods of time, wasting the resources of all parties and doing little to change the many instances of non-compliance that remain unprosecuted.[19] As one might expect, both environmental groups and polluters have therefore shown genuine interest in alternative approaches to creating and enforcing regulatory rules. The turn toward a more collaborative form of rulemaking offers the possibility of bringing polluters, experts in administrative agencies, along with citizens and environmental groups, into a form of dialogue through which they can arrive at goals that are agreeable to all.[20] Viewed in this light, the move to bring the public and other potentially excluded stakeholders into the rulemaking process has the potential to resolve the problem of non-compliance in a way that is less adversarial and more effective.

A second crucial problem defining the regulatory context that motivates recent efforts to advance collaborative, participatory, and devolved forms of regulatory rulemaking is a prevalent tension between the need for administrative expertise in contemporary environmental management and a political commitment to democratic procedure as the basis for policy legitimacy. Modern democratic forms of government need experts with specialized knowledge and skills to make sophisticated and informed judgments about the direction and means to achieve policy goals set out in legislation that elected officials approve.[21] In the environmental area, these experts staff

[18] See Klyza and Sousa (2008) for a discussion of legislative stalemate at the national level emerging from highly polarized politics.

[19] See Kubasek and Silverman (2008:52–53) and Kagan (2001) for a summary of these and other problems attributed to the adversarial nature of litigation as a strategy to achieve compliance.

[20] In the administrative law context, this form of rulemaking is commonly referred to as "regulated negotiation" or "reg-neg."

[21] See Breyer (1993) for an argument that environmental policy decisions therefore should be made by an elite cadre of civil servants.

executive branch agencies that manage the environment, such as the EPA, the Bureau of Land Management, and the Forest Service, as well as agencies that focus on a range of scientific issues relevant to environmental policies, such as the National Oceanic and Air Administration and the National Aeronautics and Space Administration.[22] Experts within these agencies conduct and oversee the studies and assessments that determine environmental standards such as the level of pollution control necessary to prevent respiratory disorders in children, the number of trees that can be sustainably cut for timber on federally owned land, and, more recently, the levels and forms of regulation that can best address carbon dioxide emissions.

Although specialized expertise is essential for drafting and implementing laws that will successfully protect human health and sustain a supply of environmental resources, reliance on specialized experts also constitutes a problem for democratic legitimacy because these experts wield an influence over the direction and extent of federally mandated environmental protection that ordinary citizens lack.[23] Citizens do maintain an equal right to vote, equal opportunities to participate in broad political discussion, and access to democratic decisions made by some majoritarian process, but an imbalance of social and economic resources produces a vast inequality of political power, threatening to undermine the neutrality and political equality that ground these formal democratic rights.[24] Thus, even if experts do not insert their personal values to shape the direction and extent of environmental policies, they may nonetheless be "captured" by anti-regulatory interests who strategically apply their substantial political power to directly influence experts or to otherwise shape the processes through which elected officials exercise oversight of administrative activity.[25] In either instance, those with specialized expertise in implementing environmental policies will be in a position to disregard the interests of ordinary citizens.[26] The threat this poses, ultimately, is the exercise of arbitrary power, in which the power of administrative agencies to modify citizens' rights and duties is inadequately checked and constrained.[27]

Viewed as a response to this problem, efforts to institutionalize more democratic forms of regulatory rulemaking are a way to recover the terrain of decision-making authority from experts who either make up a

[22] See Keller (2009) for a discussion of how the role of scientific expertise takes shape during different stages of the environmental policy process.

[23] See Christiano (2005) for an overview of this relationship between democracy and administrative agencies.

[24] Christiano (2005:211–212). [25] Eisner (2000:118–169).

[26] This threatens the political legitimacy of democratic governance, which comes from institutionalizing equal consideration of citizens' interests in the processes that establish laws generating new duties for citizens. See Richardson (2002:27–28).

[27] See Richardson (2002:28–36) for this characterization of bureaucratic domination.

non-democratically elected technical elite, or remain captured by the stakeholders they are charged with regulating.[28] By bringing citizens into dialogue with these experts and other stakeholders about the goals and strategies for achieving environmental protection, democratized forms of rulemaking at least oblige administrative experts to consider citizens' views, if not adopt them outright. In this respect they provide a way for regulatory rulemaking to navigate a more democratically legitimate path between the need for specialized expertise that informs the nature and direction of policy, and democratic commitments to establishing policies that reflect the views and interests of ordinary citizens, not only those of technical elites and special interests.

If the processes in which these participatory forms of regulatory rulemaking play out were ever characterized by ideal conditions of democratic deliberation, then they might offer a sufficient mechanism for addressing the undemocratic exercise of administrative power, if not the problem of non-compliance with environmental law. In the ideal model, stakeholders in environmental decisions would engage in a form of communication and mutual learning that transforms their preferences such that they converge upon goals all participants can accept. In the actual practice of these democratic forms of regulatory rulemaking, however, there is a significant gap between the ideal conditions of genuine democratic deliberation and the form of politics that takes place. One problem, as Howard Ernst explains, is that this model of rulemaking is "grounded in the somewhat naïve belief that education [about the harmful effects of pollution] can outweigh economic pressures and competitive forces, making coercive actions by government unnecessary."[29] To the contrary, as Ernst explains in his account of the various collaborative and participatory efforts to design a policy for improving water quality in Chesapeake Bay, local governments and industries that fall under their control do not voluntarily adopt environmentally sound practices once citizens and environmental groups make them aware of their harmful effects on the environment. Instead, because economic resources are critical to the success of politicians at the local level, the significant economic power wielded by pro-development and pro-industry stakeholders simply recreate the power imbalances that these democratic forms of rulemaking were (at least partially) created to avoid.[30] As Cass Sunstein has cautioned, some forms of democratic rulemaking might be "reflecting not the outcomes of deliberative judgments of the citizenry, but negotiated solutions among well-organized actors."[31]

[28] For a discussion of the potential for "regulatory capture" in the collaborative rulemaking context, see Freeman (1997:88).

[29] Ernst (2003:40).

[30] Baumgartner and Jones (1993:222), and Delogu (1984).

[31] Sunstein (1999:29).

Consequently, democratized forms of rulemaking can result in weaker levels of environmental protection than what is accomplished under traditional regulatory processes in which environmental groups have the option to pursue a more legal and adversarial strategy.[32] Moreover, a failure to meet compliance standards may even occur when there are formal successes in the procedural components of these collaborative approaches to rulemaking. For instance, in some cases, disagreeing stakeholders do arrive at agreement on acceptable goals. But, in order to reach this agreement, goals are often vaguely defined, making it possible for polluters to evade complying with pollution control policies when it is time to implement the specific actions that will achieve them.[33] Judith Layzer highlights this problem in summarizing evidence from seven case studies on devolved and participatory methods of decision-making in environmental policy. Layzer states that "reliance on [these] nonregulatory mechanisms has not necessarily fostered efforts to go beyond the legal minimum; rather when plans have multiple goals, development interests and their allies have sought ways to avoid compliance or comply minimally."[34] Thus, even when key features of democratic deliberation are present—such as collective agreement and ample opportunities for environmental advocates and industry stakeholders to participate in public dialogue and debate about policy decisions—these more intentionally democratic forms of rulemaking may nonetheless produce few if any tangible environmental accomplishments.[35]

This last point is worth elaborating: despite some procedural successes, democratized forms of rulemaking are still a good distance from achieving ideal processes of democratic deliberation. When a collaborative group does achieve consensus around substantive goals, the consensus may simply reflect the views of articulate and outspoken members of the decision-making group, rather than a transformation of preferences that converges on collective agreement, which is what advocates of the increased democratic process envision.[36] Likewise, these rulemaking forums also exclude or marginalize certain voices, such as those who lack power and influence necessary for negotiating on their own behalf, and those who are perceived as radical or unreasonable for assuming a position that lacks proximity to the status quo.[37] In these ways the problems of internal and external exclusion that characterize insufficiently deliberative politics at the national or state level also play out in democratized rulemaking that displaces decision authority to the

[32] See Coglianese (2001:110) and Ernst (2003).

[33] See Layzer (2008) for a discussion of several case studies in which this trend played out. See Mansbridge (1983:167) for a discussion of the imprecision that consensual decision-making generates.

[34] Layzer (2008:278–279).

[35] Ernst (2003:49).

[36] See Smith and Wales (2000:303–304).

[37] See Foster (2002) and Layzer (2008:275).

local or regional level.[38] Without doubt, much can be done to make these decision processes more genuinely democratic. However, given the broader political and economic dynamics producing non-compliance with environmental law, deliberative procedures alone—even if perfected—are unlikely to result in sufficient levels of environmental protection, characterized as minimally requiring compliance with existing laws. To put this point differently, democratized rulemaking may be successful in tempering the exercise of arbitrary power by administrative agencies, but its potential to address the problem of non-compliance with environmental laws is less plausible.

The problem of non-compliance is especially challenging because it arises at the intersection of environmental limits and unreasonable pluralism. By environmental limits I mean limits in the environment's capacity to satisfy all the interests to which domestic environmental protection is relevant. Non-compliance is occasioned by these limits because the natural environment lacks the capacity to simultaneously absorb the waste that polluters produce (and produce the resources that industries demand) and provide the level of environmental quality that protects citizens' broader set of interests. For example, in many areas of the country, the natural environment is not able to simultaneously satisfy some citizens' interest (e.g. polluters') in using air as a low-cost sink that absorbs the byproducts of industrial activities from which they attain a profit, and other citizens' interest (e.g. children's) in breathing air that does not contribute to existing or new respiratory disorders. Likewise, in many areas of the United States, the natural environment is not able to simultaneously satisfy polluters' interest in using water as a conveyance for waste produced in generating economically profitable products and services, and citizens' interest in having drinkable, fishable, or swimable water. A finite natural system simply cannot absorb an infinite amount of waste.[39] Consequently, unless we make highly contestable assumptions about the ability of technology to substitute for resources, either polluters must cut their profits to pay the cost of reducing pollution, or citizens must surrender their interest in having a certain level of environmental quality.[40] In short, because the environment has at least some unsurpassable limits, at some point there will be no "win-win" solutions to environmental conflicts over collectively shared environmental goods and services to which deliberators can agree.

We should understand the problem of non-compliance with environmental laws as emerging at the intersection of these environmental limits and

[38] Young (2002:52–63). [39] See Daly (1991, 2005).

[40] See Sagoff (1998a) and Daly (1998) for a debate about the limits of resource substitution. Jackson (2009) proposes a third way out of the conflict between environmental quality and producer profits, but this requires a more fundamental restructuring of the economic system.

unreasonable pluralism because citizens might disagree about what environmental protection should entail. Respect for reasonable pluralism in a liberal constitutional democracy requires that citizens exercise their political power by justifying their political decisions to one another with reasons that other citizens might reasonably accept.[41] This, according to John Rawls, is necessary to satisfy the criterion of reciprocity, on which the political legitimacy of government action is based. However, as Rawls also notes, "The criterion of reciprocity is normally violated whenever basic liberties are denied" because reasons cannot both satisfy the reciprocity criterion and justify denying these liberties.[42] Allowing polluters to do whatever they wish with their privately owned property as a legally protected right violates the reciprocity criterion because the consequences of the activities polluters seek to justify effectively violate legal protections established for others who suffer from pollution when it spills over into collectively shared environmental resources (e.g. air and water). By justifying their positions in terms of property rights, the polluters are not offering reasons that other citizens can reasonably accept because the reasons justifying the polluters' actions also justify the legal protections claimed by citizens who are burdened by their polluting activities. From the perspective of these burdened citizens, polluters are simply asserting that their rights (to property) should trump other citizens' rights (to be free from bodily harm). This is not reciprocity, but it does reveal the importance of having a more fundamental criterion for determining whose primary political guarantees or rights should be prioritized.[43]

Viewed in this context, democratized approaches to regulatory rulemaking are based on the flawed assumption that there are solutions to environmental conflicts that will violate the basic protections of neither the polluters nor the polluted. Such solutions may have been realistic in a world in which the environmental goods that are shared by all (e.g. air and water) were large in relation to the amount of pollution produced or in relation to the quantity of resources needed to motivate business and entrepreneurial interests to pursue monetary profits.[44] However, in a world where pollution and the demand for resources is large in relation to the environmental goods and services that are collectively shared, such ideas simply mask the genuine conflicts environmental limits pose to contemporary liberal democratic societies, especially if these societies wish to remain truly committed to giving equal consideration to the interests of their citizens.

[41] Rawls (1999:136–137). [42] Rawls (1999:138).

[43] In Chapter 5 I propose and defend an approach to establishing such priorities.

[44] As Daly (2005) argues, the "full world" we now inhabit requires a level of economic production that can stay within biospheric limits.

Thus, the problem of non-compliance arises because some views about what it means to have good relationships to the environment cannot reasonably coexist. In such circumstances, rules of democratic procedure that seek to achieve consensus around mutually acceptable goals are keyed to an unrealistic view of environmental and political relationships. Democratized rulemaking can ensure administrative agencies know what citizens want, and it can produce important kinds of learning, but it cannot prevent the flow of resources and power that polluters will use to pursue their interests either within or external to democratic procedures. For this reason, even the most idealized forms of democratic rulemaking will often result in insufficient and non-compliant levels of environmental protection. A substantive standard to guide the rulemaking process is needed because more and better forms of democratic rulemaking are unlikely to achieve compliance with existing laws, much less protect ways of living in relation to the natural environment that require going beyond them.

Because the conflicts emerging in the contemporary regulatory context are over fundamental guarantees that confound the terms of reciprocity and defy commensurability in economic terms, an alternative model of regulatory rulemaking that prioritizes substantive standards of justice over procedural goals would have the advantage of establishing both the basis for resolving such conflicts and the conditions of democratic participation necessary for procedural legitimacy in collaborative decisions. A CARR that is grounded in the capabilities approach to social and environmental justice I have advanced in preceding chapters can provide this substantive standard. This approach to rulemaking would require rejecting or amending regulatory rules when they fail to produce environmental policies that protect people's central capabilities at a threshold level.

For the purpose of developing this approach to rulemaking in Sections 6.3 and 6.4, let us assume that protecting people's capabilities at a threshold level does not entail achieving higher levels of environmental protection than existing regulatory standards require. This means that existing regulatory standards (if met) would sufficiently protect people's capabilities, and therefore, that enforcement of current environmental laws is sufficient for ensuring the CARR's substantive commitment to social and environmental justice. Given these implications, applying the CARR would entail rejecting or amending administrative decisions emerging from democratic and participatory forms of rulemaking if they fail to produce the levels of environmental protection that existing laws require, even if the relevant stakeholders agree to accept them. In the democratized rulemaking context described earlier in this chapter, this would effectively prevent powerful interests from tempering and dissipating competing interests in ways that make non-compliance with existing levels of environmental protection seem acceptable. While applications of the CARR would in this way constrain the outcomes that democratic forms of rulemaking can produce, holding administrative rules accountable to a substantive standard of capability protection should not be understood as undemocratic.

6.3 Substantive Moments in Democratic Law

The political context of regulatory rulemaking is one in which participatory processes and substantive ideals shape and constrain each other. The CARR I am proposing constrains the outcomes that democratic forms of rulemaking can produce because it requires administrative agencies to reject or amend regulatory rules that fail to protect the environmental conditions necessary for providing citizens with a threshold level of central capabilities. Despite this constraint on democratic outcomes there are good reasons why the CARR should not be understood as lacking democratic credentials. Applied in the regulatory rulemaking context, the CARR functions as a stabilizing force against structural inequalities that threaten the conditions of genuine democracy. Furthermore, the CARR can be understood as instantiating commitments already explicit in democratically produced laws. I will take up each of these points in turn.

Many democratic theorists have noted that genuine democratic deliberation is contingent on a background level of equality among participants with respect to resources, status, and other components of political power. As Jack Knight and James Johnson explain, "citizens must possess a certain level of income and resources if they are to develop the basic capacities necessary to be effective participants in democratic deliberation."[45] This condition brings the democratic character of new participatory forms of rulemaking into question because equality of this sort rarely, if ever, characterizes the contexts in which environmental conflicts arise.[46] As such, devolved forms of collaborative and negotiated rulemaking commit participants to deliberative norms of communicating and persuading others through reasoned argument amidst conditions of vast structural inequality.[47] Some citizens may be willing to submit to such norms, but even some strongly committed deliberative democrats admit that under conditions of structural inequality a more oppositional form of political action may be necessary. On this view, coercive methods of political participation may be justifiable, if only to produce outcomes amenable to a more fair and inclusive form of deliberation.[48] The CARR need not appeal to coercive methods of political participation amidst

[45] Knight and Johnson (1997:307). [46] Fung (2005:405).
[47] See Young (2001:675). [48] See Fung (2005).

conditions of structural inequality because it prevents inequalities of wealth, status, and power among participants from influencing policy implementation in ways that fail to protect people's capabilities at a threshold level. To the extent that this avoids exacerbating existing inequalities, it will also help to produce the conditions that make genuine democratic participation possible.

While these implications of applying the CARR in the rulemaking context may be far from the more mobilized form of democratic politics that some theorists advocate when structural inequalities persist, it would be short-sighted to assume that more and different forms of democratic engagement are the only democratic responses to substantive deficiencies reflecting these inequalities in environmental policy. Mobilized action, if successful, may result in stronger and enforceable environmental regulations. However, regulatory actions that bear the stamp of democratic legitimacy need not only come from a unidirectional process in which elected officials or administrators write something into law or policy that reflects the preferences of citizens. Bruce Ackerman, for example, argues that the democratic ideal of "rule by the people" does not necessarily mean that all acts of lawmaking must be viewed as acts *of* the people. He contends such a requirement implies a view of constitutional history that regards the legislature as the only institution possessing a legitimate claim to speak for citizens; that is, to represent the "People Assembled." On Ackerman's view, the US constitution creates a form of government in which the different institutions that compose it can represent citizens in different ways.[49] Responsiveness to the expressed preferences of citizens is one among several competing views of what democratic representation entails. For instance, the actions of formal democratic institutions, such as the administrative agencies that develop and implement environmental policy, can be judged as more or less democratically legitimate based on the extent to which they mobilize "express and implicit objections from the represented."[50] In institutionalizing the objections of those whose capabilities are damaged by failures to meets standards that environmental laws establish, an agency's application of the CARR bears one such stamp of greater democratic legitimacy.

The most prominent view of democracy regards political legitimacy as emerging from government's responsiveness to the expressed preferences of citizens.[51] In this view, the submission of a legislative act that reflects citizens' preferences is the archetypal democratic moment from which political legitimacy emerges. However, in the area of environmental policy, there are at least two different and distinct instances in the emergence of democratic

[49] See Ackerman (1991:181). [50] See Disch (2011:111). [51] Dahl (1971:1).

law from which politically legitimate commitments that bear on administrative rulemaking can also emerge. First, when legislators respond to citizens' preferences by drafting laws, they can go beyond what those preferences express by writing substantive commitments into the text of the relevant legislation. For instance, some environmental laws state that the regulatory standards developed in implementing those laws must produce economic benefits greater than economic costs; that is, the adopted standards must pass a cost–benefit test.[52] In these cases, many citizens may have demanded environmental protection, but this does not mean they also supported legislators' efforts to substantively constrain the level of environmental protection achieved based on an evaluation of the economic costs and benefits. Second, substantive commitments can also come in the form of directives from an institution that has democratic legitimacy due to a one-time expression of popular support for it. For instance, in 1981, shortly after he was elected to his first term in office, President Ronald Reagan issued Executive Order 12,291, which required completion and approval of a CBA for all major regulatory rules prior to their approval for implementation.

In both of these instances, a policy's economic impact is made transparent as a relevant interest of citizens, and institutionalized as an objection to economically inefficient policies. More importantly, in these instances, substantive commitments to policy goals clearly emerge neither directly from citizens' preferences, nor from genuine democratic deliberation that is oriented toward or bound by reasoned agreement. These commitments are nonetheless treated as democratically legitimate. This suggests that direct expression of citizen preferences is not the only source of democratic legitimacy. Although different theories of democracy will understand the justification for protecting certain citizens' economic interests in different ways, my primary point in the present context is to emphasize that what legislators write into laws, as well as the goals issued from institutions that have popular support, can go well beyond what is directly reflected in citizens' expressed preferences. These legislative commitments and institutionally defined goals can (and have) come to matter a great deal in defining the content of environmental protection. Even when one substantive commitment written into law, such as the commitment to protecting human health, comes into conflict with another substantive commitment emerging from a democratically legitimate institution, such as the commitment to produce regulatory rules that are economically efficient, the information these commitments produce can enable more and better democratic deliberation in the broader

[52] See Chapter 2, footnote 6, for a list of laws requiring cost–benefit analysis as part of the standard setting process.

and longer-term environmental policy debate. In this respect, a multitude of commitments creates conditions of better democratic deliberation.

When the political legitimacy of different policy goals is understood in this broader context of democratic law, using the CARR to reject or amend regulatory rules that fail to meet standards of justice need not be understood as undemocratic. As I argue in Section 6.4, like CBA, the broader substantive ideal to which a CARR appeals is grounded in political commitments that are both written into existing laws and established as policy goals by democratic institutions that have popular support. Additionally, like goals of public health and economic efficiency, the evaluative standards that a CARR establishes help to maintain the conditions of contestability that can produce more and better democratic decisions about environmental policy over longer periods of time. For both of these reasons, application of the CARR should be understood as also justifiable within the existing framework of statutory law. Other and more compelling justifications for application of the CARR can and may emerge; however, my point in Section 6.4 is only to argue that the CARR can be grounded in these same sources of democratic legitimacy.

6.4 Environmental Justice as a Substantive Moment in Democratic Law

In treating the protection of each person's capabilities as relevant to establishing and evaluating decisions in environmental policy, the CARR embraces the goal of environmental equity as a central component of social justice. Specifically, it seeks to ensure that the benefits and burdens environmental policies produce do not push any person's central human capabilities below a threshold level. If we assume the standards of environmental quality established in existing environmental laws are sufficient for protecting these central human capabilities, the CARR would require rejecting or amending any decision that allows polluters to adapt their behavior in ways that avoid meeting these standards. For example, polluters may avoid meeting standards by choosing to pay fines for their violations rather than by attaining compliance. Similarly, stakeholders in a democratic rulemaking context may agree to address non-compliance with water quality standards through voluntary reforms and incentives that motivate polluters to adopt "best practices." The CARR, in contrast, would require rejecting or amending any proposal that does not mandate actions that will *in fact* produce compliance in the event that penalties or voluntary provisions fail.[53] This ensures that the burden

[53] See Ernst (2003:69–86) for a case study relaying the failure of voluntary reforms and incentives to produce compliance with water quality standards in areas feeding into the Chesapeake

of non-compliance is not borne by those whose health and livelihoods are dependent on water quality, such as people who depend on healthy aquatic environments for commercial fishing or tourism, or for producing their drinking and bathing water.[54] Non-compliance would require action because it threatens the "ecological meta-capability", which ensures each person the environmental conditions necessary for securing a threshold level of their central capabilities, such as the capabilities for *bodily health* and *material control over one's environment*.[55]

A commitment to the goal of environmental justice that the CARR embodies is already written into some environmental laws in the same way as the goals of economic efficiency that CBA embodies. For example, just as the goal of economic efficiency embodied by CBA is written in the text of laws such as the Toxic Substances Control Act (TSCA) and the Safe Drinking Water Act (SDWA), the text of the National Environmental Policy Act (NEPA) of 1969 specifically states that it is the responsibility of the federal government to "assure for *all* Americans safe, healthful, productive and aesthetically and culturally pleasing surroundings."[56] Not only does NEPA authorize and require "to the fullest extent possible" the "policies, regulations, and public laws of the United States [are] to be interpreted and administered in accordance with the policies set forth in [NEPA]," it also explicitly recognizes that "*each* person should enjoy a healthful environment."[57] Likewise, the SDWA requires the EPA to use CBA when proposing and justifying drinking water standards, but it *also* requires the EPA to consider if the standards arrived at through CBA will create risks for particular groups that are higher than risks

Bay. In theory, environmental groups could still sue for non-compliance under existing laws if democratic rulemaking efforts fail to achieve compliance, but this would require that those opposing pollution come up with additional resources for a pursuing a legal case. Some scholars argue that the threat of such a suit is what stifled deals that the Clinton administration attempted to broker with polluters in democratized forms of rulemaking. See Hirsch (1998), Mank (1998), and Steinzor (1998).

[54] For example, see Alliance for the Chesapeake Bay (2004).

[55] In the present example, having these capabilities requires clean water and the availability of fish stocks that gives one an opportunity to pursue employment in the field on which one has built a livelihood. See Chapter 4 for a discussion of the ecological meta-capability.

[56] Emphasis added. See 42 U.S.C. § 4331, § 101(b)(2). On these grounds, for the category of government projects to which NEPA is determined to apply, agencies must already conduct an analysis of their social impacts. However, in conducting this analysis of social impacts, even if these impacts are determined to be highly negative for certain groups, NEPA establishes no formal requirement that agencies avoid or otherwise equalize the impacts. For TSCA, see 15 U.S.C. 2605 (c), the "Administrator" of the EPA is required to calculate the costs and benefits of any rule implementing the law and then compare them against each other, deeming the rule unacceptable if the costs outweigh the benefits. For SDWA, the 1996 Amendments at 42 USC 300g-1(b)(3), include a provision requiring the use of a limited cost–benefit criterion when EPA proposes drinking water standards. The Federal Insecticide, Fungicide, and Rodenticide Act (FIFRA) also makes cost–benefit balancing specific in the language of the legislation; see 7 USC 136a(a).

[57] Emphasis added. See 42 U.S.C. § 4332(1) and 42 U.S.C. § 4331(c).

the general population faces. Specifically, in setting maximum contaminant levels for drinking water regulations, the EPA must consider "the effects of the contaminant on the general population and on groups within the general population such as infants, children, pregnant women, the elderly, individuals with a history of serious illness, or other subpopulations that are identified as likely to be at greater risk of adverse effects due to exposure to contaminants in drinking water than the general population."[58] In these instances, legislators have written into law substantive commitments intended to counteract the maldistribution of individual protections that environmental policies are known to produce.[59] Clearly, legislators already have established or approved standards that hold policy decisions accountable to substantive commitments reflecting ideals of social justice, such as the concern for equity in environmental protection. A systematic application of the CARR would formalize these commitments at the rulemaking level of policy implementation.

A similar substantive commitment is established in Executive Order (E.O.) 12,898, which, as noted at the start of this chapter, was issued by President Clinton in 1994.[60] Just as E.O. 12,291 directs federal agencies to ensure that environmental regulations meet standards of the economic efficiency adopted in CBA, E.O. 12,898 directs each federal agency to "make achieving environmental justice part of its mission by identifying and addressing, as appropriate, disproportionately high and adverse human health or environmental effects of its programs, policies, and activities on minority populations and low-income populations." According to the EPA's own internal summary, E.O. 12,898 "directs federal agencies to identify and address the disproportionately high and adverse human health or environmental effects of their actions on minority and low-income populations, to the greatest extent practicable and permitted by law." Additionally, E.O. 12,898

[58] See 42 U.S.C. § 300g-1(b)(3)(C)(i). In some instances, quasi-judicial interpretations of environmental laws also have adopted strong commitments to social justice. For instance, for the purpose of allocating permits issued under the Resource Conservation and Recovery Act (RCRA), the Environmental Appeals Board (EAB) found that RCRA allows EPA to take a more refined look at its health and environmental impact assessments "in light of allegations that operation of the (waste disposal) facility would have a disproportionately adverse effect on the health or environment of low-income or minority populations." In this ruling, while the EAB warned that a finding of the alleged social or economic impacts on a community would not provide a legal basis for rejecting permit applications, EPA asserts that the close evaluation EAB authorized in this case "could, in turn, justify permit conditions or denials based on disproportionately high and adverse human health or environmental effects." See Guzy (2000:2) discussing both quotes. Also see Lazarus and Tai (1999:660–663).

[59] Although it is too early to tell what the ultimate impact will be, President Barack Obama (2011) also issued an updated executive order on regulatory impact analysis, allowing that "Where appropriate and permitted by law, each agency may consider (and discuss qualitatively) values that are difficult or impossible to quantify, including equity, human dignity, fairness, and distributive impacts."

[60] See 59 Fed. Reg. 7629 (1994).

requires each agency to "develop a strategy for implementing environmental justice" as part of a broader strategy "to promote nondiscrimination in federal programs that affect human health and the environment, as well as provide minority and low-income communities access to public information and public participation."[61] Although these goals have not been achieved in practice, they demonstrate that the ideals of justice the CARR embodies have already been embraced as substantive political commitments—in this instance, as guidance from a political institution (the presidency) that has democratic legitimacy due to the one-time electoral expression of popular support.[62]

When administrative agencies ignore the goal of preventing environmental risks from burdening certain subpopulations simply because the resulting maldistribution of environmental protection is agreed to in a democratic form of rulemaking, they are treating this form of rulemaking as though it has a legitimacy that other legislative and institutional commitments to environmental justice lack. Disproportionate environmental burdens may arise because these collaborative and participatory forms of rulemaking are not (and may never be) genuinely democratic; therefore, there are good reasons to continually seek more ideal forms of deliberation in democratized rulemaking. However, these forms of rulemaking are limited because they treat democratic legitimacy as a feature of political institutions that respond to citizens' preferences or interests rather than as a feature of political institutions that promote the interests of those they represent. Although many deliberative democrats may assume that citizens' genuine interests are only identifiable in deliberative contexts that remain isolated from elite manipulation, it is also possible that promoting the interests of citizens can entail a form of democratic representation that is more "reflexive" in mobilizing a constituency of citizens who have the capacity to "object to what is done in [their] name."[63] In this latter form of representation and in contrast to certain deliberative ideals, democracy entails contestation and struggle rather than agreement and well-structured deliberation.[64]

When aligned with this reflexive view of democratic representation, the instantiation of current legislative and institutional commitments that prevent environmental protection from burdening certain subpopulations with adverse risks can be understood as an equally legitimate form of democratic

[61] See<http://www2.epa.gov/laws-regulations/summary-executive-order-12898-federal-actions-address-environmental-justice > (accessed April 24, 2014).

[62] Because President George W. Bush did not seek to overturn President Clinton's Executive Order on Environmental Justice (E.O. 12,898), we can understand that support as ongoing.

[63] See Pitkin (1967:155) and the elaboration of Pitkin's view by Runciman (2007: 95–97) and Disch (2011: 106–109).

[64] See Young (2001, 2000:49–51).

politics. Like the institutionalized commitment to economic efficiency, a CARR—which rejects regulatory rules that fail to provide and protect a threshold level of human capabilities—can bear the stamp of political legitimacy that comes from democratic representation in which government both responds to and forms the demands of a constituency it organizes and narrates into being.[65] These commitments emerge from moments in which the representatives within political institutions that are subject to popular control institutionalize policy goals that do not directly come from the preferences of citizens, and need not directly gain their approval. In these "substantive moments in democratic law," a relevant set of interests is both defined and represented. Thus, in requiring that environmental policies meet the goals of environmental justice, the CARR can be understood as representing citizens that are disproportionately burdened with environmental risks or harms.

While the CARR's protection of certain fundamental human capabilities in the administrative rulemaking context can be understood as emerging from a substantive moment in democratic law, a crucial feature is its creation of a space for citizens to formally object to what is being done on their behalf. For citizens, the opportunity to object to the claims of environmental justice that a CARR makes on their behalf is especially crucial when making environmental policy decisions involving experts with specialized scientific skills and knowledge. Although I have proposed a model of regulatory rulemaking that requires rejecting or amending rules meeting standards of either economic efficiency or democratic procedure when these standards fail to protect the basic environmental conditions of justice, I have not yet addressed how this model can avoid reproducing the problem of expertise, which poses the threat of bureaucratic domination. Specifically, the CARR—as an administrative decision-making tool—does not ensure experts in administrative agencies cannot unduly and arbitrarily exercise power over the direction and extent of environmental protection based on their interpretation and assessment of environmental regulatory standards. Therefore, it is crucial that the CARR's mandate to ensure regulatory rules provide established levels of environmental protection does not result in a kind of expert control over policy that threatens background democratic commitments to political equality and contestability. In Section 6.5 I address this problem by proposing why and how a CARR should carve out a role for citizens in specifying the relevance of environmental protection to their own individual lives. Equally important, the development of this decision-making tool should also institutionalize citizens' capacity to object to the CARR's representation of their interests, specifically, by putting constraints on experts

[65] See Disch (2011:107).

who are charged with establishing standards of environmental quality that protect the capabilities citizens define as valuable. In these ways, the CARR can incorporate vital democratic commitments and protect environmental conditions that ultimately make it possible to maintain the conditions of democratic contestability over time.

6.5 Democracy and Justice as Constraining Expertise

If a CARR is going to hold outcomes emerging from democratic forms of regulatory rulemaking accountable to existing or stronger standards of environmental protection, it should also navigate the tension between administrative expertise and democratic procedure that gave rise to contemporary democratic forms of regulatory rulemaking. That is, the CARR should not entail a set of procedures that puts policy outcomes entirely in the hands of administrative experts, for this would just reproduce the problems of administrative control to which democratic rulemaking is responding.

As discussed in Section 6.2, the problems of administrative control concern the "capture" of administrative agencies by the industries they are charged with regulating, as well as the narrow pursuit of experts' own values rather than the interests of citizens. Two features of the CARR ensure that it does not contribute to these problems. First, in adopting a basic commitment to respecting citizens as individual agents that are capable of shaping their own lives, the CARR requires that citizens participate in specifying the central human capabilities that the relevant environmental conditions must enable.[66] Second, in order to avoid the undemocratic exercise of administrative power (i.e. by those whose specialized expertise is necessary for defining the environmental conditions that will provide a threshold level of these specified capabilities), the CARR imposes a set of constraints on experts that will hold them accountable to the objections made by the citizens whom their scientific analysis is intended to protect. I will discuss each of these components of the CARR in turn.

Citizen participation in specifying the capabilities relevant to environmental decisions at the administrative level is crucial to a CARR if this approach to decision-making is going to avoid overly paternalistic interventions in individual behavior and instead treat citizens as masters of their own personal and political lives.[67] Generally speaking, in the contemporary

[66] In doing so, citizens articulate the content of the ecological meta-capability that is relevant to their particular context.

[67] Although I am drawing on Nussbaum's list of central human capabilities to initially define the general dimensions of individual well-being and agency to which environmental protection is relevant, the importance of respecting citizens as "active agents" participating in and shaping their own destiny is central to Amartya Sen's elaboration of the capability approach; e.g. see

environmental debate the issue of paternalism arises when public policies protecting the environment threaten to overstep the proper limits of government authority, producing a level of environmental protection that undermines economic growth and/or provides a level of safety that is unnecessary for avoiding genuine risks.[68] Those who claim environmental policies exceed the acceptable limits of governmental authority fear these policies mask an effort by pro-environmental interests to coerce others into creating a world that serves their purely private interest in having a particular kind of relationship with the non-human world.[69] Thus, it would come as no surprise if some view the approach to rulemaking I am proposing—which seeks to protect the environmental conditions necessary for achieving a threshold level of each person's capabilities—as paternalistic and undemocratic. Specifically, these protections may simultaneously diminish one's individual freedom to determine the kind of relationship to nature that one chooses for one's self, and they may arbitrarily impose new and unchosen duties for citizens to relate to the environment in a particular way; for example, in a way that is excessively risk adverse or overly concerned with the environment for its own sake, independent of its contribution to human well-being.[70]

A similar concern is expressed by some who criticize Martha Nussbaum's capabilities approach to justice for seeking to protect a broad and abstract list of central capabilities that leaves too little room for citizens to define for themselves what a good human life involves. For instance, David Crocker argues that Nussbaum does not leave enough room for democratic processes to shape the list of capabilities warranting constitutional protection. Accordingly, he proposes a process of decision-making in which "fellow citizens deliberate over, decide on, and bind themselves to problem-solving policies that (most) all can accept."[71] For Crocker, Nussbaum's process of establishing the list of capabilities through "reasoned agreement on beliefs and values" does not sufficiently treat people as agents of their own lives, which "entails giving them a chance to be heard, and to be involved in collective evaluations and decisions."[72] While Nussbaum does share these goals, she also intends to characterize a generalized list of capabilities that could be the subject of a Rawlsian form of "overlapping consensus" that has the support

Sen (1999:53, 178). Consequently, some capabilities theorists argue that Nussbaum's capabilities approach is not equally committed to protecting individual agency. As I discuss further, later in this chapter and in Section 7.3 of Chapter 7, however, Nussbaum's theory of justice can also be applied in ways that manifest these same commitments while also recognizing and addressing the power dynamics that are prevalent in the politics that shape environmental policy.

[68] See Breyer (1993:11–19) for a discussion of this problem.

[69] See Guha and Martinez-Alier (1997:92–108), who make this case about the agenda of deep ecologists.

[70] See Richardson (2002:23–27) for a discussion of two general ways in which government action can implicate individual freedom.

[71] Crocker (2008:199). [72] See Peter (2003:24).

of people with diverse conceptions of what a good life involves. Furthermore, having developed her list over years of cross-cultural discussion with people in different countries and living in very different contexts, the abstract or vague content of the list of capabilities reflects a commitment to identifying broadly shared views on the conditions of a good human life.[73] Thus, I take the basic thrust behind Crocker's charge of paternalism to be that a more context-sensitive and easily revisited public discussion would produce a list of central capabilities that differs from the list Nussbaum advances as worthy of governmental protection as fundamental guarantees.[74]

In defense of Nussbaum's original list as the basis for a CARR, it is important to note that Nussbaum's capabilities approach to justice formulates the list of capabilities in a highly abstract way, with the stated intent of specifying them further in the context of local conditions and culture to which they are being made relevant. As she explains, "Indeed, part of the idea of the list is its *multiple realizability*: its members can be more concretely specified in accordance with local beliefs and circumstances. It is thus designed to leave room for a reasonable pluralism in specification."[75] In this respect, Nussbaum does allow for cultural sensitivity in the application of her theory, recognizing that "each of the capabilities may be concretely realized in a variety of different ways, in accordance with individual tastes, local circumstances, and traditions."[76] While she does not elaborate a fully participatory political process by which citizens might specify her list of capabilities, she does address how her approach to justice would walk the line between paternalism and cultural sensitivity in adjudicating legal decisions about both religion and the family.[77] In this discussion Nussbaum scrutinizes rules and rituals evolving from a particular culture or group of people based on whether or not they support the realization of a fully human and dignified life. Here she challenges the idea that values should be accepted and protected simply by virtue of having been collectively adopted or agreed upon. Because she views her project as establishing the basic commitments of a liberal constitutional democracy, she is more interested in securing a set of background conditions that put the exercise of basic political protections and freedoms fully within the reach of each citizen. For Nussbaum, protection of the central human capabilities should be understood as basic background conditions for constitutionally legitimate political institutions. These background conditions

[73] See Nussbaum (2000a:70–76).

[74] See Crocker (2008:195–196), Deneulin (2002), Alkire (2002:54). Because Amartya Sen's capability approach is intentionally underspecified, some rely on his ideas for the purpose of generating a distinct list of capabilities for each application of the capability approach. See Robeyns (2003:68–70). For Nussbaum's proposal and defense of why a universal list of capabilities is necessary, see Nussbaum (2000:34–106).

[75] Nussbaum (2000a:77). [76] Nussbaum (2000a:105).

[77] See Nussbaum (2000a:167–297).

are necessary – as preconditions – for the kind of political participation that critics such as Crocker advocate; they are also especially relevant to decision-making contexts in which the ideal conditions of democratic deliberation are not met. Administrative rulemaking in environmental policy is one such context because it is fraught with inequalities of political power that undermine conditions of genuine democratic deliberation, leaving all but the most highly homogenous and constrained forums subject to strategic abuse by the most powerful participants.

Thus, regardless of whether one is convinced by those who claim Nussbaum's theory shows insufficient respect for individuals' political agency, for the purpose of addressing environmental inequities that pervade regulatory rulemaking processes and outcomes, the substantive protections embodied in a capabilities approach to social and environmental justice have a particular advantage. That is, given the non-ideal form that democratized rulemaking in environmental policy actually takes, a CARR that starts with a commitment to protecting a highly abstract list of general capabilities ensures some set of environmental protections will be discussed and maintained amidst conditions of vast structural inequality that threaten to undermine citizens' equal participation and influence in regulatory decisions. Nussbaum's list of capabilities provides a good basis for designing policies that protect the environment because, when coupled the ecological meta-capability, it establishes a baseline substantive commitment to protecting the basic set of environmental conditions that will always be relevant to regulatory decisions, regardless of the power that special interests wield.[78] The environmental conditions a CARR protects can, of course, expand beyond providing for and protecting the list of capabilities that Nussbaum proposes, but in adopting a substantive list of capabilities as always relevant to policy decisions in the rulemaking context, proposed changes in environmental quality will always have to be considered in light of their impact on the environmental conditions necessary for protecting this substantive list of capabilities. This feature of the CARR that is adapted from Nussbaum's capabilities approach to justice is crucial in blocking the kind of strategic abuse that produces both procedural and substantive injustices.

However, the CARR should be understood as an approach to regulatory rulemaking that picks up the task of elaborating a process for further specifying the content of Nussbaum's capabilities and the ecological meta-capability, but in a way that is compatible with her commitment to the "multiple realizability" of the list of capabilities. Specifically, the CARR treats the abstractly characterized list of capabilities as the starting point in a method

[78] See Wolff and de-Shalit (2007) for an application of capabilities theory that adopts Nussbaum's list, but then adds to her list of capabilities for related purposes.

of application that incorporates an important role for citizens in specifying these capabilities so that the capabilities accurately characterize what matters to them. In the CARR, citizens must play a central role in further defining and/or expanding the central capabilities to which the environment is or should be relevant. The role of citizens in this capacity is crucial because only citizens can know the features of their lives that matter most, and, therefore, only citizens can identify the many ways in which changes in levels of environmental protection brought about by regulatory rules will improve or undermine their capabilities to do and achieve the things that make their lives meaningful.

In my community, for example, the asthma rate in local elementary schools is three times the national average and is therefore a serious health concern for children and their parents.[79] Consequently, in considering a policy that will change outdoor air quality, many members of my community would have good reason to specify Nussbaum's *bodily health* capability—which requires "Being able to have good health..."—to include *being able to avoid asthma.*[80] Likewise, if parents have responded to the asthma epidemic by not allowing their children to play outside during evening rush-hour traffic (i.e. when vehicle emissions are more likely to trigger an asthma attack), then members of my community might specify Nussbaum's *play* capability—which requires "Being able to laugh, to play, to enjoy recreational activities"—to include *being able to play outside at all times of day.* In this way, applying the CARR requires relating proposed changes in environmental quality, such as allowable levels of air pollution, to the real priorities and practices of citizens that policies changing air quality will affect.

An important concern in this context is that even when playing this central role in specifying the capabilities that matter, citizens within a community often will have to work with experts to identify the ways changes in environmental quality will support or undermine the relevant capabilities. For instance, if citizens do not know that outdoor air quality aggravates asthma, or that air quality is worse during rush hour, then, on their own, they will not succeed in identifying some of the reasons why a change in air quality matters, and therefore, why a policy improving air quality is valuable. In such contexts, a CARR cannot avoid the threat of experts exercising their specialized expertise in ways that disregard the interests of citizens; that is, in ways that favor experts' own ends, or the ends of those who wield political power, such as highly polluting industries. For instance, in either

[79] See Bethlehem Partnership for a Healthy Community (2008:15–17).

[80] As I have discussed in Section 6.4, assessing the level of protection necessary for securing this capability will require experts to learn from citizens about the actual sources of exposure in their lives.

context experts may be inclined to consistently underestimate the impact of environmental changes on people's capabilities.[81] This may be because well-intentioned experts simply do not know enough about people's actual lives (such as their pedestrian and recreational activities) to accurately assess the impact of environmental changes; alternatively, some experts may have a history of conducting research funded by polluters or other parties that have a financial stake in the outcome of a given policy decision.[82]

A CARR counteracts the potential for experts to mischaracterize the impact of changes in environmental quality on citizens' capabilities by narrowly defining and focusing the role of experts, and by establishing specific rules that allow citizens to hold experts accountable when they exercise their specialized expertise in ways that work against citizens' interests. First, in the CARR I am proposing, the role of experts should be limited to measuring the impact of changes in environmental quality on citizens' capabilities. This helps to confine the domain of experts' assessments to empirical matters concerning the relationship between environmental change and the relevant capabilities.[83] Specialized expertise will, of course, be necessary to help community members specify the relationship between capabilities and changes in environmental quality. To return to the previous example, if community members lack information about how poor outdoor air quality triggers asthma, then experts will need to provide information about why changes in air quality are related to people's capabilities for *bodily health* and *play*. More generally, the process for specifying the capabilities that are relevant to policy evaluation should be one that emerges from dialogue in which experts' understanding of the scientific dimensions of environmental change is brought to bear in helping members of a community identify specific capabilities to which those changes are relevant. Although this does leave room for experts to make scientific judgments that are not sensitive to the interests of citizens (e.g. underestimating the impact of environmental changes on people's capabilities), it need not entail leaving experts unaccountable if they betray citizens' trust.

Experts are not left unaccountable in a CARR because this approach to regulatory rulemaking has a second way of counteracting expert

[81] See Shrader-Frechette (1991:53–74) for a discussion of how experts' judgments and assumptions can pervade the highly technical process by which experts assess the probability of people's exposure to environmental risks. More generally, see Barke and Jenkins-Smith (1993) and Oreskes (2004) for a discussion of how the orientation of different disciplines within the sciences shapes scientists' perception of the risk and benefits of particular policies.

[82] See Oreskes and Conway (2010).

[83] Focusing experts' authority on questions of "empirical expertise" avoids at least some of the problems that may arise when experts exercise "substantive evaluative expertise." This latter kind of expertise, as Henry Richardson (2002:224) explains it, requires trusting experts to specify the goals legislation seeks to achieve (as opposed to the empirical impacts of environmental changes that I am proposing be the focus of expert authority).

mischaracterization of environmental impacts on people's capabilities. In addition to creating a space for citizens to take a substantive role in defining capabilities that matter to them, the CARR also formalizes mechanisms of expert accountability. Specifically, the CARR allows citizens to object to the views and actions of experts charged with considering the extent to which changes in environmental quality will impact their capabilities. This feature of the CARR is important and must occur in a process that also documents expert predictions about how environmental changes will impact people's capabilities, for this makes it is possible to identify experts that, over time, consistently underestimate how a proposed policy will undermine citizens' capabilities. In particular, when experts are found to consistently underestimate how a policy will undermine citizens' capabilities, a CARR allows communities to register and object to their analyses, and thereby prohibit unreliable experts from working on projects assessing such impacts, especially when the assessment involves changes in environmental quality impacting disadvantaged communities.[84] In this way, citizens' objections to expert analyses can trigger the involvement of new and different experts, bringing new participants into the rulemaking process, and increasing the range of expertise that is brought to bear on a proposed change in environmental protection. Likewise, while there is no reason to assume that experts who have conducted industry-funded research at one point in their careers will necessarily be predisposed to favor industry interests in their analyses of expected environmental impacts, the already documented trend of overstating compliance costs in cost–benefit analyses suggests that there are good reasons to track the institutional affiliations of experts and to document where their research money comes from.[85] An affiliation with industry, or the acceptance of industry funding, may not on its own be reason to prohibit an expert's assessment of environmental impacts on citizens' capabilities, but it could reasonably trigger an "expert alert" of the sort that subjects the analyses these experts produce to a higher level of scrutiny, or to higher standards of rigor in defending the assumptions underlying their predictions of risks to affected communities.[86]

[84] A more extreme approach would be to penalize those experts that consistently underestimate a policy's negative impact on people's capabilities. For instance, government agencies or government-contracted firms that employ those experts could be subjected to something like the "clawback provisions" that are increasingly popular in the financial investment industry. Clawback provisions allow investors to recover cash and stocks from executives receiving bonuses in cases where executives have misstated or otherwise overestimated financial assessments. See Schwartz (2008).

[85] McGarity and Ruttenberg (2002).

[86] These kinds of procedural constraints on expertise are similar to those some suggest for scrutinizing the developers involved in voluntary brownfield remediation. For example, Joel Eisen (1996) argues that because there is a potential for developers involved in these voluntary brownfield cleanup programs to engage in dishonest and deceitful behavior regarding their own environmental records and information about site contamination and remediation, state

To summarize: a CARR can constrain the significant influence experts have in shaping social goals when they implement environmental laws while simultaneously creating a place for citizens to define the environmental impacts that are most relevant to their lives. In a CARR, expertise is put at the service of what the impacted community defines as valuable. Because the capabilities that community members deem relevant must be included in the analysis, experts have less room to deny any relevant interests that conflict with their own political values, and they are less able to make errors of judgment that effectively omit consideration of policy impacts that matter to people. Furthermore, because a CARR requires looking at a whole list of distinct capabilities to which an environmental policy is relevant, experts must maintain a suitably broad focus in endeavoring to define the range of relevant policy impacts. But a CARR also narrows and focuses expertise because the task of experts in this context is to work with communities impacted by a policy to define and measure the relevant empirical relationships. The orientation of experts is thus always toward working with citizens to define the capabilities on which an environmental change will bear, and conducting the empirical research necessary for assessing those relationships. Under these conditions, if particular experts develop track records that reveal they are unworthy of citizens' trust, the CARR marks their analyses accordingly, thereby providing citizens with an opportunity to object to the role of those experts in characterizing citizens' interests and how environmental policy will impact citizens' lives. This creates incentives for empirical experts to be risk averse in their research and conclusions about how a policy will threaten citizens' interests. In these ways the CARR simultaneously lends weight to citizens' voices and limits the impact of untrustworthy experts on the policy process.

6.6 Conclusion: Socially Just Rulemaking as a Condition of Democracy

The model of decision-making I present in this chapter appeals to goals of both justice and democracy to create an iterative process of administrative rulemaking in which these goals function to draw on and limit the threat

governments should do more to track developers' performance. This would allow states to disqualify developers demonstrating a pattern of "persistent failure" in complying with remediation rules or otherwise engaging in legal and honest behavior about citizen exposure to site contamination. Eisen argues that disqualification of developers from program participation should not hinge on a faultless record. Instead, states could use "persistent failure" to characterize developers with a number of previous violations and with records otherwise demonstrating a pattern of egregious behavior.

of administrative expertise. Unlike existing economic and democratic approaches to rulemaking, the CARR prioritizes a substantive understanding of justice that protects the environmental conditions necessary to secure a threshold level of human capabilities over economic efficiency or democratic process. It holds forms of rulemaking that prioritize these latter ideals accountable to background conditions of justice as a basic political commitment. I have proposed that this form of rulemaking can help to navigate the tension between commitments to democratic procedure and the threat posed by administrative experts who arbitrarily exercise power in ways that conflict with the interests of citizens. Current democratic forms of rulemaking seek to overcome this conflict by bringing citizens into more collaborative, participatory, and devolved forms of rulemaking. While this may oblige experts to consider the views of citizens, it does not counteract the inequalities of resources and power that can ultimately determine administrative decisions. The CARR, in contrast, holds such decisions accountable to the standard of protecting the environmental conditions of human capabilities. For the sake of argument, I developed this CARR by assuming existing laws are sufficient for protecting the environmental conditions enabling human capabilities. The CARR can thus be understood as justifying the enforcement of existing standards of environmental quality with which there is significant non-compliance. A more thoroughgoing elaboration of the CARR would entail defending a stronger set of environmental protections than existing laws require. I have not developed that argument here because it would take significant space to cover the empirical literature justifying why stronger environmental protections are necessary for protecting a threshold level of human capabilities.

The ideal of social and environmental justice to which the CARR would hold administrative decisions about environmental policy accountable is already justified by the same sources of democratic legitimacy that authorize both democratic and economic approaches to regulatory rulemaking. However, I have nonetheless demonstrated how the application of a CARR can incorporate a commitment to public participation in democratic rulemaking by involving citizens in the process of specifying the capabilities to which environmental protection is relevant. While experts will inevitably be necessary for identifying how changes in environmental protection are relevant to the capabilities citizens value, I have proposed constraining experts' power to make judgments that are insensitive to citizens' interests by limiting their role to the provision of empirical expertise and by holding them accountable when they demonstrate a pattern of consistently underestimating the negative impact of environmental changes on citizens' capabilities. In this way, the CARR treats citizens as active agents in determining the relevance of the environment to the ends they personally or collectively value while constraining the potential of specialized expertise to shape policy outcomes in ways that disregard citizens' interests. Experts are charged with defining the environmental conditions necessary for ensuring citizens have a threshold level of the capabilities that citizens specify as valuable, and the CARR requires that policy decisions protect these environmental conditions as a basic political commitment that existing environmental laws have already established.

The CARR does hold regulatory rulemaking accountable to the political ideas that a capabilities approach to social and environmental justice embodies, and it should be understood as a way to secure conditions of democracy rather than as a threat to democratic deliberation. The success of genuinely democratic political processes requires citizens that are free from unhealthy environmental exposures and it requires decision-making contexts in which individuals and communities who have personally and culturally meaningful relationships to nature are fully recognized as political equals.[87] In particular, because some ways of life and cultural identities are intimately bound up with particular places, environmental resources, and the broader ecological systems that encompass them, extreme damage to these components of the environment effectively denies the validity of ways of life and practices to which the environment is intimately connected. In this sense, damage to the environment fails to treat such ways of life and cultural practices as alive, valid, and equal to the cultures and practices that society does protect; ultimately, this denies equal respect for persons, and, consequently, the ability of some individuals and groups to participate as equals in a political community.[88] As David Schlosberg has argued, such identity-based forms of disrespect and misrecognition can function to undermine one's sense of political membership, rendering political participation either unworthy of one's efforts or an unproductive use of one's time.[89]

Because a CARR requires protecting the environmental conditions that enable people's capabilities—including the capability for *political control over one's environment*—it should be understood as also protecting the conditions of effective political participation and the kind of political agency this requires. Furthermore, because environmental conditions are largely created by ecological relationships that humans neither understand nor control, the forms of misrecognition that environmental degradation can create

[87] Schlosberg (2007) does much to establish this latter link between environmental conditions and the kind of political recognition that is necessary for effective political participation.

[88] See Schlosberg (2007:26).

[89] At the level of individual psychology, such disrespect can deny one's self-worth and otherwise operate as a form of oppression that undermines the self-esteem one needs for effective participation in the political realm. At the institutional level, such disrespect manifests as a form of institutionalized subordination, wherein some individuals and cultural practices are treated as more worthy of political protection than others. See Schlosberg (2007:16–20).

are potentially non-recoverable. For this reason, environmental degradation poses a unique threat to effective political participation in highly deliberative forms of democratic politics. An approach to administrative rulemaking that protects the environmental conditions of political agency should be understood as a condition of democracy, not as a threat to it.

7

Conclusion: Climate Justice, Political Capabilities, and the Future of Human Fellowship

7.1 The Capabilities Approach and Environmental Policy

This book has explored and advanced capabilities theory as an alternative normative framework for evaluating and designing environmental policies. I have argued that the theory of well-being and the theory of justice emerging from the literature on human capabilities (Chapter 3) can respond to weaknesses in the economic approach to environmental policy assessment and decision-making (Chapter 2) that predominates in contemporary policymaking. These theories can also provide a basis for justifying policies that resolve tradeoffs among conflicting capabilities in a way that maintains at least a minimal level of capability protection for all people (Chapter 5). I have also explored the potential of these theories to address the weaknesses of efforts to reform policy design and implementation in line with democratic principles, particularly deliberative approaches to resource valuation (Chapter 4) and decentralized and collaborative approaches to administrative rulemaking (Chapter 6). The turn to deliberation and collaboration emphasizes inclusiveness as a response to problems arising in economic valuation and technocratic approaches to environmental policymaking. Problems of economic valuation concern the narrowness and reductive nature of economic methods for assessing the natural environment's instrumental value. Technocratic approaches to environmental problems are unsuccessful in addressing the distributive outcomes environmental policies can and do produce, as well as the potential for experts and political elites to disregard the interests and concerns of ordinary citizens, especially those who may be significantly burdened by environmental harms (see Chapters 1 and 2).

What emerges most prominently from my application of capabilities theory to contemporary environmental policy is the need to fully account for the relationship between the natural environment and ways of human living that contain genuine possibility and meaning. Capabilities theory offers a framework for valuing nature and reasoning about justice that can facilitate recognition of the environment's role in this capacity. Because this framework conceives of humans broadly—as having plural dimensions of well-being—it requires observation of the environment's role in enabling and realizing the conditions and activities that make up a minimally decent and flourishing human life. Equally important, capabilities theory, as I develop it, offers a framework for justifying environmental policies in terms of non-economic political values, such as social and environmental justice. It defines legitimate policy goals in terms of securing for all people some minimal level of environmental protection that makes it possible for them to share in the opportunities and advantages emerging from social and economic cooperation. The deliberative and collaborative approaches to resource valuation and administrative decision-making discussed in the preceding chapters do create an opportunity to introduce these and other non-economic values into public discussion and policy debate. However, I have argued that these approaches lack a set of substantive commitments to environmental protection that can prevent various pathologies and strategic abuses arising in the actual and non-ideal forms of democratic deliberation that continue to play out in various areas of environmental policy. The capabilities approach to social and environmental justice, by contrast, provides criteria for justifying environmental policies in the context of policy analysis and for designing environmental policies in the context of decentralized environmental management decisions. It provides criteria to evaluate democratic outcomes and to prevent the worst effects of procedural imperfections.

As I argue in Chapter 4, conceiving of human well-being in terms of people's capabilities recasts the environment's instrumental value from an object of choice that is attainable through market transactions, to a basis of human choice that is essential to a flourishing life. I propose conceiving of certain environmental conditions as an "ecological meta-capability" of humans in order to make explicit this shift in valuation. Having this meta-capability entails having the environmental resources and conditions that necessarily support the central human capabilities for people living now and in the future. When environmental conditions are understood as a meta-capability of humans, their instrumental value can be related to the various dimensions of human well-being that accurately define the lives people do and can lead. In this context, the environment's value may not be commensurable across different dimensions of well-being, but its value may be comparable *within* a category of well-being assessed across different people.

Full commensurability across *different* categories of well-being remains a proclaimed strength of the application of economic reasoning to all questions of environmental valuation, but the relevance of such commensurability diminishes when the goal of evaluation is not to determine the aggregate or net monetary benefits of an environmental protection policy. Specifically, if the goal is instead to determine whether and to what extent a policy promises to make people equally capable of attaining some threshold level of functioning across the various areas of well-being that make their lives meaningful, then the capabilities approach has clear advantages. Rather than defining how much people value resources in monetary terms, this approach to environmental valuation would define *how* environmental resources and conditions contribute to people's capabilities to live physically healthy lives of opportunity and meaning, and *who* is benefitting from policies that succeed or fail in protecting those resources and conditions.

With respect to policy justification, in Chapter 5 I advanced a theory of justice—the capabilities approach to social and environmental justice—that treats a policy as acceptable when it promises to protect each person's central capabilities at a threshold level. Applying this theory as a criterion of policy choice requires assessing the distributional impacts that policies produce and rejecting policies when they fail to meet the implied standards of social and environmental justice, that is, standards that require securing and protecting each person's capabilities at a threshold level, and the environmental conditions that are instrumental to achieving these threshold levels of protection. A form of policy assessment that relies on this criterion can help to identify patently unjust policies. However, I have argued that further theorizing is necessary for resolving the conflicts that arise when a policy is defined as unjust because it makes one person or group of people more capable, but only at the cost of pushing the capabilities of other people below the threshold that is worthy of protection. In particular, as a criterion for designing good policies rather than merely for identifying bad policies, I proposed adding "capability ceilings" to the account of capability thresholds advanced by Martha Nussbaum. Capability ceilings would establish maximum limits on the protection and provision of capabilities when these protections and provisions make it possible for people to engage in environmentally damaging activities that cause harm to others. Thus, capability ceilings are premised on a basic recognition that people's actions are connected through ecological processes, such that the exercise of one person's freedom of choice can often have environmental impacts that limit the choices of other people. Capability ceilings help to resolve conflicts in a way that equalizes these choice constraints, while protecting and providing each person's capabilities at a threshold level, and allowing for extensive and expansive protection of valuable capabilities when their realization will not cause harm to others.

Policies achieving these goals will protect and expand the capabilities of all people, not just a privileged subset.

Chapter 6 considered how this theoretical framework for evaluating and improving existing policies might be used to design procedures in the regulatory rulemaking context. In this context, administrative agencies translate the laws passed by elected officials into specific standards that determine conditions of environmental quality. Recent trends to develop and rely on democratic forms of rulemaking have the appeal of limiting the potential for experts in administrative agencies to make decisions that fail to reflect the preferences or interests of ordinary citizens. I argued, however, that these forms of rulemaking have significant limitations, not least because they often fail to meet the procedural ideals of deliberative democracy in which their political legitimacy is grounded. As a response to this problem, I proposed a "capabilities approach to regulatory rulemaking" (CARR) that will hold the outcomes of decentralized, collaborative, and participatory forms of rulemaking accountable to substantive standards of justice. I defended this approach to rulemaking as fully justifiable within the existing commitments of contemporary, democratically approved environmental law. Far from eschewing commitments to citizen participation, the CARR carves out a space for citizens to define the environmental relationships that matter to them, and a space for experts to assess the environmental conditions that must be protected in order to sustain those relationships. Although the CARR does not eliminate the potential for expert bias, it significantly narrows the role of experts, and I propose further constraints that hold experts formally accountable to exercising their judgment in a way that is worthy of the public's trust. With respect to this latter feature of the CARR, an expert's failure to protect citizens' interests would mark the relevant expert as unworthy of such authority and, therefore, as ineligible for further service in that capacity.

Overall, I have argued that, in the context of both environmental valuation and democratized rulemaking, we should understand a functioning natural environment as a condition from which human choice proceeds, and therefore, as a basis for both individual and collective choice. Adopting this view of the environment in deliberative approaches to monetary valuation of resources would entail valuing the natural environment as crucial to human capabilities, regardless of whether its value is reflected in people's subjective preferences. Adopting this understanding of the environment in democratized approaches to regulatory rulemaking would entail treating protection of the natural environment as a basic political commitment that is necessary for treating people as political equals in the rulemaking context. Therefore, just as Nussbaum's capabilities approach to justice protects a threshold level of each person's central capabilities as constitutional guarantees, my extension of her theory of justice treats the environmental dimensions of these capabilities as equally worthy of political protection. Thus, a central feature of the capabilities approach to policy evaluation and design that emerges from this theory is its assumption that a certain level of environmental protection is absolutely necessary, regardless of whether that level of protection is endorsed through purportedly democratic procedures. Policies or administrative rules that fail to protect the environment in a way that ensures each person's capabilities are secured at a threshold level are politically unjustifiable. This criterion of policy choice assumes that we should treat the ecological meta-capability discussed in Chapter 4 as a basic feature of the theory of social and environmental justice developed in Chapter 5, as worthy of the non-preference-based valuation discussed in Chapter 4, and as a constraint on the forms of democratized rulemaking discussed in Chapter 6.

Throughout my argument for why and how we should adapt and apply capabilities theory—and especially Martha Nussbaum's capabilities approach to justice—for the purpose of evaluating and designing contemporary environmental policies, I explicitly adopted a domestic point of view, focusing on policies issued at the national, state, regional, or local level in a liberal democratic society, and therefore, on environmental injustices occurring within a single liberal democratic state.[1] Of course, many of the most serious environmental threats facing humanity are global in nature. For instance, problems such as climate change, ocean acidification, and biodiversity loss, involve complex biogeochemical processes that extend across national borders. Policies addressing these problems call for a theory of justice that can be applied in a global context.[2] In closing, therefore, I will briefly highlight the relevance of the theory of social and environmental justice I developed in the preceding chapters to questions of international policy by considering the theory's implications for one of these urgent global environmental problems—climate change.

7.2 From Development Rights to Emissions Shares

A primary topic of debate in discussions of global climate justice is who should bear the burden of reducing greenhouse gas emissions to a level that will meet global targets established as necessary by the International Panel on Climate Change (IPCC), which is the body set up by the United Nations

[1] Nussbaum (2006:224–324) has already defended her capabilities approach as succeeding where other liberal theories of justice fail. Although she does not consider the implications of her theory for international policies addressing global environmental problems, this is a productive area for further development of the capabilities approach.

[2] See Rockstron et al. (2009) for a discussion of the global nature of these problems.

to review and provide direction on the most current climate science and the social and economic impacts of expected changes in climate. International treaties assigning these targets and allocating the permissible levels of emissions among different countries have lacked significant support from developing and developed countries alike, and for this reason have been relatively unsuccessful.[3] Emissions reductions pose a threat to the economic competitiveness of wealthy countries. For many poor countries, these reductions would stall or prevent a more rapid form of economic development, and therefore, constrain the emergence of economies that will bring substantial numbers of their citizens out of poverty. Amidst this apparent international stalemate, various theories and principles of justice have been advanced in proposals regarding how to allocate mitigation and adaptation costs.[4] While I do not intend to sketch a capabilities approach to global climate justice in the remaining pages of this chapter, I will consider some reasons why developing such an approach would be worthwhile.

A key feature of the capabilities approach to social and environmental justice I have advanced and applied is that it defines human well-being in terms of people's capabilities—what people are actually able to do and achieve. Although Nussbaum conceives of these capabilities as similar to individual rights that should be constitutionally guaranteed by governments, capabilities differ in offering precision and supplementation to the language of rights. In particular, understanding rights in terms of capabilities clarifies what is involved in securing a right.[5] To use one of Nussbaum's examples, while women in many nations have a formal right of political participation, they don't really have this right in the sense of having the relevant capability, "for they are secluded and threatened with violence should they leave the home."[6] Thus, although the list of central human capabilities Nussbaum advances does aim to protect and provide many of the same things secured by commonly protected constitutional freedoms (e.g. freedom of speech and religious practice), the distinct advantage of thinking about political guarantees in terms of capabilities is that the latter conceives of humans as always more or less constrained by internal traits and external conditions that determine the extent to which a given set of protections will be sufficient to achieve the goals those protections aim to put within a person's reach. This more precise and nuanced account of political guarantees that human capabilities provide is especially relevant to policies allocating greenhouse gas (GHG) emissions at the global level. Let us consider this point in the

[3] See Shue (2001) for a good overview of these issues.
[4] See Schlosberg (2012b) for an overview. [5] Nussbaum (1997b:293).
[6] Nussbaum (1997b:294).

context of one particularly well-elaborated theoretical approach to allocating GHG emissions.

In *Atmospheric Justice: A Political Theory of Climate Change*, Steve Vanderheiden builds on what is referred to as the "equal shares" approach to global climate justice, which holds that international legal agreements should meet global emissions reduction targets by assigning nations equal per capita emissions shares based solely on population.[7] In this approach to allocating emissions, the total amount of allowable carbon emissions is divided by the total world population so that every person gets an equal share of the capacity of the global atmospheric sink, and every nation gets to emit the sum of its total population multiplied by the equal per capita emissions share.[8] Vanderheiden's version of the equal shares approach applies exclusively to climate change mitigation targets and defines responsibilities for climate changes due to "luxury emissions" only occurring after the year of 1990.[9] Generally speaking, luxury emissions are emissions produced by energy use that allows people to "enjoy aspects of the good life that go beyond mere survival."[10] These emissions differ from "survival emissions," which are emissions that allow people to meet their basic needs. Vanderheiden recognizes that survival emissions are likely to vary greatly within and among nations because equal emissions among differently situated people will not translate into equal opportunities to survive. Therefore, the version of the equal shares approach to global climate justice he advances excludes survival emissions.

With respect to luxury emissions, Vanderheiden argues that *roughly* equal emissions allowances are necessary if people in poor countries are going to be able to go through a process of industrialization that allows for broader human development and quality-of-life improvements. Clearly, differences in people's ability to translate a share of carbon into welfare improvements will differ greatly with respect to survival emissions. The same variations among people may determine whether they can translate additional carbon emissions into additional further quality-of-life improvements. Consequently, Vanderheiden's "modified" equal shares approach to allocating climate emissions errs on the side of minimizing justified inequalities in emissions shares. Specifically, he argues that total inequality in per capita emissions shares should be kept relatively small, especially where "luxury emissions" are concerned.[11] The

[7] Vanderheiden (2008:225).
[8] See Jamieson (2001) and Singer (2004).
[9] Vanderheiden (2008:231).
[10] Vanderheiden (2008:108).
[11] As I will discuss further later in this chapter, this inclination toward rough equality in emissions shares stems from the atmosphere's limited and finite capacity to absorb GHG emissions, which means that unequal emissions allocations will be zero-sum, such that higher emissions caps for some will mean lower emissions caps for others. As Vanderheiden (2008:225) notes, the danger is that allowing for inequality in per capita luxury emissions shares may ultimately lead to allocations that allow for higher luxury emissions shares in wealthy countries because of infrastructural decisions that are no fault of the present generation. While citizens born into

consequences of this approach to assigning emission allowances on an equal per capita basis while attaining the targeted global reductions is that the individual shares of allowable per capita emissions will be lower than the amount of emissions many people living in developed countries currently produce. Therefore, Vanderheiden's modified equal shares approach to global climate justice would put constraints on the permissible emissions of people in developed countries so that underdeveloped countries are able to build economies that provide more than mere survival to their citizens.[12] As David Schlosberg notes, this commitment to allocating equal per capita shares for luxury emissions aligns Vanderheiden with those who argue that currently underdeveloped countries should not be punished by emissions limits that are necessary to address climate problems caused by (developed) countries that have already gone through the process of industrialization.[13]

For the purpose of formally instantiating this modified equal per capita shares approach at the level of international policy, Vanderheiden turns to Henry Shue's defense of basic (human) rights, which he uses to characterize the content of what must be protected in the allocation of roughly equal shares of luxury emissions.[14] Shue's work is important in breaking down the distinction between security rights, which are commonly treated as fundamental and requiring mere constraints on action, and broader social and economic rights, which are commonly treated as less fundamental and as requiring the positive provision of goods. In place of this typology of rights, Shue proposes a "basic/non-basic" distinction of rights. He argues that the basic rights protecting things essential to people's survival and safeguarding activities instrumental to human flourishing should be prioritized.[15] Vanderheiden uses this characterization of rights to treat social and economic development activities in poor countries that are associated with luxury emissions as part of a person's basic rights, and therefore as a priority in matters of policy. Following Shue, he then argues that the claims (of people in underdeveloped countries) on limited atmospheric space for emissions shares associated with social and economic issues are more compelling than claims "made by or on behalf of those residents of industrialized nations whose desire to continue producing excessive luxury emissions entails that development restrictions be imposed on poor countries."[16] Thus, at the level of application, Vanderheiden's approach to atmospheric justice would allocate shares

those countries may not be responsible for those emissions, because atmospheric absorptive capacity is finite, allowing for higher luxury emissions shares may effectively and unjustifiably require reductions in luxury emissions shares in other, poorer countries.

[12] Vanderheiden (2008:108, 249).

[13] See Schlosberg (2012b:447–448) for a discussion on the "development rights" approach to global climate policy.

[14] See Shue (1980).

[15] See Vanderheiden (2008:244–245).

[16] Vanderheiden (2008:252).

of emissions to meet the survival needs of all people and the social and economic development rights of people in poor nations. His approach would then cut back on the emissions of people in wealthy countries by whatever amount is necessary to free up the atmospheric absorptive space needed to protect the social and economic development rights of people in poor countries. In this way, Shue's characterization of individual rights provides a recognized legal mechanism for instantiating roughly equal per capita luxury emissions shares as a matter of international policy.

While the rights-based language provides a certain recognition and status to claims on limited atmospheric space, its weakness is that it does not provide a nuanced and substantive account of what components of a person's well-being these rights to luxury emissions are meant to protect and provide. Consequently, it does not get us very far in defining the quantity of emissions that must be made available to people in poor countries and freed up by people in rich countries.[17] The metrics and theory defining a capabilities approach to social and environmental justice is valuable for precisely this purpose. This approach to justice provides an account of well-being that can be used to specify outcomes or quality-of-life improvements that luxury emissions should make available to people. For instance, the generalized list of central human capabilities, especially when expanded to include the ecological meta-capability, which accounts for the environmental conditions of human well-being, can add conceptual clarity, as well as nuance and precision to the discussion of whether a given allocation of carbon emissions in a particular place enables people to function in socially and economically relevant ways. In this context, the list of central human capabilities can be used as a starting point for identifying the dimensions of well-being that luxury emissions are intended to protect and provide, at what level, and for whom.

Because the capabilities approach to social and environmental justice I proposed adopts a broad account of human well-being, it would define allowable per capita luxury emissions in reference to development thresholds across a range of variables that define citizens' well-being. Minimally, this would entail the use of variables such as those included in the Human Multidimensional Poverty Index, the Better Life Index, or the Social Vulnerability Index to characterize the goals that luxury emissions must enable citizens to meet.[18]

[17] Schlosberg (2012b:449).

[18] Schlosberg (2012b:449). The Multidimensional Poverty Index uses ten indicators to define the three primary dimensions of well-being measured in the Human Development Index, which are health, education, and standard of living. See <http://hdr.undp.org/en/statistics/mpi/>. The Organisation for Economic Co-operation and Development (OECD) uses the Better Life Index, which draws on 24 indicators to define 11 dimensions of well-being, ranging from health and education, to local environment and satisfaction with life, to income. See <http://www.oecd-betterlifeindex.org/>. The Social Vulnerability Index (SoVI®) 2006-10 synthesizes 30 socioeconomic variables that make communities more vulnerable to hazards, showing uneven capacity

Or, alternatively, an approach that aligns even more closely with my development of the capabilities approach is David Schlosberg's application of capabilities theory to climate adaptation policies. As I discuss further later in this chapter, Schlosberg proposes a physical mapping of vulnerabilities defined by people who are suffering the consequences of climate change, which could then be used to estimate the emissions necessary to protect the forms of social and economic development that enable people to live meaningful and flourishing lives amidst changing climate conditions.[19] Thus, whether selecting or further defining the indicators of well-being that will be used to define the quantity of permissible luxury emissions, the basic account of well-being and a good human life explicit in a capabilities approach to social and environmental justice is ripe for application to questions of global climate justice. It articulates substantive criteria that can guide, further define, and/or measure whether a proposed per capita share of luxury emissions will achieve specific social and economic development goals embodied in climate policies consistent with a global vision of justice.

7.3 From Political Participation to Political Capabilities

The capabilities approach to social and environmental justice can also inform the development of a procedural account of global climate justice. Schlosberg has already initiated development of the approach in this area by taking up the question of what it means to make people politically capable under conditions of global climate change, given that these conditions are already producing extreme vulnerability and loss to significant portions of the world's population.[20] To address policies directed toward human adaptation to climate, Schlosberg builds on his previous research theorizing a procedural account of capabilities justice, which addresses the role of misrecognition or malrecognition in producing conditions of substantive environmental injustice.[21] In this early work, Schlosberg draws on authors such as Iris Marion Young and Nancy Fraser, who call for altering institutional processes and decision-making contexts to better prevent forms of cultural and political exclusion. Such exclusions are problematized for producing vulnerability and economic inequality, as well as forms of cultural domination, non-recognition, and disrespect that subordinate people as subjects of social or political status. In moving capabilities justice beyond its common focus on "ideal" theories of justice, Schlosberg argues that theorizing and

for preparedness and response among different communities in the USA. See <http://webra.cas.sc.edu/hvri/>.

[19] Schlosberg (2012b:457–458). [20] Schlosberg (2012b). [21] Schlosberg (2007).

developing inclusive forms of political participation is crucial for improving the theory and practice of climate adaptation policies.

When establishing the importance of political participation and agency in a capabilities approach to social justice, Schlosberg and others have tended to emphasize the importance of Amartya Sen's "capability approach" to justice.[22] However, a recognition-based theory of procedural justice can provide significant content and structure for specifying or operationalizing Nussbaum's tenth capability: the capability for *political control over one's environment*. This capability requires "Being able to participate effectively in political choices that govern one's life; having the right of political participation, protections of free speech and association."[23] As such, the tenth capability does establish a general commitment to individual political participation and power. Thus, Schlosberg's account of procedural justice in climate adaptation policy can help to substantiate what it might mean in this policy context to have capabilities to participate effectively in political choices and to have the right to political participation. For instance, to return to the topic of roughly equal per capita emission shares, effective political participation in decisions about the allocation of luxury emissions may require a decision-making process that brings attention to the experiences of those who are especially vulnerable to climate change, and to "the way their status is, in part, socially, politically, and economically constructed."[24] Likewise, this decision-making process would also move attention to the instrumental importance of ecological processes in vulnerable communities; and specifically, to the way these processes are instrumental to meeting the basic needs of people as individuals and as members of distinct cultural communities. In this way, Schlosberg's procedural account of capabilities justice could be used to elaborate the content of effective political participation as a component of the capability for *political control over one's environment*. As I have characterized this content here, protecting and securing this capability requires recognition of the environment's role in making it possible for individuals to function both as individuals, and as members of a unique community—who define and experience themselves as a community.[25]

Schlosberg's work on climate adaptation also points toward important structural components of people's political capabilities in the context of

[22] See Chapter 3, Section 3.2.2. These critics argue that Sen is less prone than Nussbaum to advance particularly Western and liberal political values in defining the list of central human capabilities that make life worthy of human dignity and meaning. According to these arguments, a genuine commitment to political agency necessarily precludes the articulation and instantiation of a single list of valuable human capabilities, regardless of how "thick" and "vague" Nussbaum tries to make it. See Sen (2004, 2005:157–158) addressing these concerns himself; see Nussbaum (2003) for a response.

[23] See Nussbaum (2000a:80).

[24] Schlosberg (2012b:452).

[25] See Schlosberg (2012b:455; 2007:16–26) and Schlosberg and Carruthers (2010).

localized forms of political participation. Following Neil Adger, he argues that a general right to political participation is not meaningful unless it entails processes that give communities "some locus of control over their destinies as part of a recognition of identity and place."[26] This suggests that we should understand effective participation in policy deliberation to entail that individuals and/or communities have some concrete political power over decisions, and not just a general right to participate, which can result in being effectively ignored. For instance, much like the administrative rulemaking process I proposed in Chapter 6, effective political participation in climate adaptation policy might require that citizens themselves define the capabilities that are essential to meeting the basic goals of human development that supersede people's basic survival needs. The important point, as Schlosberg notes, is that vulnerability to climate change, and hence the share of per capita emissions necessary for both basic survival and further human development, cannot be defined in a top-down, expert-driven way: "Communities need to be thoroughly involved in both the mapping of their own vulnerabilities and the design of adaptation policies."[27] For this purpose, the accountability mechanisms I proposed to focus and constrain the role of scientific expertise in the administrative rulemaking context might be productively combined with Schlosberg's procedural account of capabilities justice to define what the capability for *political control over one's environment* means in the context of policies seeking to help specific communities adapt to global climate change.

7.4 From Mutual Advantage to Global Fellowship

Advancing a global version of the capabilities approach to social and environmental justice developed in the preceding chapters to address problems of climate change also has advantages worthy of further exploration at a more theoretical level. The approach to justice I advanced is grounded in Martha Nussbaum's non-procedural system of political justification. As I discussed in Chapter 5, Nussbaum offers an outcome-oriented system of justification that entails reasoning back and forth between our moral intuitions and the theories and principles that bear on and organize these intuitions, in order to arrive at a list of central human capabilities that are worthy of governmental protection.[28] Furthermore, she defends this list as composed of capabilities that are the subject of an "overlapping consensus" among people who may hold otherwise conflicting views of what a good human life involves. Thus, although she is committed to a Rawlsian form of "political liberalism"

[26] Schlosberg (2012b:452) and Adger et al. (2011). [27] Schlosberg (2012b:458).
[28] See Nussbaum (2006:352, 2000a:151).

that allows for the coexistence of people with diverse beliefs and goals, she does not justify protection of her list of capabilities as something that people would choose in the particular (hypothetical) social contract situation that Rawls envisions. Nussbaum's argument against the social contract justification for political principles that will guide relationships among states at the international level has to do with the "Humean circumstances of justice" that Rawls assumes when developing his theory of justice as relevant to a single society. Nussbaum views these circumstances as problematic from the start because they assume a setting for the contract in which parties who are roughly equal seek to satisfy similar interests under conditions of moderate scarcity and limited benevolence or mutual disinterest. While Rawls does not seek to generate principles of justice for application at the international level from these circumstances, Nussbaum argues that the theories offered by other scholars who develop his theory for this purpose remain similarly deficient.

For instance, Vanderheiden's equal shares approach to allocating carbon emissions builds on Charles Beitz's theory of global justice, which applies Rawls's account of a hypothetical social contract at the global level. Beitz's version of this contract does aim to diminish inequalities among the contracting parties that Rawls fails to recognize, but Nussbaum argues that this entails a more meaningful departure from Rawls than Beitz admits. As she explains, a more sufficient departure from Rawls's contract situation would entail "including from the start all who are currently unequal in power...[and] admitting from the start that the point of the contract is not, and cannot be, mutual advantage among 'rough equals.'"[29] Nussbaum's approach to global justice differs in that it starts with a substantive account of what a good human life entails and treats duties to ensure each person has the opportunity to live a good life as a matter of collective obligation, regardless of one's country of residence. The list of central human capabilities that define the substantive content of what is owed to each person operates as a freestanding conception of justice, but one that has far-reaching, cross-cultural power in commanding a broad consensus about the components of a good life.[30] Instead of assuming a hypothetical contract in which people cooperate for mutual advantage, Nussbaum regards cooperation at the global level that protects the capabilities of citizens living in asymmetrically poor countries as emerging from fellowship rather than self-interest. As beings who recognize that "a central part of our own good...is to produce, and live in, a world that is morally decent," all of us are "under a collective obligation to find ways of living and cooperating together so that all human

[29] Nussbaum (2006: 270). [30] See Chapter 3, Section 3.2.2.

beings have decent lives."[31] The importance of being able to live together in a non-instrumental ways is also embodied in the capabilities for *affiliation*, *emotions*, and *other species*, and reflects a basic commitment in Nussbaum's capabilities approach to making people capable of having relationships to the community of humans and non-humans in which people can treat these others as ends in themselves.

The apparent strength of Beitz's theory for Vanderheiden's development of a globally just allocation of carbon emissions is Beitz's principle of natural resource redistribution. Beitz argues that a hypothetical Rawlsian social contract at the international level would produce a principle of justice for allocating globally available natural resources that gives "each national society a fair chance to develop just political institutions and an economy capable of satisfying its members' basic needs."[32] Vanderheiden draws on Beitz's defense of this principle to characterize the earth's atmospheric capacity as a shared natural resource that is also subject to global redistribution. However, Vanderheiden rejects the implied allocation of this resource according to a global Rawlsian difference principle that would allow for an unequal allocation of the atmospheric absorptive capacity if it were to benefit the "least advantaged" in the global context. For Vanderheiden, the problem with Beitz's development of a global difference principle is not the flawed Humean conditions defining the hypothetical social contract, but rather the finite character of this particular natural resource.[33] Unlike other "primary goods" that Rawls subjects to distribution according to the difference principle, such as wealth and income, the atmosphere's absorptive capacity "cannot be increased by allowances for unequal shares."[34] Consequently, allocation of the atmosphere's absorptive capacity is "zero-sum": allocating more emissions to some people necessarily requires allocating less emissions to others.[35] Therefore, as I discussed earlier in this chapter, Vanderheiden argues that allocation of this global atmospheric resource must be on an equal per capita basis, and set at a level that ensures everyone the opportunity to both survive and pursue opportunities that come with basic social and economic development.

This allocation that Vanderheiden proposes is similar to the allocation required by treating a stable climate system as part of the ecological meta-capability in the capabilities approach to social and environmental justice developed in the preceding chapters of this book, and elsewhere.[36] If a stable climate is in fact "absolutely vital for the continuance of life on this planet and is instrumental to human flourishing," then it should be allocated in a way that makes people equally capable of surviving and living a

31 Nussbaum (2006:274 and 280, respectively). 32 Beitz (1979:292).
33 Vanderheiden (2008:79). 34 Vanderheiden (2008:79).
35 Vanderheiden (2008:108). 36 See Holland (2012).

minimally decent human life. Vanderheiden arrives at this position by drawing on Beitz's defense of these capabilities as "basic rights." Yet, given the problematic grounding of Vanderheiden's equal shares approach to allocating the atmosphere in Beitz's Rawlsian-based global theory of justice, adopting the capabilities approach to social and environmental justice may be a better way to bridge the gap between ideal and abstract notions of justice on the one hand, and the concrete needs of crafting climate policy on the other.[37] This approach to atmospheric justice emerges from a belief in human fellowship rather than self-interest, and as I have argued earlier in this chapter, also has the advantage of providing a substantive theory of well-being that can be operationalized by existing indicators, and a procedural account of justice that requires a politics of recognition, more genuine equality of political power, and constraints on technocratic expertise. Grounding our cross-border obligations in the ideal of human fellowship, this approach to justice advances is especially important in the global context because at present our causal responsibility for climate change forecloses the possibility of living in non-instrumental relationships to people in distant places. A commitment to human fellowship provides a stronger and more compelling source of motivation for collective political action at the international level than contractarian appeals to mutual advantage or cosmopolitan appeals to a common humanity.

[37] See Schlosberg (2012b:446) for a related point.

APPENDIX

Martha Nussbaum's List of Central Human Functional Capabilities

1. ***Life.*** Being able to live to the end of a human life of normal length, not dying prematurely, or before one's life is so reduced as to be not worth living.
2. ***Bodily health.*** Being able to have good health, including reproductive health; to be adequately nourished; to have adequate shelter.
3. ***Bodily integrity.*** Being able to move freely from place to place; having one's bodily boundaries treated as sovereign, that is, being able to be secure against assault, including sexual assault, child sexual abuse, and domestic violence; having opportunities for sexual satisfaction and for choice in matters of reproduction.
4. ***Senses, imagination, and thought.*** Being able to use the senses, to imagine, think, and reason—and to do these things in a "truly human" way, a way informed and cultivated by an adequate education, including, but by no means limited to, literacy and basic mathematical and scientific training. Being able to use imagination and thought in connection with experiencing and producing self-expressive works and events of one's own choice, religious, literary, musical, and so forth. Being able to use one's mind in ways protected by guarantees of freedom of expression with respect to both political and artistic speech and freedom of religious exercise. Being able to search for the ultimate meaning of life in one's own way. Being able to have pleasurable experiences, and to avoid non-necessary pain.
5. ***Emotions.*** Being able to have attachments to things and people outside ourselves; to love those who love and care for us, to grieve at their absence; in general, to love, to grieve, to experience longing, gratitude, and justified anger. Not having one's emotional development blighted by overwhelming fear and anxiety or by traumatic events of abuse or neglect. (Supporting this capability means supporting forms of human association that can be shown to be crucial in their development.)

See Nussbaum (2000:78–80, 2006:76–78).

6. ***Practical reason.*** Being able to form a conception of the good and to engage in critical reflection about the planning of one's life. (This entails protection for the liberty of conscience.)
7. ***Affiliation.*** (A) Being able to live with and toward others, to recognize and show concern for other human beings, to engage in various forms of social interaction; to be able to imagine the situation of another and to have compassion for that situation; to have the capability for both justice and friendship. (Protecting this capability means protecting institutions that constitute and nourish such forms of affiliation, and also protecting the freedom of assembly and political speech.) (B) Having the social bases of self-respect and non-humiliation; being able to be treated as a dignified being whose worth is equal to that of others. This entails, at a minimum, protections against discrimination on the basis of race, sex, sexual orientation, religion, caste, ethnicity, or national origin. In work, being able to work as a human being, exercising practical reason, and entering into meaningful relationships of mutual recognition with other workers.
8. ***Other species.*** Being able to live with concern for and in relation to animals, plants, and the world of nature.
9. ***Play.*** Being able to laugh, to play, to enjoy recreational activities.
10. ***Control over one's environment.*** (A) *Political.* Being able to participate effectively in political choices that govern one's life; having the right of political participation, protections of free speech and association. (B) *Material.* Being able to hold property (both land and moveable goods), not just formally but in terms of real opportunity; having property rights on an equal basis with others; having the right to seek employment on an equal basis with others; having the freedom from unwarranted search and seizure.

Bibliography

Ackerman, Bruce. 1991. *We the People, Foundations*. Cambridge, MA: Harvard University Press.

Ackerman, Bruce and Lisa Heinzerling. 2004. *On Knowing the Price of Everything and the Value of Nothing*. New York: The New Press.

Adger, Neil, Jon Barnett, F. S. Chapin III, and Heidi Ellemor. 2011. "This Must Be the Place: Underrepresentation of Identity and Meaning in Climate Change Decision-Making." *Global Environmental Politics* 11/2:1–25.

Agarwal, Bina. 1994. "Gender and Command over Property: A Critical Gap in Economic Analysis and Policy in South Asia." *World Development* 22/10:1455–1478.

Aldred, Jonathan. 1997. "Existence Value, Moral Commitments and In-Kind Valuation." In John Foster (ed.), *Valuing Nature? Economics, Ethics and Environment*. London: Routledge, pp. 155–169.

Alkire, Sabina. 2002. *Valuing Freedoms: Sen's Capability Approach and Poverty Reduction*. New York: Oxford University Press.

Alliance for the Chesapeake Bay. 2004. "Chesapeake Bay Environmental Justice Focus Groups: A Summary of Findings and Recommendations for the Chesapeake Bay Environmental Justice Task Force." Richmond, VA: Alliance for the Chesapeake Bay Richmond, pp. 1–34. Available at: <http://www.docstoc.com/docs/37673764/Chesapeake-Bay-Environmental-Justice-Focus-Groups-A-Summary-of> (accessed May 5, 2014).

Alvarez-Farizono, Begnona and Nick Hanley. 2006. "Improving the Process of Valuing Non-Market Benefits: Combining Citizens' Juries with Choice Modeling." *Land Economics* 82/3:465–478.

Amy, Douglas. 1990. "Environmental Dispute Resolution: The Promise and the Pitfalls." In Norman Vig and Michael Kraft (eds.), *Environmental Policy in the 1990s*. Washington, DC: CQ Press, pp. 211–234.

Anderson, Charles. 1992. "The Place of Principles in Policy Analysis." In John Martin Gilroy and Maurice Wade (eds.), *The Moral Dimensions of Public Policy Choice: Beyond the Market Paradigm*. Pittsburgh, PA: Pittsburg University Press, pp. 387–409.

Anderson, Elizabeth. 1993. *Value in Ethics and Economics*. Cambridge, MA: Harvard University Press.

Anderson, Elizabeth. 2003. "Sen, Ethics, and Democracy." *Feminist Economics* 9/2–3:239–261.

Applegate, John. 1998. "Beyond the Usual Suspects: The Use of Citizen Advisory Boards in Environmental Decision Making." *Indiana Law Journal* 73:903–957.

Arrow, Kenneth, Robert Solow, Paul R. Portney, et al. 1993. "Report of the NOAA Panel on Contingent Valuation." *Federal Register* 58:4601–4614.

Arrow, Kenneth, Bert Bolin, Robert Costanza, et al. 1995. "Economic Growth, Carrying Capacity, and the Environment." *Science* 268/5210:520–521.

Barke, Richard and Hank Jenkins-Smith. 1993. "Political and Scientific Experts: Scientists, Risk Perception, and Nuclear Waste Policy." *Journal of Risk Analysis* 13/4:425–439.

Barnett, Harold and Chandler Morse. 1963. *Scarcity and Growth: The Economics of Natural Resource Availability*. Baltimore, MD: Johns Hopkins University Press.

Baumgartner, Frank and Bryan Jones. 1993. *Agendas and Instability in American Politics*. Chicago: University of Chicago Press.

Been, Vicki. 1992. "What's Fairness Got To Do With It? Environmental Justice and the Siting Of Locally Undesirable Land Uses." *Cornell Law Review* 78:1001–1085.

Beierle, Thomas and Rebecca Long. 1999. "Chilling Collaboration: The Federal Advisory Committee Act and Stakeholder Involvement in Environmental Decision Making." *Environmental Law Reporter* 29(July 10):399–410.

Beitz, Charles. 1979. *Political Theory and International Relations*. Princeton, NJ: Princeton University Press.

Bell, Derick. 2004. "Environmental Justice and Rawls' Difference Principle." *Environmental Ethics* 26/3:287–306.

Benhabib, Seyla. 1992. *Situating the Self: Gender, Community, and Postmodernism in Contemporary Ethics*. Cambridge: Polity.

Benhabib, Seyla. 1996. "Toward a Deliberative Model of Democratic Legitimacy." In Seyla Benhabib (ed.), *Democracy and Difference*. Princeton, NJ: Princeton University Press, pp. 67–94.

Bentham, J. [1789] 1970. *Introduction to the Principles of Morals and Legislation*. London: Methuen.

Bessette, William. 1992. *The Mild Voice of Reason*. Chicago: University of Chicago Press.

Bethlehem Partnership for a Healthy Community. 2008. *Annual Report: July 2007–June 2008*. Bethlehem, PA: Bethlehem Partnership for a Healthy Community.

Boardman, Anthony, David Greenberg, Aiden Vining, and David Weimer. 2001. *Cost-Benefit Analysis: Concepts and Practice* (2nd ed.). Englewood Cliffs, NJ: Prentice Hall.

Brandt, Richard. 1979. *A Theory of the Good and the Right*. Oxford: Oxford University Press.

Brauman, Kate, Gretchen Daily, T. Ka'eo Duarte, and Harold Mooney. 2007. "The Value of Ecosystem Services: An Overview Highlighting Hydrologic Services." *Annual Review of Environment and Resources* 32:67–98.

Breyer, Stephen. 1993. *Breaking the Vicious Circle: Toward Effective Risk Regulation*. Cambridge, MA: Harvard University Press.

Bromley, Daniel. 1990. "The Ideology of Efficiency: Searching for a Theory of Policy Analysis." *Journal of Environmental Economics and Management* 19:86–107.

Bromley, Daniel and Jouni Paavola. 2002. *Economics, Ethics, and Environmental Policy: Contested Choices*. Oxford: Blackwell Publishers.

Brooks, Richard O., Ross Jones, and Ross A. Virginia. 2002. *Law and Ecology: The Rise of the Ecosystem Regime*. Burlington, VT: Ashgate.

Brown, Thomas, George Peterson, and Bruce Tonn.1995. "The Values Jury to Aid Natural Resource Decisions." *Land Economics* 71/2:254–255.

Buchanan, James. 1959. "Positive Economics, Welfare Economics, and Political Economy." *Journal of Law and Economics* 2:124–138.

Bullard, Robert. 1993. *Confronting Environmental Racism: Voices from the Grassroots*. Boston, MA: South End Press.

Bullard, Robert. 1994. *Unequal Protection: Environmental Justice and Communities of Color*. San Francisco, CA: Sierra Club Books.

Bullard, Robert and Beverly Hendrix Wright. 1986. "The Politics of Pollution: Implications for the Black Community." *Phylon* 47:71–78.

Bullard, Robert, Glenn Johnson, and Angel Torres. 2011. *Environmental Health and Racial Equity in the United States: Building Environmentally Just, Sustainable, and Livable Communities*. Washington, DC: American Public Health Association.

Callicott, Baird. 1989. *In Defense of the Land Ethic: Essays in Environmental Philosophy*. Albany, NY: State University of New York Press.

Callicott, Baird. 1999. *Beyond the Land Ethic: More Essays in Environmental Philosophy*. Albany, NY: State University of New York Press.

Cannavo, Peter. 2007. *The Working Landscape: Founding, Preservation, and the Politics of Place*. Cambridge, MA: MIT Press.

Carpenter, David and Rick Nevin. 2010. "Environmental Causes of Violence." *Physiology and Behavior* 99/2:260–268.

Carpenter, S., D. Ludwid, and W. A. Brock. 1999. "Management of Eutrophication for Lakes Subject to Potentially Irreversible Change." *Ecological Applications* 9/3:751–771.

Chang, Ruth (ed.). 1997. *Incommensurability, Incomparability, and Practical Reason*. Cambridge, MA: Harvard University Press.

Chichilnisky, Graciela and Geoffrey Heal. 1998. "Economic Returns from the Biosphere." *Nature* 391:629–630.

Chiesura, Anna and Rudolf de Groot. 2003. "Critical Natural Capital: A Socio-Cultural Perspective." *Ecological Economics* 44/2–3:219–231.

Christiano, Thomas. 2005. "Democracy and Bureaucracy." *Philosophy and Phenomenological Research* 71/1:211–217.

Christy, Francis and Neal Potter. 1962. *Trends in Natural Resource Commodity Statistics of Prices, Output, Consumptions, Foreign Trade and Employment in the United States, 1860–1957*. Baltimore, MD: John Hopkins University Press.

Ciriacy-Wantrup, Siegfried V. 1947. "Capital Returns from Soil Conservation Practices." *Journal of Farm Economics* 29:1181–1196.

Clinton, William J. 1994. "Federal Actions to Address Environmental Justice in Minority Populations and Low Income Populations," Executive Order 12,898, 11 February. Available at: <http://www.epa.gov/fedrgstr/eo/eo12898.pdf> (accessed April 28, 2014).

Coglianese, Cary. 2001. "Is Consensus an Appropriate Basis for Regulatory Policy?" In Eric Orts and Kurt Deketelaere (eds.), *Environmental Contracts: Comparative Approaches to Regulatory Innovation in the United States and Europe*. Cambridge, MA: Kluwer Law International, pp. 93–113.

Cohen, S. I. 2001. *Microeconomic Policy*. London: Routledge.

Cole, Luke and Sheila Foster. 2001. *From the Ground Up: Environmental Racism and the Rise of the Environmental Justice Movement*. New York: New York University Press.

Constanza, Robert (ed.). 1997. *An Introduction to Ecological Economics*. Boca Raton, FL: St. Lucie Press.

Constanza, Robert and Ralph D'Arge. 1997. "The Value of the World's Ecosystem Services and Natural Capital." *Nature* 387(May 15):253–260.

Coughlin, S. P. 1988. "Sport and the Asthmatic Child: A Study of Exercise-Induced Asthma and the Resultant Handicap." *Journal of the Royal College of General Practitioners* 38(June):253–255.

Cowling, Richard, Benis Egoh, Andrew Knight, et al. 2008. "An Operational Model for Mainstreaming Ecosystem Services." *Proceedings of the National Academy of Sciences* 105/28:9483–9488.

Crocker, David. 1992. "Functioning and Capability: The Foundations of Sen's and Nussbaum's Development Ethic." *Political Theory* 20/4:584–612.

Crocker, David. 1995. "Functioning and Capability: The Foundations of Sen's and Nussbaum's Development Ethic, Part 2." In M. Nussbaum and J. Glover (eds.), *Women, Culture and Development: The Capabilities Approach*. Oxford: Clarendon Press, pp. 153–199.

Crocker, David. 2008. *Ethics of Global Development: Agency, Capability, and Deliberative Democracy*. Cambridge: Cambridge University Press.

Cropper, Maureen. 2000. "Has Economic Research Answered the Needs of Environmental Policy?" *Journal of Environmental Economics and Management* 39:328–350.

Czech, Brian. 2006. "Steady State Economy." In Tom Tietenberg and Cutler Cleveland (eds.), *Encyclopedia of Earth*. Washington, DC: Environmental Information Coalition, National Council for Science and the Environment. Available at: <http://www.eoearth.org/article/Steady_state_economy> (accessed April 28, 2014).

Dahl, Robert. 1971. *Polyarchy*. New Haven, CT: Yale University Press.

Daily, Gretchen, Susan Alexander, Paul R. Ehrlich, et al. 1997. "Ecosystem Services: Benefits Supplied to Human Societies by Natural Ecosystems." *Issues in Ecology* 2:1–16.

Daly, Herman. 1991. *Steady-State Economics* (2nd ed.). Washington, DC: Island Press.

Daly, Herman. 1998. "Consumption: Value Added, Physical Transformation, and Welfare." In David Crocker and Tony Linden (eds.), *The Ethics of Consumption: The Good Life, Justice, and Global Stewardship*. Lanham, MD: Rowman & Littlefield, pp. 19–27.

Daly, Herman. 2005. "Economics in a Full World." *Scientific American* 293:100–107.

Daniels, Norman. 1985. *Just Health Care*. Cambridge: Cambridge University Press.

D'Arge, Ralph. 1994. "Sustenance and Sustainability: How Can We Preserve and Consume without Major Conflict?" In A. M. Jansson, M. Hammer, C. Folke, and

R. Costanza (eds.), *Investing in Natural Capital*. Washington, DC: Island Press, pp. 113–127.

Delogu, Orlando. 1984. "Local Land Use Controls: An Idea Whose Time Has Passed." *Maine Law Review* 35:261–265.

Deneulin, Severine. 2002. "Perfectionism, Paternalism and Liberalism in Sen and Nussbaum's Capability Approach." *Review of Political Economy* 14/4:497–518.

Deneulin, Severine. 2005. "Promoting Human Freedoms under Conditions of Inequalities: A Procedural Framework." *Journal of Human Development and Capablilites* 6/1:75–92.

DeWitt, John. 1994. *Civic Environmentalism: Alternatives to Regulation in States and Communities*. Washington, DC: Congressional Quarterly Press.

Disch, Lisa. 2011. "Toward a Mobilization Conception of Democratic Representation." *American Political Science Review* 105/1:100–114.

Dobson, Andrew. 2003. *Citizenship and the Environment*. Oxford: Oxford University Press.

Dobson, Andrew. 2006. "Thick Cosmopolitanism." *Political Studies* 54:165–184.

Donnelly, J. E., W. J. Donnelly, and Y. H Thong. 1987. "Parental Perceptions and Attitudes toward Asthma and its Treatment: A Controlled Study." *Social Science Medicine* 24/5:431–437.

Dore, Mohammed. 1996. "The Problem of Valuation in Neoclassical Environmental Economics." *Environmental Ethics* 18:63–70.

Driscoll, Charles, Gregory Lawrence, Arthur Bulger, et al. 2001. "Acidic Deposition in the Northeastern US: Sources and Inputs, Ecosystem Effects, and Management Strategies." *BioScience* 51/3:181–198.

Dryzek, John. 1987. *Rational Ecology: Environment and Political Economy*. Oxford: Basil Blackwell.

Dryzek, John. 2000. *Deliberative Democracy and Beyond: Liberals, Critics, Contestations*. Oxford: Oxford University Press.

Duane, Timothy. 1997. "Community Participation in Ecosystem Management." *Ecology Law Quarterly* 21:771–796.

Duraiappah, Anantha Kumar. 2004. *Exploring the Links: Human Well-Being, Poverty and Ecosystem Services*. Nairobi: The United Nations Environment Programme.

Eckersley, Robyn. 2004. *The Green State: Rethinking Democracy and Sovereignty*. Cambridge, MA: The MIT Press.

Edwards, Steven. 1987. "In Defense of Environmental Economics." *Environmental Ethics* 9/1:73–85.

Eisen, Joel. 1996. "Brownfields of Dreams? Challenges and Limits of Voluntary Cleanup Programs and Incentives." *University of Illinois Law Review* 1996:883–1039.

Eisner, Marc. 2000. *Regulatory Politics in Transition* (2nd ed.). Baltimore, MD: Johns Hopkins University Press.

Elmqvist, Thomas, Carl Folke, Magus Nystrom, et al. 2003. "Response Diversity, Ecosystem Change, and Resilience." *Frontiers in Ecology* 1/9:488–494.

Elster, Jon. 1982. "Sour Grapes: Utilitarianism and the Genesis of Wants." In Amartya Sen and Bernard Williams (eds.), *Utilitarianism and Beyond*. Cambridge: Cambridge University Press, pp. 219–238.

Elster, Jon. 1983. *Sour Grapes: Studies in the Subversion of Rationality.* Cambridge: Cambridge University Press.

EPA (Environmental Protection Agency). 2009. *Air Quality Index: A Guide to Air Quality and Your Health.* Research Triangle Park, NC: Office of Air Quality and Planning Standards.

Ernst, Howard. 2003. *Chesapeake Bay Blues: Science, Politics, and the Struggle to Save the Bay.* Lanham, MD: Rowman & Littlefield.

Espeland, Wendy. 1994. "Legally Mediated Identity: The National Environmental Policy Act and the Bureaucratic Construction of Interests." *Law and Society Review* 28/5:1149–1179.

Estlund, David. 2008. *Democratic Authority: A Philosophical Framework.* Princeton, NJ: Princeton University Press.

Faber, Daniel. 2008. *Capitalizing on Environmental Injustice: The Polluter-Industrial Complex in the Age of Globalization.* Lanham, MD: Rowman & Littlefield.

Farley, Joshua. 2008. "The Role of Prices in Conserving Critical Natural Capital." *Conservation Biodiversity* 22/6:1399–1408.

Fischer, Frank and Maarten A. Hajer (eds.). 1999. *Living with Nature: Environmental Politics as Cultural Discourse.* Oxford: Oxford University Press.

Folke, Carl, Monica Hammer, Robert Costanza, and AnnMari Jansson. 1994. "Investing in Natural Capital: Why, What, and How." In A. M. Jansson, M. Hammer, C. Folke, and R. Costanza (eds.), *Investing in Natural Capital.* Washington, DC: Island Press, pp. 1–20.

Foster, John (ed.). 1997. *Valuing Nature? Economics, Ethics and Environment.* London: Routledge.

Foster, Sheila. 2002. "Environmental Justice in an Era of Devolved Collaboration." *Harvard Environmental Law Review* 26:459–498.

Fraas, Arthur. 1991. "The Role of Economic Analysis in Shaping Environmental Policy." *Law and Contemporary Problems* 54:113–125.

Fraser, Nancy. 2000. "Rethinking Recognition." *New Left Review* 3:107–120.

Freeman, Jody. 1997. "Collaborative Governance in the Administrative State." *UCLA Law Review* 45/1:1–98.

Fung, Archon. 2005. "Deliberation before the Revolution: Toward an Ethics of Deliberative Democracy in an Unjust World." *Political Theory* 33/3:397–419.

Geertz, Clifford. 1983. *Local Knowledge: Further Essays in Interpretive Anthropology.* New York: Basic Books.

Gerrard, Michael and Sheila Foster (eds.). 2008. *The Law of Environmental Justice: Theories and Procedures to Address Disproportionate Risk* (2nd ed.). Chicago: American Bar Association Publishing.

Gillroy, John Martin and Joe Bowersox (eds.). 2002. *The Moral Austerity of Environmental Decision Making: Sustainability, Democracy, and Normative Argument in Policy and Law.* Durham, NC: Duke University Press.

Gillroy, John Martin and Breena Holland. 2008. *A Primer for Law and Policy Design: Understanding the Use of Principle and Argument in Environmental and Natural Resource Law.* St. Paul, MN: Thompson/West.

Gillroy, John Martin and Maurice Wade (eds.). 1992. *The Moral Dimensions of Public Policy Choice: Beyond the Market Paradigm*. Pittsburgh, PA: Pittsburg University Press.

Goodin, Robert E. 1992. *Green Political Theory*. Cambridge, MA: Polity Press.

Goodpaster, Kenneth. 1978. "On Being Morally Considerable." *Journal of Philosophy* 75/6:308–325.

Gore, Charles. 1997. "Irreducibly Social Goods and the Informational Basis of Amartya Sen's Capability Approach." *Journal of International Development* 9/2:235–250.

Gowdy, John and Peg Olsen. 1994. "Further Problems with Neoclassical Environmental Economics." *Environmental Ethics* 16:161–171.

Gramlich, Edwards. 1981. *Benefit-Cost Analysis of Government Programs*. Englewood Cliffs, NJ: Prentice Hall.

Griffin, James. 1986. *Well-Being: Its Meaning, Measurement, and Moral Importance*. Oxford: Oxford University Press.

Groffman, Peter, Jill Baron, Tamara Blett, et al. 2006. "Ecological Thresholds: The Key to Successful Environmental Management or an Important Concept with No Practical Application?" *Ecosystems* 9/1:1–16.

Grove-White, Robin. 1997. "The Environmental 'Valuation' Controversy: Observations on its Recent History and Significance." In John Foster (ed.), *Valuing Nature? Economics, Ethics and Environment*. London: Routledge, pp. 21–31.

Guess, George and Paul Farnham. 2000. *Cases in Public Policy Analysis* (2nd ed.). Washington, DC: Georgetown University Press.

Guha, Ramachandra and Juan Martinez-Alier. 1997. *Varieties of Environmentalism: Essays North and South*. London: Earthscan.

Guzy, Gary. 2000. *EPA Statutory and Regulatory Authorities Under Which Environmental Justice Issues May Be Addressed in Permitting* (Dec. 1. 2000). Washington, DC: US EPA Office of General Council, pp. 1–14.

Hamilton, James. 1993. "Politics and Social Costs: Estimating the Impact of Collective Action on Hazardous Waste Facilities." *The RAND Journal of Economics* 24:101–125.

Harberger, Arnold. 1978. "On the Use of Distributional Weights in Social Cost–Benefit Analysis." *Journal of Political Economy* 86/2(part 2):S87–S120.

Harsanyi, John. 1996. "Utilities, Preferences, and Substantive Goods." *Journal of Choice and Social Welfare* 14/1:129–145.

Hayward, Tim. 2005. *Constitutional Environmental Rights*. Oxford: Oxford University Press.

Heal, Geoffrey. 2000. "Valuing Ecosystem Services." *Ecosystems* 3/1:24–30.

Heinzerling, Lisa. 1998. "Regulatory Costs of Mythic Proportions." *Yale Law Journal* 107:1981–2070.

Heinzerling, Lisa. 2002. "Five-Hundred Life-Saving Interventions and their Misuse in the Debate over Regulatory Reform." *Risk, Health, Safety & Environment* 13(Spring):151–176.

Hicks, John Richard. 1939a. *Value and Capital: An Inquiry into Some Fundamental Principles of Economic Theory*. Oxford: Clarendon Press.

Hicks, John Richard. 1939b. "Foundations of Welfare Economics." *Economic Journal* 49:696–712.

Hicks, John Richard. 1943. "The Four Consumer's Surpluses." *Review of Economic Studies* 11:31–41.

Hirsch, Dennis. 1998. "Bill and Al's XL-ent Adventure: An Analysis of the EPA's Legal Authority to Implement the Clinton Administration's Project XL." *University of Illinois Law Review* 129:129–172.

Holland, Alan. 2006. "Must We Give Up Environmental Ethics." In Henk A. M. J. ten Hav (ed.). *Environmental Ethics and International Policy*. Paris, France: UNESCO, pp. 117–143.

Holland, Breena. 2008a. "Justice and the Environment in Nussbaum's Capabilities Approach: Why Sustainable Ecological Capacity is a Meta-Capability." *Political Research Quarterly* 61/2:319–332.

Holland, Breena. 2008b. "Ecology and the Limits of Justice: Establishing 'Capability Ceilings' in Nussbaum's Capabilities Approach." *Journal of Human Development and Capabilities (Special Edition on Ideas Changing History)* 9/3:399–423.

Holland, Breena. 2012. "Environment as Meta-Capability: Why a Dignified Life Requires a Stable Climate System." In Allen Thompson and Jeremy Bendik-Keymer (eds.), *Ethical Adaptation to Climate Change: Human Virtues of the Future*. Cambridge, MA: The MIT Press, pp. 145–164.

Howarth, Richard and Matthew Willson. 2006. "A Theoretical Approach to Deliberative Valuation: Aggregation by Mutual Consent." *Land Economics* 82/1:1–16.

Jackson, Tim. 2009. *Prosperity without Growth: Economics for a Finite Planet*. London: Earthscan.

Jacobs, Michael. 1996. "Environmental Valuation, Deliberative Democracy and Public Decision-Making Institutions." In John Foster (ed.), *Valuing Nature? Economics, Ethics and Environment*. London: Routledge, pp. 211–231.

Jaffe, Adam, Steven Peterson, Paul Portney, and Robert Stavins. 1995. "Environmental Regulation and the Competitiveness of U.S. Manufacturing: What Does the Evidence Tell Us?" *Journal of Economic Literature* 33/1:132–165.

James, Rosemary and Russell Blamey. 2005. "Deliberation and Economic Valuation: National Park Management." In M. Getzner, C. Spash, and S. Stagl (eds.), *Alternatives for Environmental Valuation*. London: Routledge, pp. 225–243.

Jamieson, Dale. 2001. "Climate Change and Global Environmental Justice." In Clark Miller and Paul Edwards (eds.), *Changing the Atmosphere: Expert Knowledge and Environmental Governance*. Cambridge, MA: The MIT Press, pp. 287–307.

Jamieson, Dale. 2002. *Morality's Progress: Essays on Humans, Other Animals, and the Rest of Nature*. Oxford: Clarendon Press.

Johansson-Stenman, Olof. 2002. "What Should We Do with Inconsistent, Nonwelfaristic, and Undeveloped Preferences?" In Daniel Bromley and Jouni Paavola (eds.), *Economics, Ethics, and Environmental Policy: Contested Choices*. Oxford: Blackwell Publishers, pp. 103–119.

Jones, Eileen Gay. 1997. "Risky Assessments: Uncertainties in Science and the Human Dimensions of Environmental Decisionmaking." *William & Mary Environmental Law and Policy Review* 22:1–69.

Kagan, Robert. 2001. *Adversarial Legalism: The American Way of Law*. Cambridge, MA: Harvard University Press.

Kahn, Matthew. 2001. "The Beneficiaries of Clean Air Act Regulation." *Regulation* (Spring):34–38.

Kaldor, Nicholas. 1939. "Welfare Propositions of Economics and Interpersonal Comparisons of Utility." *Economic Journal* 49/195:549–552.

Kaplowitz, Michael and John Hoehn. 2001. "Do Focus Groups and Personal Interviews Reveal the Same Information for Natural Resource Valuation?" *Ecological Economics* 36/2:237–247.

Keller, Ann C. 2009. *Science in Environmental Policy: The Politics of Objective Advice*. Cambridge, MA: The MIT Press.

Kelman, Steven. 1992. "Cost Benefit Analysis: An Ethical Critique." In Gillroy, John Martin and Maurice Wade (eds.), *The Moral Dimensions of Public Policy Choice: Beyond the Market Paradigm*. Pittsburgh, PA: Pittsburg University Press, pp. 153–164.

Klyza, Christopher M. and David Sousa. 2008. *American Environmental Policy*, 1990–2006: *Beyond Gridlock*. Cambridge, MA: The MIT Press.

Knight, Jack and James Johnson. 1997. "What Sort of Equality Does Deliberative Democracy Require?" In James Bohman (ed.), *Deliberative Democracy: Essays on Reason and Politics*. Cambridge, MA: The MIT Press, pp. 279–319.

Kraft, Michael. 2007. *Environmental Politics and Policy* (4th ed.). New York: Pearson-Longman.

Kubasek, Nancy and Gary Silverman. 2008. *Environmental Law* (6th ed.). Upper Saddle River, NJ: Pearson Prentice Hall.

Kuehn, Robert. 1994. "Remedying the Unequal Enforcement of Environmental Laws." *St. John's Journal of Legal Commentary* 9:625–668.

Kuehn, Robert. 1996. "The Environmental Justice Implications of Quantitative Risk Assessment." *University of Illinois Law Review* 1996:103–172.

Lavelle, Marianne and Marcia Coyle. 1992. "Unequal Protection: The Racial Divide in Environmental Law." *National Law Journal* 15/3(September 21):S1–S12.

Layzer, Judith. 2008. *Natural Experiments: Ecosystem-Based Management and the Environment*. Cambridge, MA: The MIT Press.

Lazarus, Richard. 1993. "Pursuing 'Environmental Justice': The Distributional Effects of Environmental Protection." *Northwestern University Law Review* 87/3:787–845.

Lazarus, Richard and Stephanie Tai. 1999. "Integrating Environmental Justice into EPA Permitting Authority." *Ecology Law Quarterly* 26:617–681.

Leeson, Susan. 1979. "Philosophic Implications of the Ecological Crisis: The Authoritarian Challenge to Liberalism." *Polity* 11:303–318.

Leinhoop, Niele and D. C. MacMillan. 2007a. "Valuing Wilderness in Iceland: Estimation of WTA and WTP Using the Market Stall Approach to Contingent Valuation." *Land Use Policy* 24/1:281–295.

Leinhoop, Niele and D. C. MacMillan. 2007b. "Contingent Valuation: Comparing Participant Performance in Group-Based Approaches and Personal Interviews." *Environmental Values* 16/2:209–232.

Leopold, Aldo. 1949. *A Sand County Almanac*. Oxford: Oxford University Press.

Levy, Marc. 2011. "Punishments of Shale Drillers: Now Need OK from Top." *Associated Press*, March 31. Available at: <http://thetimes-tribune.com/news/gas-drilling/punishments-of-shale-drillers-now-need-ok-from-top-1.1125976#ixzz1NstYtAPI> (accessed April 28, 2014).

Liu, Shuang, Robert Costanza, Stephen Farber, and Austin Troy. 2010. "Valuing Ecosystem Services: Theory, Practice, and the Need for a Transdisciplinary Synthesis." *Annals of the New York Academy of Sciences* 1185:54–78.

Lowi, Theodore. 1999. "Frontyard Propaganda: A Response to 'Beyond Backyard Environmentalism.'" *Boston Review* 24(October/November):17–18.

Lundberg, Jakob and Fredrik Moberg. 2003. "Mobile Link Organisms and Ecosystem Functioning: Implications for Ecosystem Resilience and Management." *Ecosystems* 6/1:87–98.

McGarity, Thomas and Ruth Ruttenberg. 2002. "Counting the Cost of Health, Safety, and Environmental Regulation." *Texas Law Review* 80/7:1997–2058.

Macmillan, Douglas, Lorna Philip, Nick Hanley, and Begona Alvarez-Farizo. 2002. "Valuing the Non-Market Benefits of Wild Goose Conservation: A Comparison of Interview and Group-Based Approaches." *Ecological Economics* 43/1:49–59.

Macnaghten, Phil, R. Grove-White, S. Weldon, and C. Waterton. 1998. *Woodland Sensibilities: Recreational Uses of Woods and Forests in Contemporary Britain*, Report by the Centre for the Study of Environmental Change. Lancaster: Lancaster University.

Mank, Bradford. 1998. "The Environmental Protection Agency's Project XL and Other Regulatory Reform Initiatives: The Need for Legislative Reauthorization." *Ecology Law Quarterly* 25:1–89.

Mansbridge, Jane. 1983. *Beyond Adversarial Democracy*. Chicago: University of Chicago Press.

Matthews, William (ed.). 1970. *Man's Impact on the Global Environment: Assessment and Recommendation for Action*, Study of Critical Environmental Problems. Cambridge, MA: The MIT Press.

Mazumdar, Maitreyi, David C. Bellinger, Matthew Gregas, et al. 2011. "Low-Level Environmental Lead Exposure in Childhood and Adult Intellectual Function: A Follow-Up Study." *Environmental Health* 10/24:1–7.

Menell, Peter and Richard Stewart. 1994. *Environmental Law and Policy*. Boston, MA: Little, Brown and Company.

Menon, Nivedita. 2002. "Universalism without Foundations." *Economy and Society* 31/1:152–169.

Mill, John Stuart [1859] 1956. *On Liberty: Edited with an Introduction by Currin V. Shields*. Upper Saddle River, NJ: Prentice Hall.

Mill, John Stuart [1861] 1962. "Utilitarianism." In M. Warnock (ed.), *Utilitarianism*. London: Collins, pp. 251–321.

Millennium Assessment Panel. 2003. *Ecosystems and Human Well-Being: A Framework for Assessment*. Washington, DC: Island Press.

Miller, David. 1992. "Deliberative Democracy and Social Choice." *Political Studies Special Issue: Prospects for Democracy* 40:54–67.

Miller, David. 1999. "Social Justice and Environmental Goods." In Andrew Dobson (ed.), *Fairness and Futurity: Essays on Environmental Sustainability and Social Justice*. Oxford: Oxford University Press, pp. 152–172.

Miller, Ted. 1989. "Willingness to Pay Comes of Age: Will the System Survive?" *Northwestern University Law Review* 84/4:876–899.

Mishan, James. 1982. *What Political Economy is All About: An Exposition and Critique*. New York: Cambridge University Press.

Morello-Frosch, Rachel. 2001. "Environmental Justice and the Southern California 'Riskscape': The Distribution of Air Toxics Exposures and Health Risks among Diverse Communities." *Urban Affairs Review* 36/4:551–578.

Morgenstern, Richard (ed.). 1997. *Economic Analyses at EPA: Assessing Regulatory Impact*. Washington, DC: Resources for the Future.

Morrall III, John F. 1986. "A Review of the Record." *Regulation* 10/2:25–34.

Mueller, Dennis. 1989. *Public Choice II*. Cambridge: Cambridge University Press.

Needleman, Herbert. 2004. "Lead Poisoning." *Annual Review of Medicine* 55:209–222.

Nevin, Rick. 2009. "Trends in Preschool Lead Exposure, Mental Retardation, and Scholastic Achievement: Association or Causation?" *Environmental Research* 109:301–310.

Nocon, Andrew and Tim Booth. 1989–1990. "The Social Impact of Asthma: A Review of the Literature." *Social Work and the Social Sciences Review* 1/3:177–200.

Norton, Bryan. 1986. "On the Inherent Danger of Undervaluing Species." In Bryan Norton (ed.), *The Preservation of Species: The Inherent Value of Biodiversity*. Princeton, NJ: Princeton University Press, pp. 110–137.

Nussbaum, Martha. 1988. "Nature, Function, and Capability: Aristotle on Political Distribution." *Oxford Studies in Ancient Philosophy*, supplementary volume 6:145–184.

Nussbaum, Martha. 1990. "Aristotelian Social Democracy." In R. Bruce Douglas, Gerald Mara, and Henry Richardson (eds.), *Liberalism and the Good*. New York: Routledge, pp. 203–252.

Nussbaum, Martha. 1992. "Human Functioning and Social Justice: In Defense of Aristotelian Essentialism." *Political Theory* 20(2):202–246.

Nussbaum, Martha. 1993. "Non-Relative Virtues: An Aristotelian Approach." In Amartya Sen and Martha Nussbaum (eds.), *The Quality of Life*. Oxford: Clarendon Press, pp. 242–276.

Nussbaum, Martha. 1997a. "Flawed Foundations: The Philosophical Critique of (a Particular Type of) Economics." *University of Chicago Law Review* 64/4:1197–1214.

Nussbaum, Martha. 1997b. "Capabilities and Human Rights." *Fordham Law Review* 66/2:273–300.

Nussbaum, Martha. 1998."The Good as Discipline, the Good as Freedom." In David Crocker and Tony Linden (eds.), *The Ethics of Consumption: The Good Life, Justice, and Global Stewardship*. Lanham, MD: Rowman & Littlefield, pp. 312–341.

Nussbaum, Martha. 2000a. *Women and Human Development: The Capabilities Approach*. New York: Cambridge University Press.

Nussbaum, Martha. 2000b. "The Costs of Tragedy: Some Moral Limits of Cost–Benefit Analysis." *Journal of Legal Studies* 29:1005–1036.

Nussbaum, Martha. 2001. "Disabled Lives: Who Cares?" *New York Review of Books* 48:34–37.

Nussbaum, Martha. 2003. "Capabilities as Fundamental Entitlements: Sen and Social Justice." *Feminist Economics* 9/2–3:33–59.

Nussbaum, Martha. 2004. "On Hearing Women's Voices: A Reply to Susan Okin." *Philosophy and Public Affairs* 32/2:193–205.

Nussbaum, Martha. 2006. *Frontiers of Justice: Disability, Nationality, Species Membership.* Cambridge, MA: Belknap Press of Harvard University Press.

Nussbaum, Martha. 2011. *Creating Capabilities: The Human Development Approach.* Cambridge, MA: Belknap Press of Harvard University Press.

Oates, Wallace and Maureen Cropper. 1992. "Environmental Economics: A Survey." *Journal of Economic Literature* 30:675–731.

Obama, Barack. 2011. "Improving Regulation and Regulatory Review," Executive Order 13,563, January 18. Available at: <https://www.federalregister.gov/articles/2011/01/21/2011-1385/improving-regulation-and-regulatory-review> (accessed April 28, 2014).

Odum, Eugene. 1993. *Ecology and Our Endangered Life-Support Systems.* Sunderland, MA: Sinauer Associates.

Office of Inspector General. 2004. *EPA Needs to Consistently Implement the Intent of the Executive Order on Environmental Justice,* Evaluation Report Number 2004-P-00007. Washington, DC: US Environmental Protection Agency.

Okun, Arthur. 1975. *Equality and Efficiency: The Big Tradeoff.* Washington, DC: The Brookings Institution.

O'Neill, John. 1993. *Ecology, Policy, and Politics: Human Well-Being and the Natural World.* London: Routledge.

O'Neill, John. 1996. "Contingent Valuation and Qualitative Democracy." *Environmental Politics* 5/4:752–759.

O'Neill, John. 1998. *The Market: Ethics, Knowledge and Politics.* London: Routledge.

O'Neill, John. 2007. *Markets, Deliberation and Environment.* New York: Routledge.

O'Neill, John and Clive Spash. 2000. "Appendix: Policy Research Brief: Conceptions of Value in Environmental Decisonmaking." *Environmental Values* 9/4:521–536.

O'Neill, John, Alan Holland, and Andrew Light. 2008. *Environmental Values.* London: Routledge.

Oreskes, Naomi. 2004. "Science and Public Policy: What's Proof Got to Do With It?" *Journal of Environmental Science and Policy* 7/5:369–383.

Oreskes, Naomi and Erik Conway. 2010. *Merchants of Doubt: How a Handful of Scientists Obscured the Truth on Issues from Tobacco Smoke to Global Warming.* New York: Bloomsbury Press.

Pearce, David, Anil Markandya, and Edward B. Barbier. 1989. *Blueprint for a Green Economy.* London: Earthscan.

Pearce, David. 2002. An Intellectual History of Environmental Economics. *Annual Review of Energy and the Environment* 27:57–81.

Persky, J. 2001. "Cost–Benefit Analysis and the Classical Creed." *Journal of Economic Perspectives* 15/4:199–208.

Peter, Fabienne. 2003. "Gender and the Foundations of Social Choice: The Role of Situated Agency." *Feminist Economics* 9/2–3:13–32.

Peeters, Wouter, Jo Dirix, and Sigrid Sterckx. 2013. "Putting Sustainability into Sustainable Human Development." *Journal of Human Development and Capabilities* 14/1:58–76.

Phillips, Anne. 1995. *The Politics of Presence*. Oxford: Oxford University Press.

Pigou, Arthur. 1920. *The Economics of Welfare*. London: Macmillan.

Pitkin, Hanna. 1967. *The Concept of Representation*. Berkeley, CA: University of California Press.

Prugh, Thomas. 1995. *Natural Capital and Human Economic Survival*. Solomons, MD: International Society for Ecological Economics.

Rabe, Barry. 1986. *Fragmentation and Integration in State Environmental Management*. Washington, DC: The Conservation Foundation.

Randall, Alan. 2002. "Benefit-Cost Considerations Should Be Decisive When There is Nothing More Important at Stake," in Daniel Bromley and Jouni Paavola (eds.), *Economics, Ethics, and Environmental Policy*. Oxford: Blackwell Publishers, pp. 53–68.

Rawls, John. 1971. *A Theory of Justice*. Cambridge, MA: Belknap Press of Harvard University Press.

Rawls, John. 1975. "Fairness to Goodness." *Philosophical Review* 84:536–554.

Rawls, John. 1993. *Political Liberalism*. New York: Columbia University Press.

Rawls, John. 1999. "The Idea of Public Reason Revisited." In John Rawls, *The Law of Peoples*. Cambridge, MA: Harvard University Press, pp. 131–180.

Rawls, John. 2001. *Justice as Fairness: A Restatement*. Cambridge, MA: Belknap Press of Harvard University Press.

Reagan, Ronald. 1981. "Federal Regulation," Executive Order 12,291, 17 February. Available at: <http://www.archives.gov/federal-register/codification/executive-order/12291.html> (accessed April 28, 2014).

Richardson, Henry S. 2002. *Democratic Autonomy: Public Reasoning about the Ends of Policy*. Oxford: Oxford University Press.

Robeyns, Ingrid. 2003. "Sen's Capability Approach and Gender Inequality: Selecting Relevant Capabilities." *Feminist Economics* 9/2–3:61–92.

Robeyns, Ingrid. 2005. "The Capability Approach: A Theoretical Survey." *Journal of Human Development* 6/1:93–117.

Robeyns, Ingrid. 2009. "Equality and Justice." In Severine Deneulin and Lila Shahani (eds.), *An Introduction to the Human Development and Capability Approach*. London: Earthscan, pp. 101–120.

Rockström, Johan, Will Steffen, Kevin Noone, et al. 2009. "A Safe Operating Space for Humanity." *Nature* 461/7263:472–475.

Rolston, Holmes. 1988. *Environmental Ethics: Duties to and Values in the Natural World*. Indiana: Temple University Press.

Rosenbaum, Walter. 2008. *Environmental Politics and Policy* (7th ed.). Washington, DC: CQ Press.

Routley, R. and Routley, V. 1980. "Human Chauvinism and Environmental Ethics." In D. Mannison, M. A. McRobbie, and R. Routley (eds.), *Environmental Philosophy*. Canberra: Research School of Social Sciences, ANU, pp. 96–189.

Runciman, David. 2007. "The Paradox of Political Representation." *Journal of Political Philosophy* 15/1:93–114.

Sagoff, Mark. 1988a. *The Economy of Earth*. New York: Cambridge University Press.

Sagoff, Mark. 1988b. "At the Shrine of Our Lady Fatima; Or, Why Political Questions Are Not All Economic." In Mark Sagoff, *The Economy of the Earth*. Cambridge: Cambridge University Press, pp. 24–49.

Sagoff, Mark. 1998a. "Carrying Capacity and Ecological Economics." In David Crocker and Tony Linden (eds.), *The Ethics of Consumption: The Good Life, Justice, and Global Stewardship*. Lanham, MD: Rowman & Littlefield, pp. 28–52.,

Sagoff, Mark. 1998b. "Aggregation and Deliberation in Valuing Environmental Public Goods: A Look Beyond Contingent Pricing." *Ecological Economics* 24/2–3:213–230.

Scheffer, Marten, Steve Carpenter, Jonathan A. Foley, et al. 2001. "Catastrophic Shifts in Ecosystems." *Nature* 413(October 11):591–596.

Schkade, David and John Payne. 1994. "How People Respond to Contingent Valuation Questions: A Verbal Protocol Analysis of Willingness to Pay for an Environmental Regulation." *Journal of Environmental Economics and Management* 26/1:88–109.

Schlosberg, David. 2004. "Reconceiving Environmental Justice: Global Movements and Political Theories." *Environmental Politics* 13/3:517–540.

Schlosberg, David. 2007. *Defining Environmental Justice: Theories, Movements, and Nature*. Oxford: Oxford University Press.

Schlosberg, David. 2009. "Capacity and Capabilities: A Response to the Greenhouse Development Rights Framework." *Ethics, Place and Environment* 12/3:287–290.

Schlosberg, David. 2012a. "Justice, Ecological Integrity, and Climate Change." In Allen Thompson and Jeremy Bendik-Keymer (eds.), *Ethical Adaptation to Climate Change: Human Virtues of the Future*. Cambridge, MA: The MIT Press, pp. 165–183.

Schlosberg, David. 2012b. "Climate Justice and Capabilities: A Framework for Adaptation Policy." *Ethics and International Affairs* 26/4:445–461.

Schlosberg, David, and David Carruthers. 2010. "Indigenous Struggles, Environmental Justice, and Community Capabilities." *Global Environmental Politics* 10/4:12.28–52.35.

Schuman, H. 1996. "The Sensitivity of CV Outcomes to CV Survey Methods." In David Bornstad and James Kahn (eds.), *The Contingent Valuation of Environmental Resources: Methodological Issues and Research Needs*. Brookfield, MA: Edward Elgar, pp. 75–96.

Schwartz, Rachael. 2008. "The Clawback Provision of Sarbanes–Oxley: An Underutilized Incentive to Keep the Corporate House Clean." *The Business Lawyer* 64/1:1–35.

Sen Amartya. 1980/1. "Plural Utility." *Proceedings of the Aristotelian Society* 80:193–215.

Sen, Amartya. 1982a. "Choice Functions and Revealed Preference." In Amartya Sen, *Choice, Welfare, and Measurement*. Cambridge, MA: Harvard University Press, pp. 41–53.

Sen, Amartya. 1982b. "Behaviour and the Concept of Preference." In Amartya Sen, *Choice, Welfare, and Measurement*. Cambridge, MA: Harvard University Press, pp. 54–73.

Sen, Amartya. 1982c. "Equality of What?" In Amartya Sen, *Choice, Welfare, and Measurement*. Cambridge, MA: Harvard University Press, pp. 353–369.

Sen, Amartya. 1985a. "Well-Being, Agency and Freedom: The Dewey Lectures 1984." *Journal of Philosophy* 82/4:169–221.

Sen, Amartya. 1985b. *Commodities and Capabilities*. Amsterdam: Elsevier Science Publishers.

Sen, Amartya. 1987a. "The Standard of Living: Lecture I, Concepts and Critiques." In Geoffrey Hawthorn (ed.), *The Standard of Living*. Cambridge: Cambridge University Press, pp. 1–19.

Sen, Amartya. 1987b. "The Standard of Living: Lecture II, Lives and Capabilities." In Geoffrey Hawthorn (ed.), *The Standard of Living*. Cambridge: Cambridge University Press, pp. 20–38.

Sen, Amartya. 1990. "Gender and Cooperative Conflicts." In Irene Tinker (ed.), *Persistent Inequalities*. London: Oxford University Press, pp. 123–149.

Sen, Amartya. 1992. *Inequality Reexamined*. Cambridge, MA: Harvard University Press.

Sen, Amartya. 1999. *Development as Freedom*. New York: Alfred A. Knopf.

Sen, Amartya. 2000. *The Standard of Living: The Tanner Lectures on Human Values*. Cambridge: Cambridge University Press.

Sen, Amartya. 2004. "Capabilities, Lists, and Public Reason: Continuing the Conversation." *Feminist Economics* 10/3:77–80.

Sen, Amartya. 2005. "Human Rights and Capabilities." *Journal of Human Development* 6/2:151–166.

Sen, Amartya. 2009. *The Idea of Justice*. Cambridge, MA: The Belknap Press of Harvard University Press.

Sen, Amartya and Bernard Williams. 1982. *Utilitarianism and Beyond*. Cambridge: Cambridge University Press.

Shapiro, Ian. 2003. *The State of Democratic Theory*. Princeton, NJ: Princeton University Press.

Shrader-Frechette, Kristin. 1991. *Risk and Rationality: Philosophical Foundations for Populist Reforms*. Berkeley, CA: University of California Press.

Shrader-Frechette, Kristin. 2002. *Environmental Justice: Creating Equality, Reclaiming Democracy*. New York: Oxford University Press.

Shue, Henry. 1980. *Basic Rights: Subsistence, Affluence, and U.S. Foreign Policy*. Princeton, NJ: Princeton University Press.

Shue, Henry. 1993. "Subsistence Emissions and Luxury Emissions." *Law and Policy* 15:39–60.

Shue, Henry. 2001. "Climate." In Dale Jamieson (ed.), *A Companion to Environmental Philosophy*. Oxford: Wiley-Blackwell Publishing, pp. 449–459.

Singer, Peter. 2004. *One World: The Ethics of Globalization*. New Haven, CT: Yale University Press.

Slovic, Paul. 1995. "The Construction of Preference." *American Psychologist* 50/5:364–371.

Smith, Graham. 2003. *Deliberative Democracy and the Environment*. London: Routledge.

Smith, Graham and Corinne Wales. 2000. "Citizens' Juries and Deliberative Democracy." *Political Studies* 48/1:51–65.

Smith, Kerry (ed.). 1984. *Environmental Policy under Reagan's Executive Order 12,291: The Role of Benefit-Cost Analysis*. Chapel Hill, NC: University of North Carolina Press.

Smith, Kerry and Yoshiaki Kaoru. 1990. "Signals or Noise? Explaining the Variation in Recreation Benefit Estimates." *American Journal of Agricultural Economics* 72:419–433.

Spash, Clive. 2008. "Deliberative Monetary Valuation and the Evidence for a New Value Theory." *Land Economics* 84/3:469–488.

Spash, Clive and Alex Lo. 2012. "Australia's Carbon Tax: A Sheep in Wolf's Clothing?." *The Economic and Labour Relations Review* 23/1:67–85.

Spash, Clive and Nick Hanley. 1995. "Preferences, Information, and Biodiversity Preservation". *Ecological Economics* 12/3:191–208.

Srinivasan, Sharath. 2007. "No Democracy without Justice: Political Freedom in Amartya Sen's Capability Approach." *Journal of Human Development* 8/3:457–480.

Stavins, Robert, Alexander Wagner, and Gernot Wagner. 2002. *Interpreting Sustainability in Economic Terms: Dynamic Efficiency plus Intergenerational Equity*. Resources for the Future Discussion Paper No. 02-29, Washington, DC.

Steinzor, Rena. 1998. "Reinventing Environmental Regulation: The Dangerous Journey from Command to Self-Control." *Harvard Environmental Law Review* 22:103–203.

Stewart, Frances. 1992. "Basic Needs, Capabilities, and Human Development." In Avner Offer (ed.), *In Pursuit of the Quality of Life*. Oxford: Oxford University Press, pp. 46–65.

Stokey, Edith and Richard Zeckhauser. 1978. *A Primer for Policy Analysis*. New York: Norton.

Sunstein, Cass. 1993. *The Partial Constitution*. Cambridge, MA: Harvard University Press.

Sunstein, Cass. 1999. "Consequences: A Response to 'Beyond Backyard Environmentalism.'" *Boston Review* 24/5 (October/November):28–29.

Sunstein, Cass. 2002. *Risk and Reason: Safety, Law, and the Environment*. Cambridge: Cambridge University Press.

Swanston, Samara. 1999. "Environmental Justice and Environmental Quality Benefits: The Oldest, Most Pernicious Struggle and Hope for Burdened Communities." *Vermont Law Review* 23:545–566.

Swartz, John. 2012. "Pennsylvania Report Left Out Data on Poisons in Water Near Gas Site." *New York Times*, November 3, A14.

Taylor, Paul. 1981. "The Ethics of Respect for Nature." *Environmental Ethics* 3:197–218.

Tengs, Tammy, Miriam Adams, Joseph Pliskin et al. 1995. "Five-Hundred LifeSaving Interventions and Their Cost-Effectiveness." *Risk Analysis* 15/3:369–390.

Tengs, Tammy and John Graham. 1996. "The Opportunity Costs of Haphazard Social Investments in Life-Savings." In Robert Hahn (ed.), *Risks, Costs, and Lives Saved: Getting Better Results from Regulation*. New York: Oxford University Press and AEI Press, pp. 1676–1682.

Thero, Daniel. 1995. "Rawls and Environmental Ethics: A Critical Examination of the Literature." *Environmental Ethics* 17/1:93–106.

Tietenberg, Tom. 1992. *Environmental and Natural Resource Economics* (3rd ed.). New York: HarperCollins.

Tietenberg, Tom. 1998. *Environmental Economics and Policy* (2nd ed.). Reading, MA: Addison-Wesley.

Roberts, Timmons, and Melissa Toffolon-Weiss. 2001. *Chronicles from the Environmental Justice Frontline*. Cambridge, UK: Cambridge University Press.

Trainor, Sarah Fleisher. 2006. "Realms of Value: Conflicting Natural Resource Values and Incommensurability." *Environmental Values* 8/2:3–29.

Trumbull, William. 1990. "Who Has Standing in Cost–Benefit Analysis?" *Journal of Policy Analysis and Management* 9/2:201–218.

Turner, Kerry, David Pearce, and Ian Bateman. 1993. *Environmental Economics*. Baltimore, MD: John Hopkins University Press.

US EPA Office of Air Quality and Planning Standards. 2004. *Benefit Analysis for the Section 112 Utility Rule*. EPA-452/R-03-021, January.

US EPA Office of Water. 2002. *National Water Quality Inventory 2000 Report*. EPA-841-R-02-001, August.

Van den Bergh, Jeroen C. J. M., and Jan van der Straaten. 1994. "Historical and Future Models of Economic Development and Natural Environment." In Jeroen C. J. M. van den Bergh and Jan van der Straaten (eds.), *Toward Sustainable Development: Concepts, Methods, and Policy*. Washington, DC: Island Press, pp. 209–234.

Vanderheiden, Steve. 2008. *Atmospheric Justice: A Political Theory of Climate Change*. Oxford: Oxford University Press.

Vatn, Arild. 2004. "Environmental Valuation and Rationality." *Land Economics* 80/1:1–18.

Vatn, Arild. 2005. *Institutions and the Environment*. Cheltenham: Edward Elgar.

Vatn, Arild. 2009. "An Institutional Analysis of Methods for Environmental Appraisal." *Ecological Economics* 68/8–9:2207–2215.

Vatn, Arild and D. W. Bromley. 1994. "Choices without Prices without Apologies." *Journal of Environmental Economics and Management* 26(2):129–148.

Ward, Hugh. 1999. "Citizens' Juries and Valuing the Environment: A Proposal." *Environmental Politics* 8/2:75–96.

Ward, Kevin and John Duffield. 1992. *Natural Resource Damages: Law and Economics*. New York: John Wiley & Sons, Inc.

Weber, Edward. 2003. *Bringing Society Back In: Grassroots Ecosystem Management, Accountability, and Sustainable Communities*. Cambridge, MA: The MIT Press.

Weimer, David and Aiden Vining. 1989. *Policy Analysis: Concepts and Practice*. Upper Saddle River, NJ: Prentice Hall.

Wentz, Peter. 1988. *Environmental Justice*. Albany, New York: State University of New York Press.

West, William. 1983. "Institutionalizing Rationality in Regulatory Administration." *Public Administration Review* 43/4:326–334.

Williams, Bernard. 1987. "The Standard of Living: Interests and Capabilities." In Geoffrey Hawthorn (ed.), *The Standard of Living*. Cambridge: Cambridge University Press, pp. 94–102.

Williams, Bruce and Albert Matheny. 1995. *Democracy, Dialogue, and Environmental Disputes: The Contested Languages of Social Regulation*. New Haven, CT: Yale University Press.

Wilson, Matthew and Richard Howarth. 2002. "Discourse-Based Valuation of Ecosystem Services: Establishing Fair Outcomes through Group Deliberation." *Ecological Economics* 41/3:431–443.

Wolff, Jonathon and Avner de-Shalit. 2007. *Disadvantage*. Oxford: Oxford University Press.

Wondolleck, Julia and Steven Yaffee. 2000. *Making Collaboration Work: Lessons from Innovation in Natural Resource Management*. Washington, DC: Island Press.

Young, Iris Marion. 1990. *Justice and the Politics of Difference*. Princeton, NJ: Princeton University Press.

Young, Iris Marion. 2000. *Inclusion and Democracy*. Oxford: Oxford University Press.

Young, Iris Marion. 2001. "Activist Challenges to Deliberative Democracy." *Political Theory* 29:670–690.

Index

Index